# LISTENING TO THE
# BELIEFS OF
# EMERGING
# CHURCHES

# LISTENING TO THE BELIEFS OF EMERGING CHURCHES

## FIVE PERSPECTIVES

KAREN WARD

DOUG PAGITT

DAN KIMBALL

JOHN BURKE

MARK DRISCOLL

general
editor

ROBERT
WEBBER

**ZONDERVAN**®

ZONDERVAN.com/
AUTHORTRACKER
follow your favorite authors

We want to hear from you. Please send your comments about this book to us in care of zreview@zondervan.com. Thank you.

*Listening to the Beliefs of Emerging Churches*
Copyright © 2007 by Robert Webber

Requests for information should be addressed to:

Zondervan, *Grand Rapids, Michigan 49530*

**Library of Congress Cataloging-in-Publication Data**

Listening to the beliefs of emerging churches / Robert Webber, general editor ; contributors, Mark Driscoll ... [et al.].
    p. cm.
Includes bibliographical references and index.
ISBN-13: 978-0-310-27135-2
ISBN-10: 0-310-27135-5
1. Postmodernism — Religious aspects — Christianity.  2. Non-institutional churches.
3. Church renewal.  4. Christianity — Forecasting.  I. Webber, Robert.  II. Driscoll, Mark, 1970-
BR115.P74L57 2007
230'.046209051 — dc22                                     2006032088

*Interior design by Nancy Wilson*

*Printed in the United States of America*

06  07  08  09  10  11  12  •  20  19  18  17  16  15  14  13  12  11  10  9  8  7  6  5  4  3  2  1

# CONTENTS

# ACKNOWLEDGMENTS

The writing of any book is never the product of one person. This is particularly true when a book includes the research and writing of several people. So my first statement of thanks belongs to the contributors of this book—Mark Driscoll, John Burke, Dan Kimball, Doug Pagitt, and Karen Ward.

Their contributions constitute the heart of this work. Thanks belong to them for taking the time to write, for their vulnerability, and for their honest critique of each other. Then, thanks belong to Ashley Gieschen, my faithful administrative assistant who kept in touch with everyone and made sure materials came in on time. And thanks, too, for her hours at the computer.

I also need to express my gratitude to Northern Seminary for giving me an appointment that encourages writing and research. And then, finally, and certainly not least, is the vision of Zondervan to address the issues of the emerging church. My editor, Paul Engle, was a delight to work with. Thanks for his insight, encouragement, and quick responses to all my inquiries. Thanks also to the line editor, Becky Shingledecker, and to all others who worked to produce this book and make it available to the public.

ROBERT WEBBER
**Myers Professor of Ministry**
**Northern Seminary**

# INTRODUCTION:

# THE INTERACTION OF CULTURE AND THEOLOGY

Most of us are familiar with the saying, "As culture goes, so goes the church." These words express in terse terms the close relationship between the church, its theology, ministry, and prevailing culture. For example, someone somewhere caught this symbiotic relationship between Christianity and culture in the following startling phases:

- The church started as a missionary movement in Jerusalem.
- It moved to Rome and became an institution.
- It traveled to Europe and became a culture.
- It crossed the Atlantic to America and became a big business.

Of course this is simplistic. But it does speak a truth: the church always bumps up against culture.

For two thousand years, this "Christian story" has been told in every paradigm of history and in every culture and geographical area penetrated by the Christian gospel. While the Christian faith has a fixed framework of creation, fall, incarnation, death, resurrection, church, and new heaven and new earth, this framework and the story of God it reveals is always *contextualized* into this or that culture. The faith engaged with Platonism in the ancient world, with Aristotle in the medieval world, with nominalism in the Reformation era, and with rationalism in the modern world. Now the church must engage with the emergence of a postmodern, post-Christian, neo-pagan world.

In each of the past cycles, one can observe the "last gasp of the older paradigm" and "the first breath of the new paradigm." Because we are in a time of great cultural upheaval from modernity to postmodernity, the twentieth century may be seen as the century of transition. The cycle of evangelicalism within the twentieth century may be interpreted as the last gasp of modernity and the first breath of postmodernity. For example, traditional evangelicalism (1947–1980) is the *high point* of modern evangelicalism; pragmatic evangelicalism (1980–2000) is the *last gasp* of evangelicalism in the modern world; and the emerging church is the *first gasp* of evangelicalism in the postmodern world. As evangelicalism now seeks to thrive in this new cultural context, it faces new challenges that demand new ways to think and speak the Christian message.

## Understanding the Cycle of Cultural Shifts

In order to understand this twentieth-century shift in theological thought, I suggest we draw on the historical analysis provided for us by sociologists William Strauss and Neil Howe. In their book *The Fourth Turning: What the Cycles of History Tell Us About America's Next Rendezvous with Destiny*, they assert that a sociological study of history reveals "patterns that recur over time." According to their research, "Anglo-American society enters a new era—a new *turning*—every two decades or so. At the start of each turning, people change how they feel about themselves, the culture, the nation, and the future."[1] Turnings come in cycles of four. Each cycle spans the length of a long human life, roughly eighty to one hundred years, a unit of time the ancients called the *saeculum*. Together, the four turnings of the saeculum comprise history's seasonal rhythm of growth, maturation, entropy, and destruction.

- The *First Turning* is a *High*, an upbeat era of strengthening institutions and weakening individualism, when a new civic order implants and the old values regime decays.
- The *Second Turning* is an *Awakening*, a passionate era of spiritual upheaval, when the civic order comes under attack from a new values regime.
- The *Third Turning* is an *Unraveling*, a downcast era of strengthening individualism and weakening institutions, when the old civic order decays and the new values regime implants.
- The *Fourth Turning* is a *Crisis*, a decisive era of secular upheaval, when the values regime propels the replacement of the old civic order with a new one.[2]

For us evangelicals, there is great value to the Strauss and Howe interpretation of the cycles of history. It gives us *perspective*. For example, current evangelical diversity can be organized, since 1950, through the four turnings of high, awakening, unraveling, and crisis. A brief review of evangelical faith and practice within each of these turnings will reveal that the diversity which now exists among evangelicals is due to the church bumping up against culture in each of these turnings. In each turn of history since the late forties, evangelicals have responded to cultural change in new ways. What is happening now is a new cultural change, and the emerging church is responding to the new cultural shift. In order to understand the current diversity within evangelicalism, I will comment briefly on the response of evangelicals to the cycles of culture since WWII and then look at the emerging church within the current cycle of cultural crisis.

## The First Turning: High Evangelicals (1946–1964)

The first turning is the period of American history immediately following the *crisis* of WWII. It was the age of Truman, Eisenhower, and Kennedy, stretching from 1946 to 1964. Culturally it was a time of rebuilding America. The boys came home from the war, entered school, married, settled down to the good life, to the formation of the "American dream." America was strong. Its institutions were firm. Its values were set. It was a world built on reason and science.

In this period of history, *traditional* evangelicalism was birthed. The new or neo-evangelicalism, as it was first called, broke away from its roots in the fundamentalism of the first half of the century. The new evangelicalism regarded fundamentalism as "anti-intellectual, anti-social action, and anti-ecumenical." Influential leaders called for engagement with philosophy and the intellectual ideas of the day, to the recovery of a robust involvement with social issues, and to a new form of ecumenical cooperation, especially in evangelism. New names were in the limelight—Billy Graham, Carl F. H. Henry; new institutions were born—Fuller Seminary, the National Association of Evangelicals, *Christianity Today*.

The new evangelical theology distanced itself from fundamentalist biblicism and became marked by a rational worldview, propositionalism, and evidential apologetics. These new evangelicals called for debate with the liberals, accreditation for colleges and seminaries, and for the brightest to obtain doctorates from Ivy League schools. They wanted to spar with the best, engage secularists and liberals on their own turf, and create institutions of higher learning that would command respect. And they succeeded. Traditional evangelicalism became a very "heady" expression of faith. But in its success, something very important was lost. Its academic theology lost connection with practice. Theology became an abstraction, an idea to be defended.

## The Second Turning: Awakening Evangelicals (1964–1984)

In the period of the *awakening*, culture passed through another major shift. Confidence in the American way of life began to erode. Attention shifted from institutions to the self. Strauss and Howe cite three images that particularly express the cultural shift: Apollo 11, Woodstock, and Chappaquiddick. Apollo 11 landing on the moon represented "man's technological grandeur" but was immediately challenged because "moon rockets also diverted resources from poor people"; Woodstock "challenged the social order" that had made the landing on the moon possible and now presented an anti-institutional, freewheeling, drug-inhabiting, sex-driven hippie life as the new alternative social order; Ted Kennedy's Chappaquiddick incident "exemplified America's declining standards of public decorum and private virtue—and their flight from the suffocating duties of family life and child raising!"[3] In culture, a split was in the making between ideas and the reality of life. What good is technology if the poor go hungry? The ideals of national community began to break down; in its place, the focus on self was birthed and "all hell broke loose."

Clearly this era of the Vietnam War, the assassinations of the Kennedy brothers and Martin Luther King Jr., The Beatles, the sexual revolution, the growth of an anti-American attitude around the world, the breakdown of the family, and the rise of violence and pornography made its impact on a generation of Christian leaders.

During the *awakening*, three shifts began to take place in theological thinking. The first was the shift away from scientific theology and apologetics. On a personal note, I experienced the lack of interest in these subjects during my first semester at Wheaton College. In a course called "Christian Doctrine" (later changed to "Christian Thought") I used Louis Berkhof's *Reformed Dogmatics* as my text. I had walked into that course with a traditional evangelical commitment to the way of thinking that dominated the fifties. Within a few class periods I realized I was dealing with a number of students who simply didn't care about systematic theology or apologetics (some did). In response to their interests, I set aside my textbook and turned to the arts, their primary point of interest, as a jumping-off point for a discussion of God and the meaning of life. We listened to the Beatles and other artists and read plays such as Beckett's *Waiting for Godot* and Sartre's *No Exit*, and studied the works of Francis Schaeffer. The new interest was "Christ and culture."

Then, a second shift away from the traditional approach to theological thinking came through the spread of existential philosophy. It was a new focus on experience. Formerly, evangelical experience focused on *metanoia*, a life-transforming change of direction resulting from an encounter with God's saving grace in Jesus Christ. The new experience was essentially the experience of self. The sudden appearance of the contemporary worship movement, the new charismatic movement, and the surge of the Pentecostal churches focused on "my" relationship to God—how *I* establish it, and how *I* maintain it. The contemporary movement, unlike traditional evangelicalism, became increasingly unconcerned about theological issues. It became primarily a relational movement directed toward the emotional and psychological needs of a generation torn by the social upheaval of the sixties and seventies.

The third movement of the *awakening* period was the Christian political movement. This shift burst forth under the leadership of Jerry Falwell to call for moral reform in personal life, in government, in movies and TV, in education, and in public life in general. It eventually spawned a widespread movement of civil religion.

By the early 1980s, the evangelical culture of the fifties, with its uniform emphasis on scientific theology and evidential apologetics, was challenged by new concerns — mainly the emphasis on connecting with culture, the focus on relationship, and the new moral movement which sought to change culture through political reform. We now had two evangelicalisms: the theological evangelicals of the fifties and the relational evangelicals of the seventies. In twenty years the culture of America had shifted. Enormously. And the evangelical church now reflected that cultural division. Theological thinking and relational thinking were at odds in the same community. However, another turning in culture was about to occur, and with it came the explosion of evangelical pragmatism.

## The Third Turning: Evangelical Unraveling (1984 – 2004)

The decline of the civic order had already begun in the awakening of the sixties. But now the civic order underwent a rapid unraveling. Three changes in particular should be noted. First, society, instead of "one large happy American family moving in the same direction," became a nation divided by groups, all demanding their "rights." These groups — homosexuals, feminists, blacks, environmentalists, skinheads, moralists — all wanted to be "heard," to have their rightful place in life. In addition, society began to focus on generational needs and targeted the interests of busters, boomers, and Generation X. While this division was primarily the result of the consumer society, it further divided society into contesting groups. Second, the moral values that had been attacked in the sixties began to unravel even more. The eighties and nineties became the decades of casual sex; increased availability of pornography; easy availability of abortion; public acceptance of homosexual relationships and families; the breakdown of families; the rise of latchkey children; the presence of gangs in cities, suburbs, and rural areas; the prevalence of marijuana, cocaine, and other drugs; and the increase of violence. Third, government became characterized by "fiscal excess" with large deficits, reliance on other nations, and, although the economy was booming, a widened gap between the rich and poor. "America was deep into a new era of lost purpose and shattered consensus."[4] It was in a state of "new declinism," in which a "majority of Americans, young adults especially, believe[d] that the nation's best years have passed."[5]

While institutionalism, morality, and government declined, confidence in the self and a focus on the self accelerated. While the sixties were the age of secularism in which God had been shoved to the periphery of existence, the eighties and nineties rapidly shifted to a new era of self-focused spirituality. The focus on self, which Christopher Lasch had bemoaned in *The Culture of Narcissism: American Life in an Age of Diminishing Expectations* (1979), became increasingly prominent in the spirituality of the self, promulgated by the rise of the New Age movement, the new interest in Eastern religions, the new emphasis on psychology, and the restoration of ancient pagan religions.

In this context, a "pragmatic evangelicalism" was born. It has been enormously successful, producing twelve thousand megachurches, rivaling the spiritualities of the New Age, of Eastern religion, and paganism. Pragmatic evangelicalism has literally created a new face for evangelical Christianity, and, for the most part, the pragmatics have absorbed the relational evangelicals of the awakening period. Thus, until the arrival of the emerging church, evangelicalism had been primarily divided between the traditionalists and the pragmatists.

This widespread presence of pragmatic evangelicalism has made traditional evangelicalism look like a "throwback" to a "past era," and as the traditional church, its building, its worship, and its evangelism went into decline, so did its theology. It isn't that the megachurch and the new evangelicalism reputed the old theology; it was more a case of the *transference of interest*. The theological issues of traditional evangelicalism became nonissues. The megachurch, seeker tradition, contemporary worship, and the need-driven church became post-evangelical, at least post-traditional evangelical. So pragmatic evangelicalism, responding to the unraveling of society, created new practical solutions—corporate churches, entertainment worship, need-driven programs, therapeutic faith. Theology became irrelevant. Pragmatics became prominent. The divorce between theology and practice was complete. Traditionalists maintained their intellectual theology, their evidential apologetics, their propositionalism, and their foundationalism. Pragmatists, on the other hand, were concerned with practice, meeting the needs of the people through a pragmatic agenda. They have drawn hundreds of thousands of converts around the world. They have instituted numerous small groups for Bible study and accountability. Their churches are thriving, welcoming, hospitable places, open to all groups, serving the needs of broken families, single mothers, abused spouses, alcoholics, drug addicts, and the aged. And these churches are to be commended for these and other successes in meeting needs.

The issue here is not with the results of the pragmatic evangelical, but with the lack of a theological vision for ministry. Theology became lost in the privatization and narcissism of a Christianity that focused primarily on the needs of the self. From the perspective of the emerging church and the younger evangelicals, a Christianity shaped primarily on need, private interest, and self misses the point of a biblical and historic Christianity. And it is this matter that drives the emerging church leaders of the fourth turning.

### The Fourth Turning: The Emerging Church and the Younger Evangelical Leaders (2004–)

It now appears that a new *crisis* is upon the American culture and that the emerging church is responding to that crisis. We return once again to the beginning of the cycle of crisis, stability, revolution, and unraveling. The new crisis is fueled by the emergence of a postmodern, post-Christian, neo-pagan culture and the global war on terrorism.

Fourth turnings have always been times of great upheaval, a wrenching of the social order, and the development of a new order crafted out of the old. Fourth turnings in American history include the American Revolution (1773–1794), the Civil War (1860–1865), and the Great Depression and World War II (1929–1946).

According to Strauss and Howe, "The next fourth turning is due to begin shortly after the new millennium."[6] They observe that "values that were new in the 1960s are ... so intertwined with social dysfunction and cultural decay that they can no longer lead anywhere positive ... but in the crucible of crisis that will change.[7] However, in the [coming] fourth turning we can expect to encounter personal and public choices akin to the harshest ever faced by ancestral generations."[8] In the *unraveling* of the past era, "a hero generation is born." This generation leads the fourth turning that "ends one epoch and begins another."[9]

Is it possible that the arrival of a postmodern era and the advent of the war on terrorism throughout the world marked the beginning of a new fourth turning?

Should we understand the emerging church and its new younger evangelical leaders in the cultural context of the new *crisis*? We should recognize that the current well-known leaders of the emerging church that this book features are not Millennials (born after 1982). But for reasons of upbringing, education, ministerial experience, disposition, insight, and affinity with the younger generation, they find themselves "out of sorts" with both traditional evangelical scientific theology and the pragmatism of mega-evangelicalism. Considering the new cultural context and the evangelical pattern of responding to the changing cultural realities, it can then be said that the emerging church has the potential to establish a new kind of evangelicalism that will relate to the current cultural crisis. The emerging church will form a new evangelical identity marked by new insights, new concerns, and new patterns of theological application, worship, spirituality, and ministry. I say *may* because history is best interpreted after it happens. However, if the cycles of history presented by Strauss and Howe are true and continue in the same trajectory they have followed in the past, leaders of emerging churches may very well be poised to bring about a new threshold of development that will carry a new group of evangelicals beyond the unhappy split between traditional theology on the one hand and pragmatic practice on the other.

## Introducing the Contributors and Their Theological Perspectives

Mark Driscoll, pastor of Mars Hill Church in Seattle, makes the first contribution. I have titled his chapter "The Emerging Church and Biblicist Theology" because he refers to himself as a "devoted biblicist" and notes, to prove his point, that he supports his theology with more than seven hundred verses of Scripture. Like many other pastors of emerging churches, he rejects postmodern philosophies and methodologies in favor of a hard-hitting, text-proving argument for the Christian faith. He draws on Scripture to defend the traditional Protestant doctrines of scriptural authority, the Trinitarian nature of God, and the substitutionary atonement. He regards emerging pastors who treat these doctrines lightly or who seek to interpret them in a way different than traditional thought to be shaped by cultural thought, not by the narrative of the triune God. Mark represents a passionate adherence to the particulars of a Reformed evangelical theology, and in that sense, is not typically emerging. He is a theological traditionalist leading a cutting-edge church that ministers primarily to the new emerging generation.

The emphasis of John Burke in chapter 2, "The Emerging Church and Incarnational Theology" is found in his own personal experience of coming to faith. He writes, "They accepted and loved me despite my hedonistic life-style and badgering skeptical questions." Burke wants us to treat the lost the way he was treated, so he calls us to an incarnational ministry that impacts a "hurting broken world." Burke is a "practical theologian" who serves at Gateway Community Church in Austin, Texas. He wants to know how an incarnational ministry works, not as in a pragmatic philosophy, but as in a real theology, rooted in the authority of Scripture. How does Jesus meet people in their messiness and in their journey in other religions? How can we, American Christians who are so concerned about "our" theology, step out of our Western world and see God's action for the whole world? We can only do so through "grace-giving acceptance." So that "all kinds of messy people may just feel accepted." This concern to reach out to all kinds of people is a common thread found in all emerging churches, where a "come as you are and from where you are" mind-set is practiced intentionally and incarnationally. John's concern is primarily one of application. His theology is not a system, but a person. How can we become Jesus to others? This theme of incarnating the faith by reaching into the brokenness of life is also a common emerging theme.

Dan Kimball, the pastor of Vintage Faith Church in Santa Cruz, California, challenges us in chapter 3 to be a worshiping community of "missional theologians." Dan represents a branch of the emerging church that questions a "we have an answer to everything" mentality. He calls us to remain true to the essentials of the Christian faith, such as the Trinity, the authority of Scripture, the atonement, the resurrection, the second coming, and the summary of faith in the Nicene Creed. But he advocates "mystery" even in that which is affirmed, and he calls the church to an open-ended engagement with the Scriptures, so that each person becomes a "missional theologian" able to engage the people of a postmodern culture in their questions and searching. His call to search out the mystery of faith within community is a theme one will find in many emerging churches.

In chapter 4, Doug Pagitt from Solomon's Porch in Minneapolis presents an "embodied theology." He calls us to a critical assessment of those theologies that grow out of the gnostic separation of matter from the Spirit. Those are the theologies that have separated faith from life in the world. He calls us instead to construct theology out of God's story as it dynamically connects with our story. This theology is a life lived in harmony with God and with God's agenda for the world. It is a theology that is global, local, historic, futuristic; a theology that is temporary and contextual, participatory, Spirit-led, and life-giving. These characteristics of theology are particularly important for the day in which we live, for as we transition from a modern Newtonian worldview to a postmodern world dominated by the "Heisenberg uncertainty principle," the world faces new challenges that can only be answered out of a theology that lives in an embodied community of interpretation. Doug represents a post-evangelical theology, a commitment to God's story with an open mind toward the changes occurring in the postmodern world.

Karen Ward from Church of the Apostles in Seattle presents us with a communal theology in chapter 5. She wants to bridge the gap between the abstractions of traditional theology on the one hand and the communal practice of theology on the other. She wants us to live in the community of the Trinity, to live in the atonement and inside Scripture. She wants us to be read by theology, to bring theological thinking together with everyday practice so there is no divorce between the two. Karen's ministry is in a mainline church and represents a post-liberal emerging church.

Finally, in the conclusion I offer an assessment of emerging theology represented by the five contributors to this book. These five contributors are not scholarly theologians, but practitioners. All are currently engaged in ministry at the local church level. The question of this book is, "What kind of theological reflection motivates your ministry?" My conclusion is that the emerging church reflects a growing concern to bridge the gap between theory and practice. This gap currently separates evangelical traditionalists most deeply concerned about doctrine from the contemporary evangelical pragmatists who are most deeply committed to needs. The emerging church, I contend, is on a journey that may bring theological reflection and Christian practice together once again. In the pages of this book, you will see that journey unfolding in your reading. You will note that the book is not focusing on methods of emerging ministry, but rather on the beliefs of a representative group of pastors of emerging churches.

At the conclusion of each person's chapter, you will find a response by each of the other writers. These responses demonstrate the cordial relationship that exists among emerging thinkers. There is plenty of both agreement and disagreement. What you will find beneath all the interaction is that historic evangelical sense of unity in the essentials, freedom in nonessentials, and love in all things. Finally, the bibliography provides a reading list of recently published books as well as a few forthcoming works that represent emerging thinkers.

**ROBERT WEBBER**

CHAPTER

# THE EMERGING CHURCH AND BIBLICIST THEOLOGY

MARK DRISCOLL

# THE EMERGING CHURCH AND BIBLICIST THEOLOGY

## MARK DRISCOLL

During the mid-1990s, at the same time I founded Mars Hill Church in Seattle, I was part of what is now known as the emerging church in its embryonic days. Since that time I have been encouraged by the resurgent interest of doing missions in emerging American culture. I have also been greatly concerned by some of the aberrant theological concepts gaining popularity with some fellow emerging-type younger pastors.

This chapter is my attempt to address three of the hottest theological issues in our day and to correct emerging error with biblical orthodoxy. As a devoted biblicist I am seeking to be as faithful to Scripture as possible, which explains the many Scripture references in this chapter.*

I will explore what is arguably most distinctive about Christianity, namely the nature of God's revelation, the nature of God, and the means by which God has chosen to save some sinners. The topics the publisher chose for this book are the essential elements of the Christian gospel according to the apostle Paul, who said that the second member of the Trinity, Jesus Christ, atones for our sins by his death and resurrection in fulfillment of the Scriptures.[1]

As I studied these doctrines in preparation for writing this chapter, God the Holy Spirit devastated me regarding the atoning death of Jesus. I spent many nights awake while my wife and children slept; as I visualized the agony of Jesus' death for my sins, tears soaked the pages of my

---

*All Scripture quotations referenced by Mark Driscoll are from the *New International Version*.

Bible, the same one I was reading when saved in 1990. Before we begin, I would like to thank you for taking the time to read this chapter, and I apologize in advance for having to condense so much theology. As a pastor who deeply loves his people, I wish I had more space to tell you the stories of the thousands of lives God has tranformed through these great truths, but perhaps you will simply need to come and visit our church and meet them for yourself.

## How Does God Speak? Scripture.

No one is born with a clear comprehension of who God is. So, in an effort to know about God, various philosophers and religious leaders have presented their speculations about God with seemingly endless and contradictory declarations.

But God has chosen to lift the fog of human speculation with divine revelation. Whereas speculation is the human attempt to comprehend God, revelation is God's communication to humanity with clarity that is otherwise impossible. The object of that revelation is the sixty-six books of Scripture.

### What does Scripture say about Scripture?

Before arriving at a conclusive position about Scripture, it is fitting to first investigate what Scripture says about itself. If Scripture does not declare to be from God, without error, or helpful, then it is foolish to attribute something to Scripture that it does not claim for itself. The following list is a brief selection of some of the statements Scripture makes about itself:

> Nothing to be taken from or added to (Deut. 4:2; 12:32; Prov. 30:6)
> Effective (Isa. 55:11)
> Pure (Ps. 12:6; 119:140)
> Perfect (Ps.19:7)
> Precious (Ps. 19:10)
> A life guide (Ps. 119:105)
> Soul food (Jer. 15:16)
> A fire that purifies and a hammer that breaks us (Jer. 23:29)
> True (Ps.119:160; John 17:17)
> Helpful (Prov. 6:23)
> Flawless (Prov. 30:5)

To be obeyed (Luke 8:21; James 1:22)

All we need to know God (Luke 16:29, 31)

The standard by which all teaching is to be tested (Acts 17:11)

Faith-building (Rom. 10:17)

For everyone (Rom. 16:26)

Sin-cleansing (Eph. 5:26; James 1:21)

The sword for spiritual battle (Eph. 6:17; Heb. 4:12)

The very words of God (1 Thess. 2:13)

Divinely inspired (2 Tim. 3:16; 2 Peter 1:19–21)

Life-changing (Heb. 4:12)

Life-giving (James 1:18)

Spiritual nourishment (1 Peter 2:2)

Jesus is the key focus of Scripture and the most significant religious teacher in the history of the world. Therefore, it is also prudent to examine Jesus' view and use of Scripture along with the disciples', whom he trained as teachers.

Jesus summarized the Old Testament Scripture as existing in three parts: the Law, the Prophets, and the Psalms.[2] He accepted the Old Testament Canon as it exists today, without any modifications, and he came to fulfill it.[3]

Jesus treated Old Testament narratives as straightforward facts: Genesis 1 and 2,[4] Abel,[5] Noah,[6] Abraham,[7] Sodom and Gomorrah,[8] Lot,[9] Isaac and Jacob,[10] the manna,[11] the wilderness serpent,[12] Moses as lawgiver,[13] false prophets,[14] and Jonah.[15] Regarding authorship, Jesus said Scripture was given by Moses,[16] Isaiah,[17] David,[18] and Daniel.[19]

In matters of controversy, Jesus used the Old Testament as his court of appeals.[20] And in times of crisis, Jesus quoted Scripture.[21] Jesus repeatedly taught that Old Testament prophecy had been fulfilled because it was true.[22] Jesus taught that the Scriptures could not be broken.[23]

Jesus claimed that all Scripture, including the Law, the Prophets, and the Psalms, was fulfilled in him.[24] Jesus also said the primary purpose of the Old Testament was to reveal himself.[25]

Jesus promised that the Holy Spirit would inspire the writing of the Gospels and Epistles.[26] And he said that his people would recognize his teaching.[27] This is possible because the Holy Spirit who inspired the writing of Scripture also teaches it to God's people in whom he dwells.[28]

Following his return to heaven, Jesus' students wrote the remaining books of Scripture and likewise upheld Scripture as God's unique, perfect, authoritative, helpful, and powerful revelation to humanity. The New Testament writers claim that the Old Testament is sacred Scripture.[29] Furthermore, New Testament authors quote the Old Testament roughly three hundred times.

Paul used Scripture and God's spoken word interchangeably.[30] The New Testament teaches that what the Bible says is what God says.[31] And Peter and Paul claimed that Scripture has dual authorship by both men and God.[32]

Most New Testament writers were eyewitnesses of Jesus.[33] Others received firsthand information from other reliable witnesses. Luke received his information from Paul[34] and numerous eyewitnesses,[35] Mark received his information from Peter,[36] and James and Jude were closely associated with the apostles and were probably Jesus' brothers. Paul claimed that Jesus was speaking through him.[37] Paul quotes Luke as Scripture.[38] New Testament writers claimed that their writings were holy.[39] They said that their writings were the very words of God.[40] Peter called Paul's writings Scripture.[41] Paul commanded that his letters be read in the churches and obeyed.[42] And the early church treated the apostles' teaching as authoritative.[43]

Also, at the time of its writing, upward of one-quarter of Scripture was prophetic in nature, promising future events hundreds, even a thousand, years in advance. These facts include Jesus' virgin mother,[44] birth in Bethlehem,[45] flight to Egypt,[46] entrance into the temple that was destroyed in AD 70,[47] betrayal for thirty pieces of silver,[48] clothing divided by the casting of lots,[49] crucifixion,[50] death and burial in a rich man's tomb,[51] and resurrection from death.[52]

The Bible is clearly a book of history and not just philosophy, because it continually promises concrete historical events that, in time, come to pass exactly as promised. These fulfillments of prophetic promises show the divine inspiration of Scripture and prove that a sovereign God rules over human history and brings events to pass as he ordains them. Consequently, we can trust the internal consistency of the Bible to be a chorus of faithful witnesses who sing together in harmony. Nonetheless, not everyone accepts the teachings of Scripture.

### Why is there resistance to Scripture?

In the opening pages of Genesis, we see that the serpent sought to take the sword of God's Word out of the hands of our first parents to then slay them with their own blade. He did this not by rejecting God's Word, but rather by subtly seeking to change the meaning of God's Word. Today the serpent is up to his old tricks and is once again seeking to change the meaning of God's Word through a complicated philosophical grid of rules for textual interpretation. The following chart reduces otherwise very dense and complicated philosophical debates raging in our day to a simple overview in an effort to help you see the bottom line of what all the philosophical fuss is about.

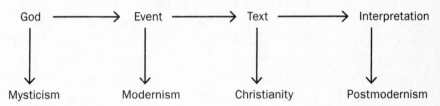

God    ⟶    Event    ⟶    Text    ⟶    Interpretation

Mysticism       Modernism       Christianity       Postmodernism

First, there is God. Those seeking to connect directly with God apart from such things as the mediation of Jesus Christ or the revelation of Scripture are guilty of non-Christian mysticism.

Second, the God of the Bible acts in events throughout human history, often miraculously. The problem with reading Scripture through modern lenses is that modernism is reticent to believe in the miraculous. Thus, modern interpreters attempt to explain supernatural events in natural terms. An example is the debate surrounding whether or not Jesus actually walked on water, or whether he walked on the shore of the water, giving the illusion that he actually walked on water. The ultimate problem with focusing on an event instead of Scripture, and examining it through modern naturalism, is that Scripture is called into question or rejected altogether.

Third, God has revealed what he has determined we need to know in the divinely inspired text of Scripture. Therefore, a proper Christian use of the Bible seeks to connect with God through understanding his person and work as recorded in Scripture. A Christian use of the Bible does not dismiss lower courts of authority such as experience, tradition, or archaeology, but reserves the clear teachings of Scripture as the metaphorical Supreme Court of final authority. Subsequently, if the Bible says Jesus walked on water, healed people, claimed he was God, and rose from death to prove his deity, then if people call themselves Christians, they are to believe these statements without modification.

Fourth, as we pick up the Bible, we must interpret the words in the text so we know their meaning. The best way to interpret Scripture is with

Scripture, since Scripture alone is perfect and the locus of final authority over us. And since Scripture instructs Christians to participate in a local church, the Scriptures themselves teach that they are best understood by being in Christian community. Also, since the church includes all saints from all ages, we are wise to study Scripture by learning from the great legacy of teachers who have gone before us, such as Athanasius, Augustine, Calvin, and Wesley.

But postmodern uses of the Bible are prone to impose on the text cultural meanings and desires that ignore or alter the meaning of the Scripture altogether. In doing so, the interpreter is elevated in authority over the text of Scripture, no longer humbly coming under Scripture, but instead rising up arrogantly over it, much like the serpent tempted our first parents with the hermeneutical question, "Did God really say ...?" For example, perhaps the most blatant postmodern use of Scripture is the growing "Christian" defense of homosexuality.

Therefore, the key to properly understanding Scripture is to come with a humility that is willing to repent of sin and reorient life toward God's commands.

### Why does our view of Scripture matter?

The opening line of Scripture introduces us to its hero, God. Throughout its pages, Scripture reveals this God. In the closing line of Scripture, we are reminded that the God who is the hero of the true story of Scripture is Jesus Christ. Thus, the written Word of God reveals to us the incarnate Word of God, Jesus Christ. And without the written Word, we cannot rightly know the incarnate Word. Therefore, our view of Scripture matters, because without a proper understanding of Scripture, we cannot truly know and love the real Jesus. In the next section we will more closely examine the Trinitarian community that he came to reveal to us.

## Who Is the God of Scripture? Trinity.

The Christian revelation of God is distinct from and superior to all other views of God. This point is controversial in our age but incredibly important for Christians to retain if we hope to maintain the uniqueness of our Christian faith.

Trinitarianism is the Christian teaching that there is one God who exists as three persons, Father, Son, and Spirit. While the word "Trinity" does not appear in Scripture, the concept very clearly does. The church father Tertullian (AD 155–220) was the first to use the word "Trinity."

## What does Scripture say about the Trinity?

To say that God exists as a Trinity does not mean that there are three Gods, or that one God merely manifests himself as either Father, Son, or Holy Spirit on various occasions. To say that God exists as a Trinity is to say that there is one God with a unified essence, who exists in three equal persons, Father, Son, and Holy Spirit. By person, it is meant that God thinks, feels, acts, and speaks. The Westminster Confession of Faith (1647) says, "In the unity of the Godhead there be three persons of one substance, power, and eternity: God the Father, God the Son, and God the Holy Ghost."

In addition to belief in only one God, Trinitarianism also recognizes the biblical teaching that the Father, Son, and Spirit are each eternally God. Throughout the Scriptures, the Father is unequivocally called God.[53]

Jesus Christ is clearly called God throughout Scripture.[54] The Scriptures are also clear that Jesus was fully human.[55]

The Holy Spirit is God throughout the Scriptures. He is all-powerful,[56] eternal,[57] all-knowing,[58] creator,[59] and all-present.[60] In the New Testament, he is also clearly declared God.[61] The Holy Spirit is not merely an impersonal force, but a person who can be grieved,[62] resisted,[63] and insulted.[64]

Additionally, though God the Father, Son, and Spirit are one, the Father and Son are two distinct persons in salutations of New Testament letters[65] as well as in other Scriptures.[66] Scripture also says that Jesus and the Holy Spirit are not the same person.[67] Likewise, the Father is not the Holy Spirit.[68]

Two of the more helpful places in Scripture where we see the Trinity at work are the baptism of Jesus and the work of salvation. At Jesus' baptism, God the Father spoke from heaven about Jesus who was coming up out of the water while the Holy Spirit descended upon him like a dove.[69] Regarding salvation, it was God the Father who predestined us,[70] God the Son who died for our sins to secure our salvation, and God the Spirit who sealed us as God's possession.

## Why is there resistance to the Trinity?

There is resistance to the doctrine of the Trinity because of the pressure from our pluralistic culture for all religions to sand off their edges and arrive at a vague spirituality that is shallow enough to embrace all faiths. But the fact remains that Jesus Christ is distinct from and superior to all other religious leaders and their religions, and philosophers and their philosophies.

| Name | Belief | Adherents |
|------|--------|-----------|
| Atheism | There is no God or gods/goddesses. | Marxists, naturalists, pure materialists |
| Agnosticism | It cannot be known whether or not there is a God or gods/goddesses. | Rationalist philosophers such as David Hume and Immanuel Kant |
| Pantheism | Everything in the material world is God. | Paganism, some forms of New Age spirituality |
| Polytheism | There are many gods/goddesses. | Buddhists, Hindus, Mormons, religious pluralists |
| Monotheism | There is only one God. | Jews, Muslims |
| Trinitarianism | There is one God in three persons, Father, Son, and Spirit. | Christians |

Additionally, the Bible says that any "gods" other than the one true God are not "gods" at all.[71] However, demons may also pose as gods and elicit worship, possibly even through counterfeit signs, wonders, and miracles.[72]

Lastly, the refutation to all false views of God is the incarnation of God, Jesus Christ, which disproves the atheist denial of God, the agnostic denial that God can be known, the pantheist claim that creation is God, the polytheist claim that there are many gods, and the monotheistic claim that God is anyone other than Jesus.

## Why does our view of the Trinity matter?

There are multiple reasons why the doctrine of the Trinity is essential to the Christian faith. But perhaps three reasons are most urgent to note in our day.

First, the doctrine of the Trinity reveals a God who exists as a loving community throughout eternity. And since we are made in the image of the Trinitarian God, if we lose the doctrine of the Trinity, we lose the root system from which we nourish community, love, and friendship.

Second, the doctrine of the Trinity helps to safeguard Christianity from being reduced to yet another world religion because our God is uniquely distinct.

Third, because Jesus is the "image of the invisible God," if we lose the Trinity we also lose Jesus Christ.[73] In the next section we will transition from who God is to what God has accomplished through the death of Jesus.

## Why Did Jesus Die on the Cross? Atonement.

Many people warmly recollect the kind deeds of Jesus, such as healing the sick, caring for the poor, and feeding the hungry. Many people also appreciate Jesus' teachings related to doing good deeds and being loving. But it is the death of Jesus and what it accomplished that is the most controversial aspect of Jesus' life and ministry, because it is the most important.

### What does Scripture say about Jesus' atonement?

To understand the doctrine of Jesus' death on the cross, also known as the atonement, we must connect it to the doctrines of God's character, God's creation, human sin, and the responses of God to sin and sinners. To do this we will briefly examine four essential truths of Scripture.

**Truth 1: We are sinful.** All of the individual and corporate shortcomings of God's perfect intentions for creation, whether intentional or unintentional, or through omission or commission, qualify as sin or the effects of sin. The first sin was committed by Satan,[74] who led a rebellion against God.[75] After Satan and demons were cast out of heaven, Satan tempted our first parents, Adam and Eve, to join his sinful rebellion against God. Adam was the representative and father of humankind, and when he sinned and fell out of favor with God, so did every person who would ever live.[76]

Every person since Adam is a sinner, both by nature and by choice.[77] Everyone (except Jesus Christ) is, from conception, sinful by nature and corrupt to the very core of their being, and therefore incapable of doing anything that pleases God.[78] Thus, everyone (except Jesus Christ)[79] sins [80] by breaking God's holy laws[81] because they are sinners in their hearts.[82]

The fall was the descent of the human race and the rest of creation[83] into a state of rebellion against God. Despite depravity, we retain dignity because we remain image-bearers of God even though that image is marred by sin.[84] This marring includes the mind,[85] the will,[86] the emotions,[87] and the physical body.[88]

While unredeemed people are not absolutely sinful (they could do evil things with greater degree and frequency), they are totally sinful in that their every motive, word, deed, and thought is for their glory rather than God's.[89] Consequently, those who do not belong to God are incapable of pleasing God.[90]

**Truth 2: God is holy and just.** In saying that God is holy, Scripture teaches that God is absolutely separate from any evil.[91] In saying that God is just, Scripture teaches that he must deal with sin and sinners and does so justly.[92]

**Truth 3: God hates sin.** Scripture plainly says that God does not delight in sin,[93] hates and detests sin,[94] and hides his face from sinful people.[95] Scripture also teaches that God is so profoundly troubled by sin that he feels both sorrow[96] and anger over sin.[97]

God's hatred of sin has been explained with the glib statement that God hates sin but loves sinners. And while Scripture does declare God's universal love for all people, it also says that God hates some unrepentant sinners.[98]

**Truth 4: God deals with all sinners and sin through Jesus.** In examining the accomplishment(s) of Jesus' death and resurrection, it is essential that we embrace the totality of what Scripture says on the subject, rather than slip into the sin of reductionism. Reductionism occurs when one aspect of Jesus' work on the cross is presented by itself at the expense of clearly seeing the totality of his work and all aspects of what he accomplished. The atonement is the great jewel of our faith, and like all jewels, it has many glorious sides that I will briefly explain.

- Jesus died in the place of sinners, sometimes called penal substitution.[99] Though Jesus was sinless,[100] he died for our sin,[101] and death is the penalty for sin.[102]
- Jesus' death and resurrection prove his divinity.[103]
- Jesus died to ransom many people.[104]
- Jesus died as the new covenant sacrifice.[105]
- Jesus died to forgive sins.[106]
- Jesus died to accomplish the justice of God.[107]
- Jesus died to reveal the glory of God.[108]
- Jesus died to demonstrate the love of God.[109]
- Jesus died for God's good pleasure.[110]
- Jesus died to reveal the wisdom and power of God.[111]
- Jesus died to justify sinners.[112]
- Jesus died to propitiate God's wrath and expiate our sin.[113]
- Jesus died to redeem sinners[114] from sin,[115] condemnation,[116] the curse of the law,[117] the Mosaic code,[118] and Satan and demons.[119]
- Jesus died to reconcile people to God and each other.[120]
- Jesus died to triumph over Satan, demons, sin, and the world.[121]
- Jesus died to ransom sinners by paying their debt to God.[122]

- Jesus died to take our sin and impute his righteousness to us.[123]
- Jesus died as our example for holy living.[124]
- Jesus died to take all people as his possession, known variously as unlimited atonement, Arminianism, or Wesleyanism.[125]
- Jesus died to forgive the sins of the elect, which is known as Calvinism or limited atonement. This point is expressed in varying ways, such as Jesus died for many people but not all people,[126] Jesus died only for his sheep,[127] his church,[128] the elect,[129] his people,[130] his friends,[131] and all Christians.[132]

At first glance, the positions of unlimited and limited atonement are in opposition. But that dilemma is easily resolved by noting two things. First, the two categories are not mutually exclusive. Because Jesus died for the sins of everyone, that means he also died for the sins of the elect. Second, Jesus' death for all people does not accomplish the same thing as his death for the elect. This point is complicated, but is, in fact, taught in Scripture. First Timothy 4:10 says, "we have put our hope in the living God, who is the Savior of all men, and especially of those who believe." And 2 Peter 2:1 teaches that Jesus bought heretics whom he will judge and destroy, saying, "But there were also false prophets among the people, just as there will be false teachers among you. They will secretly introduce destructive heresies, even denying the sovereign Lord who bought them—bringing swift destruction on themselves."

Simply by dying for everyone, Jesus purchased everyone as his possession, and he then graciously forgives the elect who repent of sin and applies his wrath to the non-elect who are unrepentant of their sin. As a result, Jesus' death was sufficient to save anyone and only efficient to save those who repent of their sin and trust in him. Therefore, Calvinists like me do not believe anything different than our Arminian brothers and sisters; we simply believe what they believe and more. I call this position unlimited limited atonement. And regarding this point, I do believe it is a secondary matter and don't fuss with faithful Christians over it.

In summary, the accomplishments of Jesus' death are multiple and not singular, and thereby defy reductionism. And while some people struggle to reconcile the varying aspects of the atonement, such work is unneeded because the purposes of the atonement are complementary and not contradictory. Having established the objective reasons for Jesus' death and resurrection, we will now examine the subjective reasons why some people reject his atonement.

## Why is there resistance to the atonement?

Scripture plainly predicts that the death of Jesus on a cross for our sins would be seen by many as both foolish[133] and offensive,[134] particularly to those who are enemies of the cross.[135] As promised, questions are raised today challenging the acceptability of the scriptural teachings about the atonement:

- Is the notion that we are evil sinners offensive to "good" people?
- Is the belief that the Father saved us through the Son sexist?
- Is the Father punishing the Son an endorsement of child abuse?
- Is God a sadist and Jesus the willing masochist?
- Does our world need an angry and violent God?
- Does Jesus' willingness to suffer excuse abuse?

Subsequently, since offending someone is perhaps the most scandalous of present-day cultural "sins," and many Christians don't want to sound foolish talking about the sinless, homeless Jesus who was God, born to a virgin in a barn, and who died for their evil existence, there is always an attempt by some to give Jesus an extreme makeover so that he is more trendy with the times. Paul foresaw this error and warned us against seeking to alter the gospel to please non-Christians,[136] because some people are destined to trip over Jesus and not be saved.[137] Instead of ignoring the cross or substituting another symbol for our faith, God's people are to boast in the cross[138] unashamedly[139] because we are simply fools for Christ.[140]

What I find particularly troubling is the attempt by some pastors and teachers to dismiss the plain, literal meaning of Scripture through what has come to be known as a trajectory hermeneutic, or a redemptive historical hermeneutic. These terms simply mean that the Bible borrowed its concepts from pagan culture and that Christianity was syncretized with pagan beliefs. But since our culture has evolved beyond the primitive times of the Bible, we are well served to form a new theology to accommodate present-day pagan culture so Jesus is more acceptable and less offensive. Summarily, since all theology is culturally embedded, no truth is binding on all peoples, times, and places. In short, this is theological evolution that believes much of Scripture is primitive and no longer fitting for people who are more advanced, refined, and embarrassed by such things as gender roles and the violence that litters Scripture.

For example, I have argued with some well-known pastors who believe that redemption was a theory taken from the pagan slave market. But the Bible clearly teaches that the concept of redemption is not taken from paganism, but rather from Exodus, where the real God crushed Pharaoh and the false gods of Egypt to liberate his people and allow them to worship him freely.[141]

Some also argue that propitiation was a pagan concept whereby the capricious pagan gods had to be appeased and kept happy with offerings and sacrifices (sometimes human), and Jesus therefore was shown to have died to appease the angry wrath of a mean God. Again, Scripture says that God alone created blood sacrifice for forgiveness of sins, negating any relation to paganism. In the great chapter on atonement, Leviticus 17, God says, "I have given it to you to make atonement" (v. 11).

Paul, like Moses, is emphatic that the gospel message of Jesus' death for our sins[142] is not something he made up or borrowed from pagan culture, but instead the result of divine revelation from God alone.[143] The gospel message comes from God to the culture, but does not emanate in any way from the culture, though it must be effectively communicated to all cultures. Because of this, the truth of the gospel is binding on all peoples, times, and places. Any gospel that does emanate from or that accommodates pagan culture is a false gospel with demonic inspiration.[144]

The curious paradox of the atoning death of a bloody Jesus rising above the plane of human history with a mocking crown of thorns is that he is offensive in an attractive way. It is the utter horror of the cross that cuts through the chatter, noise, and nonsense of our day to rivet our attention, shut our mouths, and compel us to listen to an impassioned dying man who is crying out for the forgiveness of our sins and to ask why he suffered. Tragically, if we lose the offense of the cross, we also lose the attraction of the cross so that no one is compelled to look at Jesus. Therefore, Jesus does not need a marketing firm or a makeover as much as a prophet to preach the horror of the cross unashamedly.

## Why does our view of the atonement matter?

Salvation is defined as deliverance by God from God and his wrath.[145] As we survey the Old Testament, we find more than twenty words used to express "wrath" as it applies to Yahweh. These are used so frequently that there are nearly six hundred occurrences to consider. A survey of the New Testament also reveals God's wrath, though with less frequency.[146]

God is holy and righteous, and our sins against him cause his wrath to burn against us, which can continue forever.[147] Nonetheless, in his mercy, God does grant salvation. Salvation is solely a work of God.[148] And salvation is only possible in this life, with no possibility of salvation after death through such things as reincarnation.[149] Salvation is made possible through Jesus Christ alone and there is no possibility of salvation apart from him.[150]

From God's perspective, salvation is accomplished by God choosing some people for salvation.[151] From our perspective, salvation is accomplished by repenting of sin and turning to Jesus Christ in faith.[152] Salvation is accomplished by God's grace alone.[153] The result of salvation is a life lived to be increasingly like Jesus until we see him face to face.

However, not everyone will spend eternity in heaven with Jesus. Jesus speaks of hell more than anyone else in Scripture and plainly states that non-Christians will be in hell as long as Christians will be in heaven. Echoing Daniel 12:2, Jesus says, "Then they will go away to eternal punishment, but the righteous to eternal life."[154]

Logically, a sin against an eternal God is an eternal offense requiring an eternal payment. And this payment will either be made by God's enemies in eternal hell,[155] or by the life, death, and resurrection of Jesus our eternal God.

Some, however, will argue that God should save all people. But God has the right to give grace as he determines[156] and has done so throughout history.[157] Some will accuse God of being unfair, but if God were completely fair rather than merciful, then *all* would go to hell and none would go to heaven as is the case with fallen angels who have no possibility of salvation.[158]

While the postmodern fascination with the present has caused some to dismiss the importance of eternal destiny, Scripture has no such shortsightedness. For the purposes of brevity, the following Old Testament truths about hell are worthy of note:

- Hell is unending, conscious, loathsome torment.[159]
- Heaven and hell will have people in them forever.[160]

Also, Jesus had much to say about hell, including the following:

- The pain in hell will be excruciating, causing "weeping and gnashing of teeth."[161]
- The torture in hell comes from Jesus.[162]
- Jesus is coming to throw people into the fiery furnace of hell.[163]
- The physical pain of hell is like being burned in a fire.[164]
- Unrepentant sinners will be thrown into a fiery hell.[165]

- Hypocrites will be butchered and spend eternity in pain.[166]
- God will send unbelievers to the same fate as Satan and demons.[167]
- Jesus said the eternal torment of Isaiah 66:22–24 is literally coming.[168]
- The punishment of hell is like a painful beating.[169]
- Hell is a place of unending torment.[170]

Lastly, the apostles also speak of hell in the following terms:

- Jesus will repay unrepentant sinners with everlasting destruction.[171]
- Jesus today holds the unrighteous in punishment.[172]
- Jesus will rule over hell as well as heaven.[173]
- Hell is like spending eternity in a fiery lake of burning sulfur.[174]

In conclusion, the Bible is one story about the Trinitarian God who created us, mercifully endures our sin, and sent Jesus Christ to live and die in our place, thereby saving us from eternal wrath if we repent of sin and trust in him alone. This is the true gospel revealed to us by God through Scripture.

What is at stake is nothing less than the gospel of Jesus Christ and people's eternal destinies. If in our day culture rises up in authority over Scripture in the church, any god rises up other than the Trinity, and any gospel is preached other than the death and resurrection of Jesus for our sins, then we literally have hell to pay for emerging into false teachers with false doctrines, false gods, and false gospels that assure false hope.

Some people will argue that these traditional doctrines are no longer useful in our postmodern age of pluralism. Yet I can assure you that after preaching on these themes for ten years in one of America's youngest, most liberal, and least Christian cities, that the unchanging gospel is still changing lives, especially those of young lost people. For example, I preached a three-month series on the atonement with the sermons lasting well over an hour, and I saw our attendance swell by over eight hundred in the first three weeks as people wept throughout the sermons, confessed their sins, and gave their lives to Jesus.[175]

Likewise, more than one hundred churches planted across the country through our Acts 29 Network are seeing tens of thousands of lives changed by these doctrines.[176] Therefore, a new theology does not need to emerge, but rather a renewed faith in and passion for the timeless truths of Scripture that empower us to live like Jesus for the benefit of other people.

# RESPONSE TO MARK DRISCOLL

## JOHN BURKE

I think Mark just made this book worth buying. Not that the rest of our chapters have no value, but when I think about the theology of the emerging church and the challenge of ministering in a postmodern context, I realize we must remember who it is we represent and how we form our Christian beliefs. Mark has done a great job laying out for us some key foundational beliefs on which to build churches that can hold out hope to our broken world. We don't all have to agree on the nuances of every doctrine (Mark and I differ on some), but we must decide whether we will appeal to Scripture as our primary source of truth about God. If not, are we truly following the way of Christ?

As Mark states, a Christian use of the Bible does not dismiss lower courts of authority, such as experience, tradition, community, or science, but Scripture acts as the final court of appeals. Not just because the Bible claims to be from God, but also because God has done something concrete in history to verify that these are indeed his authoritative words that will not pass away—and this is the main point I try to make in my chapter.

I don't think Mark is saying there is no room for doubt or questioning, but I can hear people reacting against him with this concern. While I agree with most everything Mark is saying in principle, one of the past abuses of Scripture the emerging church reacts against is the inability to allow people space and time to process beliefs. I wonder if some emerging leaders distance themselves from Scripture as a reaction against a misuse of God's Word—using the Bible in a defensive or aggressive way or browbeating people into unquestioning belief-compliance for the sake of being "true to Scripture."

The emerging church must find its way through the narrow straits of following truth in a postmodern world by holding to the most clear, compelling revelation from God available—that found in the Bible. I've read the scriptures of most of the world's religions, and no other gives prophetic, historical confirmation of its words. Yet we must avoid using the Bible in pharisaical ways that produce nothing but stale religiosity and more isolated Christian subcultures. Mark has done a masterful job concisely articulating some critical beliefs, but the emerging church must build on this foundation beyond belief-compliance.

This is why it is important that we provide space and room for questioning theology, yet direct one another back to Scripture in doing so. Beliefs are important, as Dallas Willard points out in *The Divine Conspiracy*. But assenting to the correct doctrinal beliefs alone can create that stench of the Pharisees if we're not careful, because what people *say* they believe is not always what they *actually* believe. Maybe the reason our generation seeks God through Buddhism or Eastern mysticism before considering Christianity is because so many professed Christians don't actually believe what they say they believe. They say, "Lord, Lord," but don't do the Lord's will (Luke 6:46). Ultimately, how we live reveals what we truly believe.

Mark challenges the emerging church to return to beliefs that Scripture articulates, and I agree with this challenge. But the test of our theology (beliefs) must be relational, not propositional. Jesus said that all the commandments of Scripture can be summed up in two: Love God and love people. Now, what that actually means is far beyond what our society's definition of "love" can encompass, but it still requires that we test the effectiveness of our beliefs through a grid of relationship. Would people close to me say I love God and follow his Spirit humbly and willingly more this year than last year? Would the people I live with say I'm becoming a more life-giving person to be around? If not, what good are our propositional beliefs?

Jesus said we can't change ourselves into the loving, joyful, peace-filled beings God created us to be: "I am the vine; you are the branches. If you remain in me and I in you, you will bear much fruit; apart from me you can do nothing" (John 15:5). So God causes the growth, as Paul reminds us in 1 Corinthians 3, but we create the soil or environment that either allows or hinders spiritual growth ["We are God's co-workers," Paul says (v. 9)]. But as Willard points out, we are creatures of habit, and unless we utilize disciplines and relationships to form new habits by which we will more readily "stay connected" in our moment of impatience or arrogance or self-promotion or judgmentalism, we won't change.

This is why beliefs, true beliefs that are formed in the cauldron of questioning and wrestling with Scripture in community, are so important.

Spiritual character is developed by responding to God. This response is influenced by habits, which are formed by practices, which come from beliefs. Beliefs form our practices. You can claim propositionally that God is sovereign and quote the five points of Calvinism, but if you worry about not having enough money when you actually have more than 95 percent of humanity, you don't believe Jesus' words in Matthew 6, that if you seek God's kingdom, you have nothing to worry about—but you can't help it, it's habitual. So your practice of obsessing over how to get more reinforces the habit of worry, and it keeps you from responding to God's Spirit.

I point this out because Mark has done a masterful job pointing us back to the source of our beliefs as Christ-followers. But we must continually help one another go beyond propositional assent to those beliefs (scripturally sound doctrine) to make sure we don't say "Lord, Lord," yet fail to practice what Jesus said. We must allow people space to question and struggle with beliefs, and we must help people understand why God's truth is good and beautiful and beneficial. Then we will truly believe God's words and put them into practice, and he will grow us up in love.

I know Mark came to faith living far from God and his church. He became convinced of the truths of Scripture and the way of Jesus without having the baggage of past church abuses to drag along behind him. Sometimes I wonder if the emerging leaders who are distancing themselves from Scripture are doing so more in reaction to a fundamentalist background that perhaps smelled more pharisaical than of the life-giving aroma of Christ.

I didn't grow up with that baggage, so I don't understand it completely. But as Mark has said, we cannot turn away from the revelation of God or some of the clear teachings of Scripture (and yes, some of what Mark has laid out we will not all agree on and can wrestle with for the rest of time, while maintaining unity in the faith). But we must also not fall into the trap of the educational model, thinking that teaching and testing assent to correct doctrine yields fruit—it alone does not.

I think this is the narrow strait the emerging church must navigate through our postmodern world. We must prayerfully lead our churches to produce people whose beliefs make them fiercely alive with God, not veering too far right into the rigidity of pharisaism, not steering too far left to find ourselves shipwrecked on the wide beach of postmodern relativism. "Instead, we will hold to the truth in love, becoming more and more in every way like Christ, who is the head of his body, the church ... so that the whole body is healthy and growing and full of love" (Ephesians 4:15–16 NLT).

# RESPONSE TO
# MARK DRISCOLL

## DAN KIMBALL

Sharing a little of what I know of Mark will explain what I think of his chapter. I first met Mark in 1997 when I picked him up at the San Jose Airport. He was one of the speakers at Leadership Network's "Gen X 2.0" event, and it was my job to make shuttle runs to the airport. As I began chatting with Mark in the car, I sensed he was not the usual type of pastor but stood out among other church leaders. He shared how he had recently launched a brand new church, which at that time already had around two hundred people. Within the space of a forty-minute ride, Mark shared how he also was taking a class at a seminary, and how by the end of the course, he was actually helping to teach. We talked a little about theology, his personal viewpoint as a Reformed Calvinist, and what his church believed. This introduction to Mark led me to conclude that he is a very sharp, intelligent thinker, one who jumped into talking about theology very naturally. At the same time, Mark was not just a theological thinker cloistered into a Christian subculture, but he was very aware of our emerging culture. I discovered during our drive that we both appreciated the band Social Distortion, and that he was quite savvy on many of the bands on the music scene today.

About a year later, my wife and I visited Mars Hill Church in Seattle for the worship gathering one Sunday night, and afterward we went out to dinner with Mark. At that time, the church was meeting in a rented building with around four hundred people, double the size from the year before. I looked at some of the church literature revealing their conservative Reformed theology, and I believe some of what was written back then is very similar to what is actually written in Mark's chapter here. Another time soon after that, we were both speaking at an event in Anaheim, and as we were driving to dinner with some others, a theological topic came up on which I disagreed with Mark (I think it was something about the five points of Calvinism). He jokingly said, "Kimball, don't make me jump back there and slap you." If I had kept pressing and arguing, I wouldn't doubt he would have leapt into the backseat and actually fulfilled what he threatened me with! Mark certainly takes his theology very seriously.

Recently I was in Seattle again and met Mark at the fairly new and large Mars Hill Church campus and saw where several thousand people now worship each week. I couldn't help but envy the building's creative design. Mark pointed out yet another building nearby that they were purchasing for expansion. We went out to dinner and got caught up in the conversation and even talked a little theology.

Much had happened at his church since that first encounter in the van nine years earlier. As I listened to the thrilling stories of how lives were being changed in his church, it was the same Mark with the same intelligence, the same zeal and passion for Scripture, and the same passion for evangelism. Because of this passion, and in order to communicate his Reformed theological beliefs, he has contextualized them into today's culture. So, as I read his chapter, I saw the same steadfastness and consistency in his beliefs and felt like I was once again hearing Mark talk from 1997. Perhaps the only difference is that he now has more solidity and clarity with a much larger church. He is Reformed to the core, and as long as I have known him, nothing seems to change in this regard.

I fully resonate with Mark's beliefs on core doctrine that aligns with the Nicene Creed. We both have a very strong passion for evangelism and for those outside the faith. We both beat the drum of those in the church being missionaries right here and now—not just overseas. When I hear Mark speak or write about this, it feels like he is reading my mind and heart. However, I don't necessarily feel the same as Mark about the extent of certainty and steadfastness in other theological systems, such as a locked-in system of Calvinism and all that comes with it. Augustine and Calvin were coming from distinct cultural backdrops, and we cannot forget how culture shaped their writing and conclusions. I admit that it must be comforting to have such detailed doctrinal opinions with a specific theological system, but it can also be a weakness if taken to the extreme and held with absolute certainty. I love what theologian Ben Witherington III states in his book *The Problem with Evangelical Theology*:

> The Augustinian-Lutheran-Calvinist juggernaut kept Evangelicalism focused on soteriology or the way of salvation. Dispensationalism renewed our focus on and thinking about the future in eschatological ways. Wesleyanism/

Pentecostalism stressed the experiential dimensions of Christian thought and life and the need for holiness of heart and life. However, each of these contributions came at a price—individualism and determinism in the case of the Augustinian heritage; systematic ahistoricism in the case of Dispensational reading of prophecy; and the raising of experience to a norm, sometimes even above the Bible, in the case of Wesleyanism/Pentecostalism.[1]

Witherington believes that when we take extreme theological positions on anything, the extreme part of it actually is the weakest part of the theological system. (You will have to read Witherington's book to get the details and full argument.) I agree with the historical core beliefs Mark lists. However, when we go beyond core beliefs with such certainty about a specific system of theology that was developed a long time after the Nicene Creed, that is where we differ. I lean toward more historic Nicene Creed orthodoxy, and I still remain overall conservative in my theology. Yet I do allow mystery and exploration in some areas of theological belief.

Despite some disagreement, I highly respect what God has done through Mark's leadership in the way so many people in Seattle have put their faith in Jesus. It is amazing and thrilling to hear those stories of people becoming disciples of Jesus and having their lives changed by the Spirit. Mark's passion for seeing his church become a church of "missionaries" is something that ignites my heart, and I look forward to hearing even more stories in the future of how God will be working through the people of Mars Hill Church. Mark is a brother in Jesus and a friend. Through the years, I have gotten to know the personal and compassionate side of Mark, which occasionally can be overshadowed by his abrasive communication style. We both also like wearing black, which increases my sense of kinship with him.

# RESPONSE TO MARK DRISCOLL

## DOUG PAGITT

At times I found it difficult to read Mark's chapter.

Mark and I have known one another for more than eight years. I have stayed at his house, held his children, worked on events with him, and learned from him. But we are very different on many things, most notably this discussion on theology, theological method, and understanding.

In the time I have known Mark, I have not seen his theology change; it has hardened in some ways but is basically the same as when I met him. Much of what is in his chapter I had seen in material at his church in the late 1990s. And it is familiar to me from my study of systematic theology in seminary. Mark has refined the Reformed tradition into distinctive patterns of thought. This is clear to me in his use of charts and binary conclusions ("if this, then that"). I will not get into specific differences but will simply say that we see the Bible differently and the role of Christianity in the world differently.

Mark places great emphasis on Christianity's explanation of God's effort to save sinners. He says, "I will explore what is arguably most distinctive about Christianity, namely the nature of God's revelation, the nature of God, and the means by which God has chosen to save some sinners."

So, for Mark, that serves as the unifying theological concept of his perspective, and as he wrote, he built into and from that presupposition. I find God's hopes, dreams, and plans for the world to include the eradication of sin and freedom for humankind through Jesus, but those are not the primary point of the gospel. Mark and I have discussed these matters, so I know he will disagree with me on this and even feel that I am not hearing him accurately. I think much of our difference comes from the fact that in many ways we are telling different stories of Christianity. We seem to be calling for different starting and ending points. This could be reason to just turn from one another and part ways, but I am not choosing that path. I feel that we need to engage with one another, even through the difficulty that accompanies such an effort.

This difficulty does not mean we cannot express our differences. We just need to do so without harmful innuendo or divisive intent, but we do need to share openly and plainly our perspectives (remembering always that even our most firmly held beliefs were formed in a certain context and situation, and therefore are perspectival, though Mark would perhaps disagree with that assumption).

I will mention a few areas of concern that haunted me in my reading of Mark's chapter.

I am troubled by Mark's use of the Bible in what seems to be reference approach. Placing Bible passages in and around an argument is not in and of itself a proper way of being informed by the Scriptures. Because I have familiarity with Mark's way of thinking, it is easy for me to be cynical, finding weakness too easily. I will not go further other than to point out that declaring oneself a "devout biblicist" does not mean that one uses the Bible in an appropriate manner. Laying claim to part of the Bible as support for one's theological perspective needs to be done in a careful manner. Mark and I might well differ on the appropriateness of his doing so in this chapter.

I also have concern about Mark's feeling that he needs to and is equipped to correct the theological faults of others, saying, "This chapter is my attempt to address three of the hottest theological issues in our day and to correct emerging error with biblical orthodoxy."

Why does Mark feel that it is his job to do the correcting? To really consider this a legitimate option would mean that he would be "correct" on these matters, and that all who think more broadly on such issues of Scripture and atonement are in his care to correct. This is a ludicrous assumption.

I have concern about Mark's view of the broader church and church history. The way he presents his ideas is to assume that any other view is in error. The truth of the matter is that most Christians in history do not hold the views presented in this chapter. This would mean that all those other views are not biblical and are in severe error. This troubles me and does not match what I see in the world today or am familiar with in the history of people of Christian faith.

Less importantly, his view does not seem to be changing or changeable. Mark writes that theology is a different task from reading the Scriptures, to which I agree. But at the same time, he suggests that any cultural influence on our understanding of the Bible is akin to the "serpent ... up to his old tricks ... once again seeking to change the meaning of God's Word through a complicated philosophical grid of rules for textual interpretation." This seems to me to suggest a "The Bible says it, I believe it, that settles it" approach.

I think such a view denies the reality of the development of language and the pressures of culture. I am not advocating a postmodern reading of the Bible for everyone (unless that is your culture and then there is nothing more one can do), but I am suggesting that people cannot legitimately operate with no cultural lens. It is troubling to suggest that those who do read the Bible in context are being deceived. I guess Mark's thinking would hinge on the "complexity of the rules," but he does not seem to have trouble with the complex cultural issues of the third or fifteenth centuries, which were marked by the development of Augustinian-Neo-Platonic thought and the cultural issues of the Reformers—they were certainly not doing theology in a culturally neutral environment. I understand that the "Read the Bible and get the meaning" approach is part of Mark's own personal history of faith, but that does not give it credibility as a theological system.

Finally, Mark's approach seems to be filled with issues of power. I found a sense of struggle in it, struggle for things to be set, to be a certain way, for one view to win. This concerns me, for I believe that such a way of seeing the world so often oppresses people who think differently or are different from us. This view represents to me the kind of thing that makes Christianity unattractive and impotent to all outsiders. And I do not think this is a case where the gospel is offensive. The offensiveness of this view may have little to do with the gospel and more to do with one view of the gospel in competition with all other understandings.

I do hope for good things for Mark and the people of Mars Hill Church. I trust that God will continue to shape their community and use them for the benefit of all the world—may it always be so.

# RESPONSE TO MARK DRISCOLL

## KAREN WARD

What struck me first in Mark's chapter was how he begins with a serious, no-nonsense outline of his goals, which were to zero in on and address three "hot issues"—Scripture, the Trinity, and the atonement. After clearly stating his goals, he dives right in, so let me do the same.

### Re: Scripture

It is significant to note that Mark begins his section on the role of Scripture by quoting and listing scriptural references about the topic. That says much. For Mark, Scripture itself is key for interpreting Scripture. From that premise he goes on to discuss Jesus' use of Scripture, because Jesus lies at the heart of the Word, and Scripture points to the work and merits of Christ.

Another of Mark's analogies that struck me was that of Scripture as the Supreme Court, a court superior to the lower courts of experience, culture, and archaeology, asserting that "Scripture alone is perfect and the locus of final authority over us."

It is clear to see that Scripture is the common daily bread of our community at Church of the Apostles as it is for Mark's community. But at the same time, we choose to draw on some different aspects and strike a different posture regarding how Scripture is authoritative.

I reference Scripture as the "big S story," a founding partner in a relational dance, as my friend Rachel Mee Chapman says, "in the overlap" of text, community, and Spirit.

As such, my take on truth is that it is *personal*, and my view of authority *is dynamic*. For me, Christian truth takes flesh in the *person* of Christ, who in the name of the Father and in the power of the Spirit, leads Christian communities into truth and into him, as he is truth. And regarding the authority of truth and Christ, I do not see proof resting in Scripture alone, but in Jesus himself (his life, death, and resurrection) as attested to in Scripture and as reflected upon, wrestled with, and discerned within Christian community, by the leading of the Spirit.

## Re: Trinity

Here I find myself sharing very strong common ground with Mark, and I echo his comments: "First, the doctrine of the Trinity reveals a God who exists as a loving community throughout eternity. And since we are made in the image of the Trinitarian God, if we lose the doctrine of the Trinity, we lose the root system from which we nourish community, love, and friendship."

The Trinity is deeply foundational to our view of God at Church of the Apostles, since the Trinity is the source of all human relationality. The five-foot icon of the Trinity at Apostles (handmade by one of our own apostles) is beloved among us. This icon expresses our love for the Trinity, not primarily as a doctrine we espouse and defend, but as the reality of *how God is*, as told to us in the narrative of Scripture, and as the reality of *what we are to become* in our life and witness as a Christian community.

I'm glad to discover with Mark this common theological grounding in the Trinity. So now I find myself wondering how Mark might relate to use of Rublev's icon of the Trinity (and icons in general) as an artistic and multivocal way to convey theological truth within Christian community.

## Re: Atonement

I resonate with Mark's firm holding to the atonement of Christ as Lord and Savior. I affirm no other Savior than Jesus Christ, yet at the same time, I feel no need to know with certainty the final destination of those of other faiths who either have no knowledge of Christ or who do not accept the Christian claims of the atonement. My view of God is high enough to leave such matters to God, while at the same time never downplaying the twenty-four/seven calling of Christians to make bold our witness to the gospel of Jesus Christ.

However, I do seem to have a different ethos than Mark concerning atonement. We both agree on the central importance of atonement, but we each have our own views on "how it means." For Mark, it seems that having a correct doctrine of atonement is absolutely critical, while my writing centers on atonement as more of a *verb*, a happening to and within God that invites a happening to and within us.

## In Conclusion

I am struck by how this chapter reflects Mark's deep passion for the truth of God as revealed in the Scriptures and played out in the death of Christ for our salvation.

I sense that Mark is a pastor who is always "on message" and "on mission," and his writing pulses with his urgency for truth and his desire for a no-fat, no-saccharine, no-filler approach to biblical truth and Christian life. When I read his words, I think, "Wow, if Gold's Gym were a Christian church, then Mark would be the lead manager, nutritionist, and personal trainer."

Mark's writing inspires me to get more of a workout with Scripture and Christian doctrine in ways that challenge, pull, and stretch me to build up my endurance and the endurance of my faith community for the long haul.

Finally, it has not escaped me (or Mark, probably) that many think of us as "yin and yang" poles on the "emerging" continuum, so I smile with the knowledge that God, in wisdom (or perhaps in serendipity) has seen fit to locate our respective faith communities less than two miles apart within Seattle. So, who knows ... maybe someday, the Spirit will arrange for me to run into Mark at the Jolly Rancher pub in Seattle and have a chat at this middle space between our worlds, because I have no doubt that Mark loves God in Christ as I do, and I have heard that like me, Mark enjoys a good beer.

# THE EMERGING CHURCH AND INCARNATIONAL THEOLOGY

JOHN BURKE

# THE EMERGING CHURCH AND INCARNATIONAL THEOLOGY

## JOHN BURKE

'm not sure where I fit into this discussion. For a number of years now, I've lived with the tension of not feeling completely comfortable in any of the Christian camps or subcultures. Brought up in a highly liturgical, strongly Reformed mainline tradition, I left the church faithless (not their fault I'm sure—I just was not one of the elect ... yet). I found faith in a parachurch small group because they accepted and loved me despite my hedonistic lifestyle and badgering skeptical questions. Church attendance came more from obligation than vision.

While working in an extremely modern-style college ministry in the nineties, our lack of success in trying to reach the first postmodern generation caused me to question our methods. Something visceral was missing—those who prayed to accept Christ didn't join us in following him. I attended what Robert Webber calls the representative traditional evangelical seminary (Trinity University) while working at a representative pragmatic modern church (Willow Creek Community Church). At the church, I was working to start Axis, a church within a church for the emerging generation.

In 1999, my family left Chicago to start a church in Austin to reach this emerging, postmodern, post-Christian world, and yet, I have not fully fit into the emerging camp either. But even though I'm not sure where I fit, I am confident of what I've seen. I have watched God raise up a healing body out of a very broken, postmodern generation that is seemingly far from God. It's this awesome work of God, seeking and saving and restoring all kinds of people into a community of Christ followers, that has had the most profound impact on me. I feel indebted and shaped by all of the faith communities with whom I've interacted, and yet I've witnessed God's most powerful work among this community of the newly redeemed. This is the eclectic background from which I write about pastoral theology in the emerging church.

As I pondered what to write, I remembered the very disturbing incident involving Peter in Matthew 16. Having just won the praise of Jesus for a God-inspired proclamation of Jesus as Messiah, Peter gets rebuked for being the voice of Satan. I pray I will not fall into the same deception. A very real temptation exists to carve out an identity by differentiating myself from what is traditional or pragmatic or modern. Jesus rebuked Peter, saying, "You do not have in mind the concerns of God, but merely human concerns" (v. 23). I think this is a valid warning for the emerging church that is shaping theology in our postmodern world.

We must be very wary of reinventing theology for the sake of being the new, "new thing," which is very much a trend of the cultural flow in which we swim. Case in point, when I first started ministering to this emerging generation, it had no label. In the mid-nineties, "Gen X ministry" became the vogue buzzword. Come the new millennium, you were late-nineties if you were talking about Gen X anything; you had to be doing "postmodern ministry." A few years later, the term "postmodern" feels old, and the new "new thing" is the "emerging" or "emergent" church. I think it's a legitimate concern that we have these labels and buzzwords since we can get swept along in our over-marketed, overly trendy cultural flow.

For this reason, I believe we must firmly anchor any emerging theology in the revealed Scriptures, and we must subject our interpretations to a broader community, including traditional and pragmatic communities on whose shoulders we stand, and from whom our faith was passed down. Having said this, the church must wrestle theologically with the questions of the emerging global culture. If not, we will further retreat into isolationism and obscurity and miss the amazing opportunity God has given us to minister to people longing for what the body of Christ has to offer.

Honestly, I'm not that interested in internal church debates about who has the right or wrong form of theology or Christian practice if the outcome doesn't impact a hurting, broken world. Jesus came to seek and save what was lost, to restore all things. So I write mainly from a concern that his church be his body, on his mission, in his world. How does our theology help or hinder us in accurately re-presenting Jesus to our world?

## The Questions of a Global Village

Last summer, our family did our own version of National Lampoon's *Vacation*. We took our kids across 4,300 miles of pavement to see the Grand Canyon and Yosemite National Park. I found myself awestruck by the beauty and grandeur of God's creation, something I had expected. However, I had not anticipated the global intersection we would cross.

As I walked with my daughter onto the scenic precipice jutting over the Grand Canyon, I began to notice all the languages people were speaking: German, French, Spanish, Russian, Japanese, Hindi, and Slavic languages I couldn't recognize. We began to count distinct languages and country dialects, and we tallied up representatives from over twenty countries that crossed our path that day. In Yosemite, we sat next to French winery owners at dinner, and we stood in line behind Romanian visitors to go rafting. I found myself awestruck by the global intersection happening around God's natural revelation.

As we reflect on theology in the twenty-first century, the church in America must consider the unique intersection and opportunity to which we have come in our travels. Though nothing about the human predicament is new, we do find ourselves in a world unlike any other before us. We must grapple with questions raised by a global village. The questions come as a result of worldwide communications, global travel, and the media shrink-wrapping and exporting an increasingly common global culture (MTV beams into 140 countries). We find ourselves at a global intersection around God's special revelation: "How do we accurately re-present Jesus to a global diversity of religious cultures?"*

Historically, theological refinement has come about by wrestling with God's revealed Word in light of the questions of the world. Starting with Acts 15, the church had to grapple with the theological questions posed by a formerly pagan, Gentile world, while holding to the revealed Scriptures.[1] "Does God demand circumcision for salvation?" "Do Gentiles have to abide by our Jewish kosher laws?" The questions of a world intersecting with the message of Christ forced their theological reflection.

---

*This intersection is new for the American church, which historically has not had to interact with such diverse religious views. But this challenge is not new to the worldwide church, which grew amidst the religious pluralism and relativism of a Greco-Roman world. But this is the first time diverse religious cultures are so aware of one another globally, and it's the first time since Babel for a shared global culture to emerge.

Fast-forward to the fourth-century church wrestling with the theology of the Trinity. Church historian Bruce Shelley quotes one bishop describing the whole city of Constantinople seething with dialogue and questions about the Trinity: "If in this city you ask anyone for change, he will discuss with you whether God the Son is begotten or unbegotten. If you ask about the quality of bread, you will receive the answer that 'God the Father is greater, God the Son is less.' "[2] The councils and creeds attest to the theological struggle the church went through to answer a world of questions.

The Reformation of the sixteenth-century church could not have occurred in a vacuum. The world around the church swirled with secret questions about religious authority and the nature of salvation. Into this vacuum stepped the Reformers, filling it with a theology of salvation by faith in Christ alone and the theology of the authority of Scripture.

And we must not forget the seventeenth-century Galileo lesson. Sometimes our theological interpretation of Scripture must subject itself to answering the questions of a skeptical world, or we can make grave mistakes by holding to a theological conclusion that denies the truth.

Theology must seek to answer the questions of the culture without conforming to the culture. We must let our culture's questions help us better conform to truth and God's revelation. So what theological questions must the emerging church in a global village wrestle with?

Since starting Gateway Church, we've interacted with thousands of people from all over America, mostly individuals under forty years old, mostly those unchurched prior to exploring faith at Gateway (I've chronicled many of their stories of overcoming barriers to faith, and showing how the culture of the church can help or hinder, in the book *No Perfect People Allowed*).[3] These people grew up in a postmodern, post-Christian, global village. Here is a sampling of the most commonly asked questions written down at what we call our "Free-For-All-Q&A Sunday":

- If there is no correct religion, why is Christianity the only way?
- What happens to people who have never heard of Jesus?
- Are all Jews, Muslims, and Buddhists doomed to hell?
- What happens to people raised in other religions?
- Do you think God loves those who are not Christians?
- Why just Jesus? What about Buddha, etc.?
- Are all religions the same?
- Isn't it arrogant to believe Christianity is the only path to a full spiritual life?

Theologically, the emerging church must wrestle with what the Scriptures say God has revealed about the uniqueness of Jesus in relation to the world's religions. Why must we wrestle with this question? Because instead of helping people find their way home to Jesus as the only one who can save, we often put up barriers to belief by the way we communicate what Scripture reveals.

We need to weigh heavily the conclusion of the first-century Jerusalem Council, when Jesus' half-brother James declared, "It is my judgment, therefore, that we should not make it difficult for the Gentiles who are turning to God."[4] How can the emerging church honor Jesus, stay true to Scripture, and best answer the burning questions of our global culture? I believe our answer must be both incarnational and propositional.

## Theology of the World's Religions

There is a Jain parable of an elephant and four blind men that describes a common view of the world's religions in our global village.* Four blind men happened upon an elephant one day. One of them felt its trunk and said, "An elephant is like a hose." Another felt its side and said, "No, an elephant is like a wall." The third blind man put his arms around its leg and declared, "An elephant is like a tree." Finally the fourth blind man grabbed its tail and insisted, "No, an elephant is like a snake."

Many people today think this accurately explains the descriptions of God from different religions. Many have learned that all of the world's religions are trying to explain the same God, but in our limited ability to truly comprehend, we all describe God a little differently based on our cultural limitations. The emerging church must grapple with the fact that this perspective is the starting assumption for our global village.

The Barna Research Group and others note that the current generation is actually the first generation in American history in which a majority of those seeking faith begin their spiritual journey with a faith group other than Christianity.[5] Thus we must understand how to be wise as serpents but innocent as doves in helping them understand what Scripture reveals.

### All Bad? All Good?

Do the Scriptures reveal that the religions of the world are all bad, all good, or a twisted blend of both? Some evangelical Christians respond as

---

*Jainism is an Eastern religion founded around 500 BC.

if everything about Buddhism or Islam is demonic to the core—all bad. Other emerging evangelicals almost seem to answer the question to the other extreme. I don't believe either extreme is biblical or helpful in seeing God's kingdom come to our world.

If you know the history of religion or philosophy, you know that most all cultures for all times have tried to answer several basic questions. The religions of the world tell us a story of our blind search for meaning and purpose. Since the dawn of civilization, humanity has searched to explain our relationship to the cosmos and how best to live this life according to this internal moral compass we all have. And most religions do say similar things about right and wrong.

It's uncanny how similar a moral code most every major religion has—almost like this innate understanding of right and wrong comes from within. Which, of course, exactly matches what the Bible teaches. "(Indeed, when Gentiles, who do not have the law, do by nature things required by the law ....They show that the requirements of the law are written on their hearts, their consciences also bearing witness, and their thoughts now accusing, now even defending them.)"[6] C. S. Lewis summarizes this common moral law found in religious traditions in *The Abolition of Man*.[7]

Personally, I think Christians can be true to Scripture, explaining that religion is our attempt to answer questions about God or human evil or the way out of suffering. Different cultures and people have answered the questions differently. And when people ask the question, "Don't all religions basically say the same thing?" we can affirm that they *do* all say the same thing about what's right and wrong—the moral law.

Matt came to our church very skeptical. He grew up in Seattle in a nonreligious family. He said that among his friends, "Nothing was absolutely true for us. We all kind of saw the religions of the world as different viewpoints of corrupt institutions. I didn't see any difference or relevance in any of them." Yet he and his wife found themselves sitting in church one Sunday as I talked about this common moral law and how it teaches us all that we need God's help.

That was the turning point for Matt: "As I sat listening that Sunday morning," he recalls, "something clicked. As John walked through each moral law the religions of the world teach us, it hit me like a ton of bricks ...we know what is right and wrong! We always have! And yet, we fail, over and over again. It is said the definition of insanity is to expect a different result from the same input. I was tired of fighting and failing. For the first time, I had the thought, 'I want to know God.'"[8]

## What about Idolatry?

Some truth *can* be found among the religions of the world, and acknowledging this in our global village can remove barriers to faith. But what about idolatry? The world's religions do not say the same things about God's identity. And doesn't the Old Testament speak more of other religions as idolatrous and ultimately as the worship of demons in ignorance?[9] Without a doubt. But evil can only twist what is good and from God; evil cannot create good.

Our propensity to worship something is good, but the things we mistake for gods, thinking they can give us life (whether the handmade idols of India or handmade material goods of the United States) all constitute idolatry. Recall the idolatry of the rich young ruler in Matthew 19—he did not keep the first commandment because his wealth came before God, as Jesus pointed out. God says anything we put before him feels like adultery—unfaithfulness of God's beloved creatures toward the One who loves them most.[10]

Some Christians feel the need to assert a stance of condemnation toward all non-Christian religions. When asked, "Well, what about other religions?" the only biblically justifiable answer for some Christians is, "They're wrong, they're idolatrous." I would suggest that though this may be true in part, Paul gives us a better approach that removes barriers to faith rather than reinforcing them.

In the book of Acts, we see how Paul lived out his missional approach of "becom[ing] all things to all people"[11] by pointing out the living God at work in an idol-worshiping culture. In Acts 14, Paul tells the polytheists in Lystra that God has been at work among them all along: "He has not left himself without testimony: He has shown kindness by giving you rain from heaven and crops in their seasons; he provides you with plenty of food and fills your hearts with joy."[12] So now, turn from your idols to the living God, Paul pleads with them. He created you and is the source of any joy you experience!

In Acts 17, Paul finds himself in Athens, distressed by the myriad of idols everywhere. Yet how does he communicate to those of other religions in order to build bridges to faith? When brought before the city council asking questions about Jesus among the gods, he begins not by condemning their idolatry, but by pointing out their worship of an Unknown God. Paul proclaims that this God they ignorantly worshiped is *the* God who made the world, who has now revealed himself through Jesus.

Paul knew that if their eyes were to be opened, they needed to see that, buried in their misguided, mythological religion, were traces of worship of the one true God. He quotes the truth about God conveyed through their religious sayings, "'For in him we live and move and have our being.' As some of your own poets have said, 'We are his offspring.'"[13]

Really, Paul? Children of God? You could argue that Paul is being theologically fuzzy, yet I believe Paul really understood how to help people from other religious persuasions see God's hand leading them toward his full revelation. He assumes that all their religious pursuits were partly in ignorance, but now they can know this Unknown God who has clearly revealed himself in Jesus (Paul uses the Greek name for God, *Theos*, which would be like a Christian referring to God as "Allah," which means "God" in Arabic). And Paul is saying that the God of Jesus is the Unknown God they've ignorantly worshiped in the past!

## Other Religions — Other Tutors?

Paul declared that the purpose of the law of Moses was to point out to us our need for justification by faith: "But before faith came, we were kept in custody under the law, being shut up to the faith which was later to be revealed. Therefore the Law has become our tutor to lead us to Christ, so that we may be justified by faith."[14] Maybe Paul understood the religions of the world, even in their misguided idolatrous twist, as partial tutors to lead people to Christ. Maybe we can point out that all people of all religions, Christians included, struggle to fulfill the moral law, and so we all need God's help made available through Christ.

The emerging church can affirm the mysterious ways God has always been at work, drawing people to himself out of various religious backgrounds, like God did with Nebuchadnezzar the Babylonian king,[15] Rahab the prostitute from pagan Jericho,[16] the Queen of Sheba from Africa,[17] the Iranian astrologer, and the magi who found the Messiah's birth written in the stars.[18] This same God still works behind the scenes pursuing those from all religious backgrounds.

A woman named Joy tells of the mysterious way God drew her from her experiences among the world's religions.

> For several years, I explored Buddhism through meditation and yoga. I studied Tai Chi Chuan and karate, would go see psychics, and read many New Age–style books on spirituality. One weekend, I attended a conference in Austin with a Buddhist Lama who had studied in India. The moment I walked into the room, I could feel a very peaceful, lov-

ing presence. It made a strong impression on me. He seemed very open, authentic, and loving, with a great sense of humor. My Buddhist mentors had helped me see so much truth about myself, and I loved them dearly, but I was still trying to figure out if this was the path for me. As I talked to the Lama that day, I just couldn't find the solid foundation for denying all desires [a tenet of Buddhism], and I didn't feel like totally losing my self-identity to become one with everything. There were traces of truth that attracted me, but something was missing. I kept making the same mistakes in life and didn't know how to deal with the condemning feelings I had carried for so long.

Not long after the conference, I was in meditation class and the leader directed us to focus our minds by picturing a Buddha. I tried, but couldn't. Only a half-image would appear in my mind. Then suddenly and uninvited, an image of Jesus appeared in my conscience. I wasn't a Christian and still knew almost nothing about Jesus, yet there he was! That day I decided I really needed to understand more about Jesus.[19]

Joy came to our church, and because we acknowledged God's work behind the scenes, she overcame barriers and found faith in Christ. Today, four years later, she serves as a small group leader and is on staff as an administrator for our Christian spiritual formation classes.

Can the emerging church build the kinds of bridges to those pursuing other faiths or coming from other religious backgrounds like Paul did? Does our theology have room for a God who works behind the scenes, even in other religious pursuits, drawing people to Christ?

## Scripture in a Global Village

In our postmodern world, drifting in the current of relativism, when Christians say Christianity is true or right, people often have a knee-jerk response. Having had many of these conversations, I think something like this goes through their minds, "Oh, no—this is one of those ignorant, arrogant, religious-snob types who thinks they're always right." They assume a claim like this comes from ignorance of the global world we live in, or else from sheer arrogance.

Because most people I interact with assume religious belief is a preference thing—like preferring blue over green—for them, arguing that blue is better than green (or Christianity is right and other religions are wrong) feels like foolishness. For that reason, we must avoid arguments about religion and get back to the basics of knowing God.

Christians can agree with the postmodern culture in at least one thesis: "No human has a lock on all truth." Maybe our modern systems of theology have blinded us to this reality by causing us to think we really have Scripture systematized, and therefore, have God all figured out. But our knowledge really is biased by our cultural upbringing, and nobody knows it all (or has a 100 percent accurate concept of God).

The twelve disciples found that their entire understanding of the Messiah's kingdom inauguration had been shaped by a bias for political deliverance more than by a careful reading of the prophesies of a Messiah who would suffer. Years after the resurrection, Paul had to rebuke Peter for cultural bias still creeping into his faith.[20]

So we can agree with the postmodern culture, that all humans find themselves adrift on a sea of relative, incomplete knowledge, blinded somewhat by cultural biases. We cannot know much at all about God unless God reveals himself to us. And here the uniqueness of the Scriptures comes to bear. Postmodern relativism creates a wonderful theological bridge from our culture to the amazing revelation of God. Because in many respects, the Jain parable nails it—we *are* all blind. And on our own, none of us can accurately describe God beyond a blind guess. So the more fundamental question is, "Has God revealed his identity?" Now we're on level ground with all the world's religions.

We see the uniqueness of the Scriptures when we ask the simple question, "Do any of the world's religions *even claim* in their sacred texts that God has revealed himself?" Mortimer Adler, a world-renowned philosopher and editor of the Encyclopedia Britannica, wrote a book as a philosophical seeker, called *Truth in Religion*. In it, he points out that if you read the sacred texts of the world's religions at face value, only three actually claim that the creator God has revealed himself or his will directly in history: Judaism, Christianity, and Islam.

We can point this out to our global village by respecting the world's religions, yet show that the sacred writings of most world religions do not claim to be God's self-revelation. From here, we can show how God confirmed his revelation in history by foretelling the life and death of his Messiah throughout the Old Testament, confirming it in both New Testament and extra-biblical history.*

---

*People rarely ask why the Qur'an would not also be considered God's revelation. When asked, I explain that the revelation of the angel to Muhammad (from which the Qur'an is believed to originate) validates Jesus as Messiah, yet contradicts the prophecies and extra-biblical history of Jesus, claiming that Jesus did not die on

## Our Anchor in a Sea of Relativism

One fear I have for the emerging church is that we will cut loose from the anchor of the authority of the Scriptures in hopes of relating to our relativistic culture. I fully understand the force of the current of postmodernity, and I struggle at times trying to explain those aspects of God, as revealed in Scripture, that are just plain hard to swallow. But I keep coming back to what I see as nothing short of God's fingerprint of authentication in the prophecies of the Messiah. And I believe the emerging church must keep coming back to why we can have confidence in the authority of Scripture.

God declared to Moses that the way we could differentiate God's self-revelation from human invention would be through prophetic foretelling. "You may say to yourselves, 'How can we know when a message has not been spoken by the LORD?' If what a prophet proclaims in the name of the LORD does not take place or come true, that is a message the LORD has not spoken."[21] God reminded the people of Israel, "I am God, and there is none like me. I make known the end from the beginning, from ancient times, what is still to come."[22]

Every year, I take our church through the prophecies of the Messiah. I walk through the historical validation that can be shown, not just from the New Testament writers, but from extra-biblical history as well. Every time I study it, I am more amazed at how much assurance God has given us that he superintended the writing of the Scriptures. Our faith can find anchor, not just in tradition or simply the story we find ourselves in (though these are important). Our faith can find anchor in the confidence that God has revealed himself through the Scriptures, and finally through his Messiah spoken of in the prophecies.

What I'm about to say may seem like preaching to the already-convinced, but I think it's important in the flow of our relativistic culture to reconsider what we anchor to and why. Studying the prophecies each year as I interact with skeptics, I'm reassured of God's authority that undergirds the Scriptures. I find the evidence of history so compelling, it bends my knees in awe of God's mysterious, confirming, prophetic voice. From confirmation in the Talmud that the Messiah should have come by AD 7, to

---

the cross. "They denied the truth and uttered a monstrous falsehood against Mary. They declared: 'We have put to death the Messiah, Jesus the son of Mary, the apostle of God.' They did not kill him, nor did they crucify him, but they thought they did" (Qur'an 4:157).

confirmation of the Messiah's death in secular history right before the temple's destruction, to confirmation in the rebirth of Israel in our day—only God could have foretold these things as he did in Scripture.

Knowing assuredly that God foretold the Messiah in Scripture, I then look at the way Jesus treated the Scriptures. I assume that if God could so miraculously foretell the coming of the Messiah, surely he could accurately preserve the message of the Messiah. Jesus treated the Hebrew Scriptures as mysteriously inspired by God, saying, "How is it then that David, speaking by the Spirit, calls him 'Lord'?"[23] Luke states, "And beginning with Moses and all the Prophets, [Jesus] explained to them what was said *in all the Scriptures* concerning himself."[24]

Jesus said, "Do not think that I have come to abolish the Law or the Prophets; I have not come to abolish them but to fulfill them. Truly I tell you, until heaven and earth disappear, not the smallest letter, not the least stroke of a pen, will by any means disappear from the Law until everything is accomplished. Anyone who sets aside one of the least of these commands and teaches others accordingly will be called least in the kingdom of heaven, but whoever practices and teaches these commands will be called great in the kingdom of heaven."[25]

Jesus indicates that he is the fulfillment of everything written in the Hebrew Canon, and that everything written should be heeded as lasting until the end of time. I don't think Jesus intended a wooden interpretation of Scripture, devoid of symbol, poetry, or imaginative speech—he often taught using parable and story. But we do need to hold to his view of an all-encompassing authority found in the Scriptures. I think the emerging church will find itself stranded on the shoals of postmodernity if we separate from Scripture as our final authority. Yes, communities of faith need to interact and inform interpretation, but it cannot be the tradition or the community that becomes the final authority—only the Scriptures can claim that, and only because of God's validating prophetic fingerprint and the Messiah's words.

If you are tempted to treat the Scriptures lightly, go back to the basics and study the prophecies and their fulfillment in Jesus and in history. Study the ways the prophets treated the Scriptures and the way Jesus treated the Scriptures rather than merely reacting against or buying into what your tradition has said. Every generation gets tempted to be wise in its own eyes and stumble over the simplicity of faith. Jesus prayed, "I praise you, Father, Lord of heaven and earth, because you have hidden these things from the wise and learned, and revealed them to little children."[26]

## Postmodern Revelation

As leaders of the emerging church, we must submerge ourselves in the Scriptures, staying humble before God, and praying we won't be deceived as we seek to be all things to all people that some might find faith. And we must not be afraid to let our relativistic world know that they too can tie off to the anchor of God's revelation. I've found that the most postmodern relativists long for this kind of grounded assurance from God. That's what Leigh's story shows.

Leigh moved from Massachusetts to Austin to marry Steve. When she and Steve first came to Gateway, their resistance was high. Like many of her generation, Christianity was the last stop on her eleven-year tour to find God. Leigh recalls:

> I had tried Hindu meditation retreats, Unity churches, and very new-agey churches still searching for truth. It felt too nebulous. Gateway wasn't like that, it was clearly a Christian church, but I felt that if God led me to Gateway, maybe there was something I needed to understand about Jesus. Still, on the inside, I was kicking and screaming intellectually. I felt very put off that you had a group of missionaries. To me that seemed like going where you weren't wanted, changing people's cultures, pushing your beliefs on others. I didn't want to be exclusionary. I didn't want to start quoting Scripture at people. I didn't want to feel like anybody else was wrong. I didn't want be like "those Christians." I have very liberal friends. If I had anything to say about Jesus, except that he was a teacher among many, I would be labeled a freak. But I was looking for a community of people who cared about each other, and I could sense that with Gateway. So after a month, I got involved in a mom's group. I had a real attitude, but whenever I'd come back at them with my issues, I didn't get an attitude back. I sensed genuine humility from the leader, who constantly encouraged me to be myself and question openly. She welcomed me like a friend and tried to understand my point of view while explaining the Bible's point of view with integrity.
>
> I didn't know anything about the Bible except I had been told it had been changed over the years, a book of myths. I remember praying to God saying, "If there's really something to this Jesus thing, I'm gonna give you thirty days, and I'll just focus on Jesus. If this is what you want for me, come lead me and guide me." I started reading the Bible for the first time, and I know it was the Holy Spirit guiding me, because I not only understood it, I couldn't get enough of it. I couldn't wait to read more about Jesus every night.

I kept giving God thirty-day extensions to convince me. During that time, the church did a series called "Prophecies of the Messiah."[27] Those messages changed everything for me. That was the key to my intellectual resistance. Seeing God's fingerprints in prophecy, confirmed by history, made me realize this is real—even for people who think the way I think. Suddenly I wanted everyone in the world to hear this. I bought tapes to give away to friends. I was telling everybody. It just made so much sense. Not long afterwards, I worked through the pre-baptism study, and that's really when I understood the grace of God offered in Christ. I asked him into my heart and my life. After eleven years of searching, there has been a change in me this year that's hard to describe. There is a happiness and relief I hadn't expected. I have a focus I didn't have before. Now that I see God through Christ, God's identity has become clearer to me, and I now know how I can relate to God.[28]

The emerging church must stay anchored to the authority of Scripture, but we must do a better job explaining to our global village why the Scriptures can claim God's authority. When we do, it makes a world of difference.

## Jesus for a Global Village

I believe the American evangelical church needs to make a subtle, yet important, theological shift away from an "our God" mentality. The Pharisees of Jesus' day had this mind-set. They "had God" and the Gentiles, the nations, did not. They lived "God's way," but those outside their religious culture were "sinners." An "us-them" attitude pervaded the religious institution of Jesus' day. But the Lord rebuked them, saying, "Go and learn what this means: 'I desire mercy, not sacrifice.' For I have not come to call the righteous, but sinners."[29] The irony of this statement gets lost; the religious leaders weren't righteous. They would soon crucify him! Jesus came for all people who realize how desperately they need God.

God is the creator of all people, whether those people recognize it or not. Living in St. Petersburg, Russia, the year after the fall of seventy years of atheistic communism, I remember how astonishingly few atheists I met. Most people believe in a Creator. We must approach the people of today's global village, letting them know their merciful Creator has done something *for them*.

If you trace God's intentions revealed from Abraham to Jesus, he's always had all the nations in mind. God told Abraham he would bless *all nations* on earth through him.[30] Solomon understood God's will for the new temple by praying "that *all the peoples* of the earth may know your name."[31] Isaiah foretold God's plan for the Messiah, saying, "The LORD will lay bare his holy arm in the sight of all the nations, and *all the ends of the earth* will see the salvation of our God."[32] Paul recognized that through Jesus, God extended an invitation to all people across our globe: "This is good, and pleases God our Savior, who wants *all people to be saved* and to come to a knowledge of the truth. For there is one God and one mediator between God and human beings, Christ Jesus, himself human, who gave himself as a ransom *for all people.*[33]

## Have We Profaned His Name?

Something is really wrong! There's a reason American villagers first check out the way of Buddha before the way of Christ. Something about our theology has led to a misrepresentation of Jesus. George Barna has been reporting trends of the church in America for some time now. Barna says, "Of more than 70 moral behaviors we study, when we compare Christians to non-Christians we rarely find substantial differences."[34] And if you ask non-Christians for one word that comes to mind when they hear the word "Christian," the most common answer is "judgmental."

So on the one hand, our global village hears Christians proclaim that Jesus is the only way and the right way, and all other ways are wrong. And yet following Jesus makes no difference whatsoever in the way these so-called Christians live and treat people, except that it makes them more judgmental and hypocritical.

This slap in the face must be addressed by reconsidering how the church has viewed herself in North America, because obviously, something's not as God intended. We've profaned the name of Jesus, so that his name gets associated with the opposite of the good news he came to proclaim.[35] How do we re-present Jesus accurately to our global village? What needs to change?

We need a new job description as the church, Jesus' body in the world. As I understand Scripture, we're misrepresenting Jesus if the world hears our message as a message of judgment. Not even Jesus came into the world to judge the world: "As for those who hear my words but do not keep them, I do not judge them. For I did not come to judge the world, but to save the world. There is a judge for those who reject me and do not accept my words; the very words I have spoken will condemn them at the last day."[36] There will be a day of judgment, but today is not that day and we are not those judges. So if our job description is not to judge the world, nor to change it by some political system (like the disciples mistakenly assumed Jesus would do in their day), then what should we be about?

## Come As You Are

Jesus told a parable of the kingdom of heaven, saying that God is like a king who prepared a great wedding celebration and invited his guests, but they were too busy to come, and some were even hostile toward the king. "Then he said to his servants, 'The wedding banquet is ready, but those I invited did not deserve to come. Go to the street corners and invite to the banquet anyone you find.' So the servants went out into the streets and gathered all the people they could find, *the bad as well as the good*, and the wedding hall was filled with guests."[37]

Jesus goes on to say that not all invited will come, and some will not be fit to stay (they will not clothe themselves with God's righteousness that comes through faith). But the servants don't make those decisions, the king does. The servants go out and say, "Come as you are—both good and bad—the party's open!" The church must reclaim our job as servants of the king, extending to our global village an open invitation, and we must give the task of judgment back to the Judge, for his appointed time. Very simply, we need to show grace-giving acceptance more than behavior-centered judgment to an unbelieving world.

The problem with practicing this theology comes down to messiness. If we really live out grace, not just as words we say, but as a way we treat people, all kinds of messy people may just feel accepted enough to crash our church-party, and that would feel a lot different than the party of near-perfect people some of us have come to enjoy. But that's how grace works—by making beauty out of ugly things.[38]

If you owned a Rembrandt covered in mud, you wouldn't focus on the mud or treat it like mud. Your primary concern would not be the mud at all, though it would need to be removed. You'd be ecstatic to have something so valuable in your care. But if you tried to clean the painting by yourself, you might damage it. So you would carefully bring this work of art to a master who could guide you and help you restore it to the condition originally intended. When people begin treating one another as God's masterpiece waiting to be revealed, God's grace grows in their lives and cleanses them.

We have watched gay people, radical feminists, atheistic Harvard grads, homeless crack addicts, couples living together, porn addicts, and greedy materialists come into our church, hang out around the body of Christ, find faith, change, and grow to wholeheartedly follow Christ (but for some it takes a long time, and some never change). Could those people, good and bad, come to your church? Can you picture it? When you consider these people entering your group, what are the first thoughts that come to mind? Thoughts that focus on what you think needs to change? Or thoughts that focus on their worth as people? Do you see the mud or the masterpiece?[39]

When Kylie Kent came to our church, her defenses were up. Kylie worked for the attorney general's office overseeing programs for domestic violence and sexual assault. As a feminist, all she had seen and heard gave her the impression that faith in Jesus was a very oppressive, intolerant, unloving, man-made religion. Listen to how the experience of acceptance and grace changed her mind:

> As an adult, I was never involved with church at all, except occasionally on holidays. I felt that religion was just a man-made belief system created by desperate people to fill some sort of void within. When I thought of Christianity, I thought of bigots and gay-bashers. My hometown of Topeka, Kansas, is also the home of a nationally known street preacher. On every major intersection, he and his congregation held high their signs proclaiming, "God hates fags" in the name of Christianity. I knew I would never align myself with people like these. After attending Gateway for over a year, asking questions openly, researching, and soul-searching my current beliefs, I was able to see Jesus and Christianity in a whole new light. Studying Jesus' life and teachings at Gateway also helped me realize that Jesus modeled something totally different than what I saw modeled growing up. Jesus loved and served others. He is the ultimate servant. He is not judgmental; he is the greatest advocate for social justice! All people are welcome to come to Christ, no matter who they are or where they have been. I couldn't believe the truth about Jesus had been so obscured. When I came to understand the nature and character of Jesus, I gave my heart to Christ and was baptized.[40]

Kylie started our Comfort and Hope ministry, showing grace to survivors of sexual abuse or domestic violence. But as you can see, she had to let grace soak in to believe it. Can we invite people to "Come as you are" and hang out in our churches long enough to experience grace incarnate?

## A Theology of Messy Ministry

Jesus' ministry felt messy, didn't it? Didn't Jesus' body live among the "sinners" of his day? Wasn't Mary Magdalene a demonic? Weren't Matthew and Zacchaeus thieving tax collectors? Wasn't Judas a traitor who looked like a follower? Didn't Jesus entrust him with the finances? Didn't Jesus treat Judas as an insider even though he never truly submitted his heart to God?

So why would we have a hard time inviting broken, sinful, messed-up people (who need God's grace as much as we do) to come and live among us in the church? Jesus was given for them! They need to hear that, see that, feel that. They need a touch from the body of Christ, which requires that we actually get close to them.

But that's so messy! Many in churches today do not have a practical theology of grace that could accommodate our broken world. The tendency is to give people about six weeks to change themselves, then we start trying to nudge and push and shove them into the acceptable kinds of people whom we can truly welcome to the party. Maybe we need to reconsider our theology of how people change.

Paul said, "I planted the seed, Apollos watered it, *but God has been making it grow.*"[41] Jesus said, "I am the vine; you are the branches. If you remain in me and I in you, you will bear much fruit; apart from me you can do *nothing.*"[42] Stop and ask yourself whether you really believe the words of Scripture you just read, that God alone makes people grow. That no amount of teaching, Bible study, classes, disciplines, or condemnation-engineering can change people. God alone changes people, and only when they are willing. If this is true, what implications does this have on the role of the church? Our job primarily is to create the right soil, the right culture, which helps people connect and stay connected to God. Does our theology and practice create the soil where people really change and grow? This will be a critical question for the emerging church.

According to Jesus, the emerging church shouldn't look like a tidy garden. Consider his parable:

> The kingdom of heaven is like a man who sowed good seed in his field. But while everyone was sleeping, his enemy came and sowed weeds among the wheat, and went away ....The owner's servants came to him and said, "Sir, didn't you sow good seed in your field? Where then did the weeds come from?" "An enemy did this," he replied. The servants asked him, "Do you want us to go and pull them up?" "No," he answered, "because while you are pulling the weeds, you may uproot the wheat with them. Let both grow together until the harvest. At that time I will tell the harvesters: First collect the weeds and tie them in bundles to be burned; then gather the wheat and bring it into my barn."[43]

If God is okay letting it all grow up together, believers right alongside unbelievers, in a sometimes-tangled mess, can our theology accommodate that? Can our churches stop defining the church as certain people who sit in certain seats on a given day of the week? Jesus never defined the church this way.

Can we tell our global village, "Jesus was given for you," so come as you are, and together, God can change us all into what he intended us to be? The emerging church has great news for our whole global village. I pray we will faithfully re-present Jesus at this important historical intersection.

# RESPONSE TO JOHN BURKE

## MARK DRISCOLL

I met John briefly some years ago when we were both launching our churches. I have since heard nothing but tremendous things about the work God is doing through him and his church. Subsequently, I have a tremendous amount of respect for John because he is not merely a man espousing concepts, but a pastor seeing lives changed.

As I read John's chapter, I felt much like I did in reading Dan's. Both John and Dan are solid evangelical men of God with whom I resonate on most everything. In particular, I appreciated John's warning against pastors chasing faddish trends, as well as his obvious love for Scripture and church history. I also appreciated his warnings against practicing our faith in isolation and against conforming to that which stands contrary to the teachings of Scripture. Lastly, John's acceptance that ministry is messy and that final judgments are to be reserved for Jesus alone at the end of time helps to explain why lost people are attracted to his ministry.

Overall, I believe John and I are essentially in agreement on nearly all of his points. However, there was one point I felt was either unclear or unwise. In his discussion of how Christianity is to interact with world religions, he appealed to the essential similarity of all religious moral codes. In one sense, I understand that, like C. S. Lewis and Ravi Zacharias, he is arguing for a transcendent moral law.

But Jesus stands against religion and morality as enemies of the gospel because, as Martin Luther said, religion and morality are the default mechanisms of the human heart to pursue righteousness apart from him. Therefore, it is essential that Jesus not be presented in terms of morality or religion because Jesus' mission was not to establish religion or morality. Instead, Jesus came to provide for us, through the cross and empty tomb, an eternal way of life that the self could never produce through either religion or morality.

To articulate this more clearly, I will show that all religions do not have in essence the same morality, and then I will explore the declarations of Jesus regarding himself, which condemn all other religions. Indeed, Jesus so towers over human history that he alone is the only religious figure who appears in every major world religion. Not because he represents one of those religions, but rather because he rises above them as the one true, sovereign God.

First, the assertion that all religions possess essentially the same morality is patently false. Many examples could be given but a few will suffice. In Nigeria, when a young girl is forced into sex with a gang of men, she is then flogged for having premarital sex while the men are unpunished according to their Islamic law. In Ireland, a fourteen-year-old girl was disowned by her Islamic family for having sex with a thirty-five-year-old man; he was in no way punished because she alone was held responsible, despite the fact that their relationship was statutory rape. Numerous countries practice female infanticide since varying religious groups consider boys superior to girls, not believing that both genders are equal image-bearers of God. Some animist and Islamic religious adherents practice female genital mutilation on their daughters, solely to eliminate their married sexual pleasure, a practice that has been done on some 130 million females. In various Muslim countries, a reported five thousand women and girls are strangled, shot, beaten to death, stabbed, hacked to death, or, in some cases, burned, for being sexually active outside of marriage, while the men they sleep with are rarely punished. And each time I fly in an airplane, I am forced to remove my shoes before passing through a metal detector because there is a fear that an advocate of radical Islam may have explosives in their shoes, intended to murder innocent civilians and usher the extremist into an eternal paradise filled with virgins. Simply, the moral code of all religions is not the same.

Second, Christianity is not a religion like the other world religions. Christianity is the resurrected Jesus Christ ruling and reigning over all times, peoples, places, and religions. It is imperative that we remain steadfastly committed to articulating the reasons why Jesus is distinct from and superior to all other religions and religious leaders. To do this, we must simply allow Jesus to speak for himself.

Jesus said he was God (John 8:58–59; 10:30–33; 14:8–9). Throughout the history of the world there have been numerous people who claim to speak for God, but there has also been a surprisingly short list of people who have actually claimed to be God. For example, such religious leaders as Buddha, Krishna, Muhammad, and Gandhi did not claim to be God. But Jesus clearly and repeatedly said he was God.

Jesus said he came from heaven (John 6:38; 16:28). Rarely, someone will claim that they have been taken into heaven for a brief experience of its grandeur. Examples would include people who claim to have had a near-death experience; and the founder of Islam, Muhammad, who claimed that on one occasion he was taken from earth to heaven. But Jesus claimed to have come down from his eternal home in heaven, a claim that has never been made by the founder of any other world religion.

Jesus said he was sinless (John 8:46). In the history of the world, no one else has claimed with any credibility that they are without sin. As the old adage goes, no one is perfect. Even those religious leaders who are widely recognized as the most devout and morally upright (e.g., Muhammad or Gandhi) claimed they were indeed sinners. But Jesus declared that he was, in fact, sinless.

Jesus forgave sin (Mark 2:5). While much of the resources in our world are spent dealing with the effects of sin (e.g., war, illness, death, depression, crime, poverty), there is still no way for people to have their sins forgiven so that they might be cleansed of their stains. At best, some religions try to teach their adherents what they can do to pay God back through such things as good works and reincarnation; they still lack any concept of forgiveness. But Jesus forgave sin because he is God.

Lastly, Jesus said he was the only way to heaven (John 11:25; 14:6). While there are many religious and spiritual teachers who claim they can point one to heaven's path, they themselves do not claim that they are that path. But Jesus promised that he was the way to eternal life in heaven.

In conclusion, I do believe that John would essentially agree with me on these points. But I believe it is important to clearly state that Christians must be careful not to make concessions about the similarities between Christianity and other world religions, because Jesus is nothing like any other man-made religion based on salvation by morality. It is paramount that we preserve the clarity of our gospel of grace, which comes from Jesus alone.

# RESPONSE TO JOHN BURKE

## DAN KIMBALL

I know the content of John's chapter is from the heart of an evangelist who has extreme passion for those outside the church. I love this about him, and during the times we have been together, I quickly concluded that he does not speak about evangelism from theory. He speaks as one fully engaged in the lives of non-Christians. He is passionate about seeing those outside the church become followers of Jesus. That is why the examples and illustrations he uses in his chapter are from people in his church who have come to Christianity from other belief systems. His theology is backed up by the Spirit of God changing lives. He is the real thing, and he is in real ministry to post-Christian people who have grown up outside the church. In John's chapter, I think he raises the exact theological questions that any missional pastor or leader would have to. You cannot avoid these questions if you are in relationships and conversations with real people outside the church.

I find it strange that a lot of pastors aren't wrestling with these issues as John is. Many don't ask these questions, nor do they articulate such clear thinking or have a heart of compassion as John does. It seems that too many pastors become callous and don't treat those outside the church and from other faiths with consideration, showing only interest in proving them wrong. Quote a few Bible verses about Jesus being the only way, and if they don't like it, then move on to the next person. This isn't necessarily intentional, but it is all too many pastors know as the normative American way of evangelism. Since we aren't living anymore in a Judeo-Christian America, we can no longer just think of people of other faiths as "over there somewhere." People of other faiths and spiritual beliefs are right here, all around us. We see them daily and look at them eye-to-eye, talking as neighbors, peers at work, school teachers, doctors, and others. They aren't just in photos from around the world in *National Geographic* or a travel magazine.

So it is wonderful that John is really trying to understand what people of different faiths believe and why they do so.

I hope in reading his chapter that you will be excited about what God is doing through John at Gateway Church. I hope you will be excited hearing how a pastor who is theologically conservative can still appreciate and love people of other faiths and backgrounds, yet still hold to Jesus as the way of salvation. I hope that more and more pastors and Christian leaders can approach things with a "theology of messy ministry" as John put it in his chapter. With so many emerging generations growing up outside the church, too much is at stake not to.

I really don't disagree with anything John wrote. I can only admire his missionary zeal. But more than just having zeal, John then puts this zeal into action as he is involved in lives of people outside the church. And as a result of actually being involved in lives, he has been forced to grapple with the theological questions he raises in his chapter. And not just grapple with them and have easy answers, but admit that we need to do some deep theological thinking. John then compassionately and intelligently communicates his theology to the very people asking the questions. And as a result, the Spirit uses such thinking to bring many to faith in Jesus. May there be more pastors and leaders who take John's lead and think through the theological questions raised in his chapter as any true missionary would.

# RESPONSE TO JOHN BURKE

## DOUG PAGITT

I really like John Burke. I had the privilege of meeting him when he was in the process of starting Gateway. My wife Shelley and I even attended their first public worship service—I still remember the sermon John preached that morning some seven years ago.

As is evident from John's chapter, he is deeply embedded in the life of his community. It is clear to me that he loves not only the people of his church, but the people of the broader community of Austin, caring deeply for all humanity.

I have recommended Gateway to many people who are looking for healthy, authentic communities of faith in the Austin area.

I think John brings a wonderful contribution to this conversation. His thoughts and suggestions about how the church represents Jesus in the midst of the global world are very helpful. I know from personal conversations with John that his desire to help people connect with God has come at times by paying a great price from some who feel that he is far too open on certain controversial issues, and I know that John is not seeking controversy but faithful ministry.

I understand that the responses in this book aren't so much for pointing out places of agreement, for which there are many, but to engage in some dialogue on issues of difference. I hope my disagreement does not create the impression that I am hostile toward John or his chapter, because the few areas we differ on pale in comparison to what we agree on, and also to what an inspiration he is for me.

My engagement with his chapter came around three issues: scriptural authority, the desire for uniqueness, and a more subtle issue of "cultural freedom."

John makes a series of fine arguments for the authority of Scripture for people who already hold to the Christian story. It seems to me that authority of the Scriptures comes after faith, and is not a precursor for it. This was the situation in the life of at least four of the authors of this book, and I am sure for most of the people in our communities. I find it interesting that John wants the Scriptures to be able to stand as authoritative for those outside the faith.

John writes, "The emerging church must stay anchored to the authority of Scripture, but we must do a better job explaining to our global village why the Scriptures can claim God's authority."

I wonder if we would not do better to help people connect with God, and then as they are part of our communities, add the internal issues of translating thousands of years of history, story, instruction, and meaning from the Bible. It seems that our history would allow for such a thing. There was serious consideration and debate well into the Reformation over the canonization of certain books of the Bible. So then, are we not asking people of our day to come to certainty on issues that those who preceded us in faith did not require?

This raises another question I had while reading this chapter. John makes the statement, "Thus we must understand how to be wise as serpents but innocent as doves in helping them understand what Scripture reveals." I think I understand what John is getting at, but don't we really want people to see what God is revealing in our world? And do we not put the emphasis on the wrong place when we begin with focusing on Scripture, especially in this way which seems to put the impetus on Scripture as the revealer?

John makes a persuasive argument for making important the uniqueness of Scripture and Jesus. But I wonder if that emphasis is not a result of a culture that finds value in distinction, thinking, "We are better because we are different from the other." It seems to me that what Paul argues in the significance of Jesus was not that the Gentiles were different from the Jews, but that they were part of the same promise—this is the heart of the book of Romans for instance. To be faithful to the New Testament struggle of the Jew/Gentile issues, we ought to learn from the message of that day. Jesus was seen as the fulfillment of the promise of God whereby the old day of distinction had passed. This is also the statement of Peter in Acts 10, that God doesn't show favoritism. Peter confirmed to Cornelius that he was indeed part of the story of Jesus, and that his goodness recognized by God put him on the path of Jesus. I do not think this removes the special ways of the Christian life that Cornelius was being called to, for the angel did not say, "No worries, Cornelius"; rather, "Go and get Peter and hear what he has to say to you."

Interesting that John's perspective is built on uniqueness and difference, rather than commonality. This was what Peter did with Cornelius, and what Paul did in Romans: "You see that which was promised to the Jews is also for the gentiles, for there is no difference" (paraphrase of Romans 10:12). It is hard to find an argument of today that would have that kind of significance and implication.

There seems to be an undercurrent of the idea that we ought not be caught up in our culture to such a degree that we would diminish the gospel.

John writes, "Theology must seek to answer the questions of the culture without conforming to the culture. We must let our culture's questions help us better conform to truth and God's revelation."

I think this notion, while sounding good, is simply not possible. Every time we use language, meet in a place, or make decisions, we are full participants in our culture. This idea that we can stand outside of culture in some sort of neutrality is not possible. So it seems to me that we need to be a part of the cross-cultural practice of engaging with our faith from our culture, in relationship with another culture, but not allow ourselves to think that we are somehow unbiased.

One of the reasons I was excited to be involved in this dialogue was to go through the practice, and fun, of sharpening ideas and refining my own understanding of what I believe (and I hope to be helpful to the readers as well, but that seems to be out of our hands). I certainly found John's contribution helpful to me, and I am guessing it will be beneficial to many others.

# RESPONSE TO
# JOHN BURKE

## KAREN WARD

John Burke is the only person in this book whom I have not had the honor to meet, unlike the others whom I have known for quite a number of years. So my reflections are limited to what I have read in his chapter, and it feels kind of "un-emerging" for me to write a response when all I have to go on is a paper trail and no other writing or personal experience.

With that said, I agree with John's assertion that he is not concerned about debates over who has the right or wrong theology "if the outcome doesn't impact a hurting, broken world" since "Jesus came to seek and save what was lost, to restore all things."

I resonate with John's view of emerging Christianity within an emerging global village, and I especially appreciate his acknowledgment and willingness to take on and examine the problematic tendencies of evangelicalism (harboring parochial cultural perspectives, seeing divine truth as totally knowable and "locked in" by human beings, and clinging to forms of unexamined biblicism that often come off as arrogant and patronizing). These are the very things that have caused the majority of North Americans to paint the evangelical church (and often all Christians) with a negative brush.

His words are telling: "We need a new job description as the church, Jesus' body in the world. As I understand Scripture, we're misrepresenting Jesus if the world hears our message as a message of judgment. Not even Jesus came into the world to judge the world.... There will be a day of judgment, but today is not that day and we are not those judges. So if our job description is not to judge the world, nor to change it by some political system (like the disciples mistakenly assumed Jesus would do in their day), then what should we be about?"

Another aspect I can say amen to is his use of some stories from the lives and experiences of those who attend or attended his church. As I organized "my chapter" not to be *my* chapter but to be a reflection on the theologizing that is ongoing in my community, I can relate to allowing the experiences of people to be an important avenue for how theology takes flesh.

The power of "story" in authentic emerging churches is huge. We can learn to see ourselves connected to God's story only in so far as we have opportunity to tell and reflect upon our own stories, as faith and transformation are birthed by the Spirit in the overlap where God's story and our own human stories meet.

That is why John's community and Church of the Apostles' community have developed their own unique ways of placing a priority on providing space and opportunity to hear each "voice" of the community, as this enables our "day to day" martyrdom (our bearing witness to the lordship of Jesus) to take place.

I also appreciate the call to people to "come as you are" to Christ, and that faith and practice is a "messy" enterprise, that we dare not try to sweep under the rug or clean up in a false way, but see as a gift that comes when a global Christian stew is brewed by every culture of Christians, fresh and from the heart.

And finally, I love his mention of the wedding banquet parable, as this story is near and dear to how we at Church of the Apostles see church, as a community of those who have taken up the invitation that Christ provides to participate in the breaking of the Reign of God in the world.

Because of John's words, I would like to meet with him and have a face-to-face conversation about the global horizons of theology over some South American yerba mate, Morroccan mint tea, or fine Belgian ale. Cheers.

CHAPTER

# THE EMERGING CHURCH AND MISSIONAL THEOLOGY

DAN KIMBALL

# THE EMERGING CHURCH AND MISSIONAL THEOLOGY

## DAN KIMBALL

I am glad there is finally a book addressing the theology (or theologies) of various emerging churches. It has been strange to read in magazines, books, and blogs all the chatter by people about the "emerging church" and what *they* all believe. As you will read in this book, there is great diversity in belief. Each leader and each church is diverse in their theology. There are Baptist emerging churches as well as Episcopalian, Reformed, non-denominational, and many others. Many emerging churches would be considered conservative and many would be considered liberal. (I actually have a hard time even using the terms "conservative" and "liberal" anymore, as they are so subjective.)

### Why I Use the Term "Emerging Church"

Even the term "emerging church" is somewhat misleading to many people. When I wrote the book *The Emerging Church: Vintage Christianity for New Generations*, I used the term because I first saw the organization, Leadership Network (*www.leadnet.org*), using it. They used to describe themselves as "advance scouts for the emerging church." I liked this use of the word "emerging," because it felt like an adventurous exploration of new horizons, which the Spirit of God was leading amongst churches in our emerging culture.

The dictionary defines the word "emerging" as "what is coming to the surface." So I began using the words "emerging church" to describe churches that are exploring what it means to be the church as we enter emerging cultures. This is not unlike what missionaries do. If missionaries do not rethink things as they enter a culture, they probably aren't very effective in the mission. I never thought the "emerging" way of thinking to be merely a specific "style" or "methodology" of ministry. I also never thought of it to be a specific theology (although the roots of all we do in church are theologically based). I see the idea of the emerging church as more of a mind-set about theology. I view the term "emerging church" as describing those who notice culture is changing and are not afraid to do deep ecclesiological thinking as we're on an adventurous mission together for the gospel of Jesus.

I also don't think that the "emerging" way is the new great way, or that if you aren't "emerging" you are submerging, sinking, and useless. Or that some are "in" and some are "out," depending on if you are emerging or not. We all have different places in the mission God has given us in our specific church contexts. One is not better than another; they are all just different depending on the local context. I have always believed that there will be new expressions of the church as culture changes. The New Testament church emerged and primarily met in homes and had a certain small structure of plural leadership. Through time, the early church moved into buildings and the format of worship changed and became more formal. Time went on and the church struggled through theological issues, which resulted in writing formal creeds. The Reformation moved the centerpiece of the church from the table to the pulpit due to theological issues it was facing (architecture does reflect values and even theology). Changes in the church like this will continue to emerge throughout history.

So I don't see what is happening now as anything but the continuing emergence of the church since its birth. There was actually another book called *The Emerging Church*, written in 1970 by Bruce Larson and Ralph Osborne. They spoke of what was emerging in the church at that time period. The cover of the book has a somewhat psychedelic-looking 1970s-style plant on it, reflecting the graphics of that emerging time period. Probably in the year 2035 there will be another book called *The Emerging Church* written by someone who is around six years old right now, talking about what is emerging in the church at that time. Interestingly, Larson and Osborne in the 1970 "Emerging Church" book wrote, "If the church be true to its Lord, it may never properly say that it has 'emerged.'"[1] I couldn't agree more.

## I Am Still a Conservative Evangelical, but Not "One of Those" Conservative Evangelicals

Despite what I just said here, some may read this chapter and think I am not really "emerging" theologically—but still am a conservative evangelical. You may have heard the terms *post-protestant* or *post-evangelical* to categorize whether or not someone really is emerging theologically. I don't personally care for labels like this, because I don't really think of myself in any specific category. I see myself as a pastor and leader in a local church community, on a mission striving to be true to Scripture, but also engaged in the culture and thus enjoying wrestling with theological issues our culture raises. But since we do frame things in categories and labels to some degree, I would say I still am a conservative evangelical. But when I say those words "conservative evangelical," all these bad images come into my mind. Christian leaders on television saying that SpongeBob is gay. Christian leaders on the Larry King show awkwardly squeezing John 3:16 into every other sentence. Radio preachers slamming homosexuals as being the source of all evil in the world today and saying they are out to get your kids. Christians wearing "Jesus would vote Republican" buttons around election time. Overly opinionated Christian leaders who talk as if they have access to God's truth and know all answers, and believe everyone else is wrong but them. Judgmental finger-pointing Christians focusing on the negatives in the world.[2]

I also think of conservative evangelicals as Christians who are generally afraid of discussing any new expression of theology and who are immediately closed to any new ideas. This always puzzled me, why many conservative evangelicals go into such a "defend and protect" mode when it comes to hearing and discussing other theological views and thoughts. I don't know why anyone should be afraid of discussing other theological views; we should always be open to questioning in healthy ways what one believes. If not, it seems like we are not confident in what we believe and are afraid of what we might discover. So, am I one of these conservative evangelicals? Oh, no. Please, no. But am I a conservative evangelical in terms of how I view theology in our church? After you read this chapter, you may say I still am, and that is okay.

## Not Just Re-Fluffing the Pillows Either

Another very important thing to know is that I am not a conservative evangelical who only tries to fix the outer wrappings of a church with each generation. If we are only trying to be "relevant" (a word churches love to use), by adding candles and coffee, using art in worship, and playing hip music, this is not good. Those are only surface fixes. If we merely tweak the surface level of things, we are missing the whole point of cultural change and what the emerging church is about. That is only a re-fluffing of the pillows. I believe true emerging churches must go deep within, and from the inside out, rethink, reshape, and revalue how we go about everything as culture changes. We must rethink leadership, church structure, the role of a pastor, spiritual formation, how community is lived out, how evangelism is done, how we express our worship, etc. It's not just about what we do in the worship service, but about *everything*. This includes our local ecclesiological expression and ethos, as well as our mind-set about theology. I strongly feel the emerging church must love to wrestle with theological issues and not be afraid to immerse herself in all types of discussions and viewpoints. We should be open to change and let ourselves be challenged in our thinking, not simply feel that the way we were taught is the only theological finality. If that is the case, then I don't believe you would be "emerging" as described in this book, but you would just be re-fluffing the pillows on the exterior surface level of things.

Speaking of pillows, in this book, you are reading viewpoints of different leaders in emerging churches. You will see discrepancies, since the point of this book is to discuss each other's differences. So I assume we will discuss and even challenge one another in our responses. But this is not fisticuffs fighting. This is more like a fun pillow fight, you could say. I'm not sure grown men and women have pillow fights, and I think Doug Pagitt with his long arms would wipe most of us out with a swing of his pillow, but I think you understand what I mean. I have seen and read ugly, bitter, cutting ranting on blogs and in books. This book will not have that. Something for the reader to know is that all of us contributors are friends. I have spent time with each person writing in this book, and I tremendously respect them all. Writing our opinions in this format is difficult, because it is only words without facial expressions; no cup of coffee or a pint of Guinness is on the table as we chat theology here. So, it is hard to write and then critique, as I know we do have different beliefs. But I approach this with great humility and wish this was more of a roundtable discussion. I am certain that if I were to ask the other writers, they too would prefer such a discussion—as we are not in combat here; we are expressing our own theological journeys and ideas. We are talking about holy, mysterious things here and should tread lightly and prayerfully.

When anyone speaks or writes about theology and church, they are emerging from some sort of background and culture that frames what they say. It is important to know someone's formation of thinking and experience to understand how they arrive at what they do. So in the rest of this chapter I will tell some of my personal background by sharing:

- what I originally believed theologically,
- the tension that caused me to rethink my theology,
- what I now hold to as some essential doctrines that I am comfortable saying are truth, and
- how we are fleshing out the importance of theology in our emerging church.

## Oh, How I Loved the End-Times Charts About Jesus

I grew up outside of the church with a vague concept of "God," knowing Jesus was somehow related to God as "his Son" but having no idea what that meant. It always confused me to think God had a son. My parents would occasionally drop my brother and me off at a church, but I found it horribly dull and boring, and I can't remember much from my time there. One thing I do remember at that church was getting caught by the pastor when my friend and I found their circuit breaker and turned off all the power in the middle of a church service. I also remember giggling intensely while smearing Vaseline on the choir seats, and then watching from the balcony as the choir members sat down.

I did have someone witness to me in a shopping mall when I was a freshman in high school. Out of fear, I prayed with him to trust in Jesus so I wouldn't go to hell (he really played up the going to hell part, which as I look at it now, was kind of weird for a grown man to do to a ninth-grader). I do wonder if that actually was the point of conversion for me, but I don't know.

After that time, I didn't really do anything since I didn't know any Christians and had no idea what it meant to follow Jesus. I went to Colorado State University to study landscape architecture and urban planning, and that is where I first found the "charts." I was staying at my girlfriend's family's house for a weekend visit. In the guest room, her dad had a copy of a Tim LaHaye book called *The Beginning of the End*. I had never heard of Tim LaHaye, and this was long before the Left Behind series of books came out. I laid there in bed thumbing through the book, and it was an amazing experience.

I had a very fuzzy understanding that "Armageddon" was about the end of the world, and that according to some movies I had seen like *The Omen*, the Antichrist would have the number 666. I never imagined that to be real or serious, but this book showed what the Bible taught about the end times. I had not read the Bible at all and had never even known that the Bible says Jesus will return. But the book contained images of Jesus in the clouds, with arrows pointing downward saying when and where he would return. Here were details about battles and geographical maps of where these future battles would take place. There were fairly confident descriptions of what the Antichrist would be like. It was really a head rush reading this stuff. So while lying in bed reading this book in the wee hours of the night, by the fifth chart, I became an instant premillennial, pretribulational dispensationalist.

When I left my girlfriend's home that weekend, I actually took the book with me. I didn't ask to borrow it. I wanted to keep reading it and was embarrassed to ask to borrow a religious book, so basically I just stole it. I feel guilty as I type this now. I still actually have it on my shelf in my church office. So, if you are Sherri's father, wherever you are, forgive me, and I owe you a book! When I got back to campus, I began finding anything I could on this topic, and over time, I became acquainted with theologians such as Charles Ryrie, John Walvoord, and those who were deeply entrenched in what I ended up learning was dispensational theology. I loved how there was such confidence in these systems of theology, as it gave me a sense of security and comfort to have answers. I was so into the theology of it all that I even had a goal of memorizing Charles Ryrie's book *Basic Theology*.

After I graduated from college, I traveled out of the country for almost two years and even spent a few months in Israel—a critical geographic location in all the end-times charts. So it was thrilling to be there and see the places where things will happen one day. When I returned to the United States, I found a wonderful Bible-teaching church—an evangelical, dispensational, conservative church. All that I had been reading aligned with this church, and it was where I first started serving as a volunteer and eventually went on staff as youth pastor. During this time, I also completed a master's degree at Western Seminary, which for the most part also held to these same theological views. I was really into theology and finding answers, and on a regular basis, I would read books into the late hours of the night. I even remember one of the very first times I went on a date with Becky (whom I would later marry). Instead of paying strict attention to her while we had lunch, I spent the time scribbling out theology charts on a napkin.

## Moving from Dispensational Theology to Missional Theology

So it was easy at first to slip into a church culture that for the most part had very neat and tidy theological viewpoints. If there was a question, there was a confident answer to give, explaining it in three points. I discovered that the Christian subculture of an evangelical conservative church really didn't want to explore or re-explore anything theologically. Most people there came from churched evangelical backgrounds or Catholic backgrounds. There was already a "buy in" for most things, and people didn't question what the pastor said. The church was confident, explaining God in a lot of detail. What he likes, what he doesn't, what we should do, what we shouldn't do. They explained everything very rationally and wrapped things up neatly. For the most part, the church's job was just to make things easier to understand and then to lead people to say a sinner's prayer of salvation the evangelical way, if they hadn't formally done that before, maybe coming from a Catholic background. But after a while, a tension developed within me.

Because I came into the church from the outside, I have always had a heart for evangelism to those still outside the church. But it didn't mean that I wanted to wait for them to come to the Christmas musical or outreach event. Instead, I would spend time with these people, for instance, on high school campuses talking with students. What this did for me was to keep a fresh perspective of what is going on outside the church. What are the questions being asked in our emerging culture? How is the church perceived from the outside? Coming into the evangelical Christian subculture from not having grown up in a church was quite an experience (which is a whole other story in itself). I started noticing the overall lack of theological tension, about really wrestling theologically with key cultural issues of today. It was also unsettling to see the lack of theological questioning that churched people generally have about what they hear from the pulpit. Rather, they rely upon the preacher without wrestling with issues that a missionary would. Our culture is now flooded with pluralistic religions and mixed spiritual beliefs. Our culture is spinning out of control with sexual, religious, and moral confusion and choices. How do we respond to the somewhat parallel words of Jesus and Buddha? How do we answer the pro-gay theological arguments given today? What about euthanasia? What about women in ministry? It calls for not just a quick answer as it is easy to quote a verse and then say "case closed" and have those in the church who already believe that nod their heads in approval. But quite often, that is what I would experience. Here's the Bible verse or two that proof texts a complex situation—or determines almost an entire end-times theology. But is it really that easy to answer these types of theological questions with such certainty? I wondered why people weren't wrestling more with these issues in the conservative evangelical church. How can people be satisfied with these little, wrapped-up, tidy, black-and-white answers, when the issues are far more complex?

## Not Safe to Ask the Theologically Dangerous Questions

I think because I came in from the outside, plus always having had friendships with non-Christians, I was becoming more and more aware that our theology needs to be missional in engaging culture and exploring the questions of the day. But so many churches don't seem to be open to wrestling with anything, predetermining everything from a former systematic theology textbook the pastor of the church used in seminary. What I also found in most conservative evangelical churches is that there wasn't any room to ask questions, and if you did, you would be under suspicion.

I fully believe that if someone is truly engaged on the mission field among emerging generations here in our own country, he or she cannot help but think theologically about all types of questions and ethical issues. But the tidy and somewhat shallow answers I would hear weren't satisfying to me, nor could I give these easy answers with a Bible verse or two or three with respect and integrity to others. Yet, I felt alone. It seemed that so many conservative evangelical Christians were more concerned with the pragmatic felt-need answers to problems in life, than they were in thinking about theology behind the felt-needs tips they were given. If whatever the pastor says "works" in my life and protects me and my family from the evils of culture—this is all I need. I don't need to think theologically about it. Since the focus of so much preaching in the church was primarily on personal felt-needs for day-to-day living for the already conservative Christian, and since solving their felt-needs was the primary concern of most church-goers, deeper theological discussions weren't needed. If the pastor gave a confident, logical, and tidy reason for things, no one questioned it. Now, I know that felt-needs are very important, and I want felt-need teaching to help me in daily living. So I am not against teaching that has strong application for daily living. However, the more I engaged in the emerging culture, it just didn't allow me to give the packaged and somewhat simplistic answers you could get away with within the church subculture. People outside the church were asking deeper theological questions than were people inside the church.

This caused a dilemma. I knew for myself and the mission I was on that the boundaries of answers needed to be expanded. But what do they expand to? In the same way I sensed that maybe the particular dispensational theological system I believed was not the absolute correct one. I didn't want to solve things by simply jumping straight into another traditionally conservative theological system of belief. I also didn't feel that what are known as more liberal churches would provide the answers, as some don't hold to the authority of the Scriptures in the way that I do—and I knew that was not going to change for me. I believe the Scriptures are divinely inspired and will always remain a constant for me. I understand that in some churches there is so much theological liberty, that it almost seems that anything goes, as long as you are loving. That doesn't ring true either, as there are plenty of very loving Buddhists and atheists. Since I was confused about where to turn, instead of turning anywhere, I just began rethinking how I was taught to think about theology. I started asking questions I hadn't raised beforehand.

## Seeing Theology More Like a Mysterious Adventure Than As a Mathematical Puzzle

It seemed that maybe we as human beings ended up coming up with a lot of very concise theological answers about things that maybe we just can't be quite as certain of. (However, at the same time, I do believe we absolutely need to be certain about some things as I will explain later.) Perhaps we are supposed to approach theology more with a sense of wonder, awe, and mystery than like trying to solve a mathematical puzzle. Perhaps we need to admit that our own personal biases and backgrounds do taint how we view theology. Therefore we better not be too prideful in how dogmatic we get with some of our conclusions as they very well may be our own tainted ones.

My assumption is that we all have pure motives when we think about theology, and of course we have the Spirit to guide us. Even so, we are inherently sinful (Romans 6:6; 7:17–18) and our hearts can be deceitful (Jeremiah 17:9). Knowing this, why do we then so confidently think our particular theological conclusions from our denominational brand are always *the* true and perfect ones? I am not talking about core theological beliefs such as those in the Apostles' Creed or the Nicene Creed. I fully understand that when the early creeds were crafted, they were addressing theological issues of that day and culture. When the Apostles' Creed was drawn up, the primary theological issue was Gnosticism, which denied that Jesus was truly Man, so we see this reflected in this response. When the Nicene Creed was drawn up, the primary theological issue was Arianism, which denied that Jesus was fully God, so we see this reflected in that response. Culture and issues of a culture forced them to think and make statements of faith about these things. They were also sin-tainted human beings struggling to draw conclusions, but it was not done in isolation. Through time, people have wrestled with and tested these core doctrines in the Nicene Creed, and they apply in any culture of any time period. We would be struggling with these same questions today if they hadn't back then. It wasn't just cultural theological response that would later change. These were statements of belief that remain core doctrines which I believe we should cling to and hold onto firmly. These are mysterious things still to be in wonder and awe about, but they are doctrines that we can have confidence and faith in and believe are truth no matter what culture or time period we are in.

## Beyond the Nicene Creed

At the same time, when we move beyond what the Nicene Creed discusses, I feel that it is not as easy to be saying so confidently that we have things all figured out. I wonder quite often if, beyond the Nicene Creed, we end up shaping some theology or even choosing what theology we believe because of personality and temperament. For example, the more someone needs control in their life, the more they will need to have very distinct answers for everything. We can subtly feel we can control God by controlling our theology and having the need to control and have answers for all mysteries. Or someone who may fear the chaos and uncertainty life brings feels better when a more detailed system of theology is there to direct them fully and provide strong answers for them. Some people are more steady and passive and don't want to think about things and make decisions. Instead, they just want to be told what to do and think—therefore, having someone distinctly tell them what to believe is all they need in order to be satisfied.

It's the same way with how we view Jesus. It is interesting even in the same church, to ask individuals how they perceive Jesus. Quite often, people describe Jesus to match their own temperament and personality. For the outgoing gregarious extrovert, Jesus was someone who was outgoing and happy and made jokes. For the more introverted, Jesus was serious and deep and introspective. Try this sometime in your church. It is fascinating.

I raise all of this because my personal dilemma led me to reexamine what I believe and why. Where did it come from? Did I believe something just because I read Tim LaHaye's viewpoint and then accepted it and did not question it again? Did I believe something because the theology book I used in seminary biased me toward one particular way? Was it only because of being in a certain church and denomination that I believed what I did? I didn't feel the need to rethink core Christian doctrines too much, such as those in the Nicene Creed. But moving beyond the Nicene Creed, I began to recognize there is much that is mysterious and uncertain.

Let me take a rather hot issue as an example. I was in a church for many years that very strongly stated that women should never be pastors. As a young Christian in the church, I simply accepted that as fact. I heard some of the verses about why women shouldn't be pastors, and these people taught with great authority and confidence. I didn't think about it too much, as everyone in the church believed the same thing. But then I met a female pastor, which forced me to think about this more deeply. She was very wise and could teach wonderfully. She had a great marriage and seemed to be very much in love. Then the questions started coming. Why can't she teach? She taught better than most men. If we allow females to talk and share with men in a home Bible study, why can't we allow them to share more formally in a classroom? Or from the pulpit? They didn't have pulpits in the early church, so why do we see speaking from one as different from when a female shares what she is learning in a home setting? Then you look into the spectrum of theological books written on this subject and see wise and godly leaders with PhDs say that women can be pastors, and they give very convincing explanations of why the Bible says this is allowed. But then you read other wise and godly leaders with PhDs who say that women cannot be pastors and give careful explanations from the Scriptures why the Bible says this is not allowed. There are really strong arguments on both sides. Who is right and who is wrong? I was speaking at a conference recently to several hundred church leaders and asked them to raise their hand if they allow females to be pastors and elders in their church. About half raised their hands. Then I asked who doesn't allow females to be pastors and elders in their church. The other half raised their hands. I then said "One of you is wrong! But look at each other. You both love God, and you are faithfully following the Scriptures to the best of your ability. You both pray and ask the Spirit of God to lead you to truth, but this is an issue that seems to be less of an absolute in our human ability to know for sure."

## Being Comfortable in Saying Both "I Don't Know" and "This I Know"

My dilemma of grappling with cultural change moved from questioning dispensational theology to questioning a lot of things beyond end-times issues. I moved to asking: What is the church? Why do we say we "go to church" when we are the church? What are "elders"? Why do elder boards feel more like corporate boards than what we find in the Bible? Was the title "pastor" ever used for church leaders in the Bible? Why do we preach the way we do? How did we end up giving these thirty-five-minute, four-point sermons with everyone sitting in rows staring at you on a stage? Why do we sing songs for worship the way we do? Where did all this come from?

Through all this, I ended up moving from a personal doctrinal state-ment with twenty things I would rigidly hold to—to about ten things. I became more of a Nicene Creed believer and then left more to mystery after that. Please understand, that as I say I left more to mystery, it doesn't mean I don't believe you can't come to solid conclusions about many things in addition to the Nicene Creed. There are many things not mentioned in the Nicene Creed that I believe are clear, such as Jesus' teaching about marriage, the authority of the Bible itself, the role of the Spirit in personal sanctification, etc. But at the same time, I have grown comfortable and secure in saying "I don't know" about some things (many things, in fact).

As in any culture and in any time period, with the emerging church, there are some theological issues that are raising more questions than others. We will always be grappling with theological questions and issues depend-ing on the culture and time period. Even so, we can still have an anchor of belief and a foundation of essential core doctrines. For me, it is the Nicene Creed. If our church today, as a community together, was never to know of the Nicene Creed and then opened the Bible to explore and study it, we probably would end up with the same conclusions. So that is why I believe there are essential core doctrines God has revealed in Scripture that we can firmly hold on to. I believe doctrine is important (1 Timothy 4:16), so let me explain a few of the doctrines I believe.

## Believing the Bible Is Inspired and a Compass and Anchor for Us

When I used to hold the Bible in my hands, I viewed it as the ultimate "answer-everything" book and ultimate "how-to" manual. I was basically taught to dissect the Bible, to take it apart piece by piece like dissecting a laboratory animal. I experienced the Bible being used like a textbook or an auto manual, where you looked up certain problems and how to solve them. When you found the page with the verse, you would then say, "If God's Word says it, I believe it, and that settles it." Unfortunately, so many people never question their pastors when they preach and use verses in this way. Or another extreme is when we go verse by verse through books of the Bible, never understanding the context of the whole book, or even the whole story the verse falls into. I am personally saddened to talk to Christians who have been raised in churches hearing lots of sermons from the Bible, but who rarely can tell you much about the Bible story itself, the historical context of when a book was written, etc. So, the irony is that in a time when we have so many Bibles out there, so many translations, so many radio preachers, it seems most Christians don't really know the Bible.

When I attended Multnomah Biblical Seminary, I was able to meet almost weekly with the founder, Dr. Mitchell. When asked a question, he would look at his students with a blank stare and would jokingly reply, "Don't you folks ever read your Bibles?" He also would use a verse from Amos: "'The days are coming,' declares the Sovereign LORD, 'when I will send a famine through the land—not a famine of food or a thirst for water, but a famine of hearing the words of the LORD'" (Amos 8:11). And he would apply it to people today. Now, I know that knowledge of the Bible itself does not make a disciple of Jesus. There are some people who know the Bible but are some of the most cold and callous people I have met. Or people that fill their heads with Bible knowledge and become arrogant and puffed up. But nevertheless, the emerging church needs to revere, teach, respect, discuss, and study the Bible. I think all the more in our emerging culture, do we need to create a culture of hungering for the Scriptures. Following are some of the reasons I feel so strongly about the Scriptures:

- *Jesus believed the Bible was important.* If we desire to be disciples of Jesus, know that disciples model themselves after their teacher. So, foremost, I want to know what my teacher valued and practiced. Jesus took the Scriptures very seriously as a major part of his life. Of course, when Jesus was on earth he only had access to the written Hebrew Bible, but when you look at the pattern of his life you see how important the Scriptures were to him. He began his public ministry by reading Scripture (Luke 4:16–21). When Jesus was tempted, he quoted Scripture that he had memorized (Luke 4:1–12). Jesus was constantly quoting Scripture when teaching (Matthew 5:21, 27, 31; Luke 18:20; Mark 2:25; Luke 7:27). Even on the cross, he quoted

Scripture (Matthew 27:46). After his resurrection, he quoted and taught Scripture (Luke 24:25–32). He spoke about the importance of Scripture (Matthew 4:4; Luke 11:28).

- *The Scriptures themselves claim to be a very important part of knowing and loving God.* We see that the Scriptures claim to produce faith (Romans 10:17). They help us with temptation (Psalm 119:11). They nourish us (1 Peter 2:1–2). They guide us (Psalm 119:105). They are a mirror to our soul (Hebrews 4:12). They give us spiritual insight (Psalm 119:30; James 1:25). They teach us wisdom and equip us for this life (2 Timothy 3:14–17). The overwhelming evidence again, is that the Bible is a major part of spiritual formation.

- *The Scriptures are inspired.* Throughout the Bible, you see where it says that God was behind the writing of the Scriptures. The classic passage is 2 Timothy 3:16 where it says that Scripture is "God-breathed." My best understanding of this is that God super-intended the human authors, using their unique personalities for God's purpose. Passages like 2 Peter 1:21 say the Holy Spirit carried the authors along. Jesus backs this up in Mark 12:36 where he says the Holy Spirit is the author of what David wrote in the Psalms.

How exactly the Spirit carried the authors along, I don't know. But by faith, I believe that the Spirit oversaw and directed the authors to compose what they were supposed to. Of course there are alleged contradictions we may never understand in this life, and through time there has been human corruption in copying Scripture. On our part, we must have faith to trust that God oversaw the formation of the specific books of the Canon. But the Bible is our light, our source, our guide, our compass. A compass gives direction but doesn't go into specifics. I see the Bible as a spiritually-inspired compass, where it gives us strong direction and even gives specifics about many things. But at the same time, there are some topics and things we wish we could have specific answers to, but they remain more of a mystery. It gives direction rather than acting as a how-to answer book. But the Bible gives enough direction so we don't get totally lost, and it helps us stay on the path and go in the right direction, no matter what culture or time period we live in.

I really believe the Bible does need to be given more prominence, something I feel we must absolutely cling to with passion. I believe we need to be teaching the Bible in the emerging church with depth and zeal, saturating our churches with Scriptures in everything we do. I personally believe emerging generations are hungry for Scripture, what Dr. Mitchell alluded to as a "famine for the Word of God." One of my prayers for our church is that people would fall in love with the Scriptures (not worship the Bible, but understand that through the Scriptures we grow to love and worship God all the more). The Scriptures are intended for transformation, not just information, nor just for how-to helps in our lives.

Bono of the band U2, in a *Rolling Stone* interview, stated that he sees the Bible as what "sustains" him. He also called the Bible an "anchor" and a "plumb line."[3] I like Bono's anchor analogy. When we are in a boat that is anchored, we have freedom to drift around, but there is a limit to the drifting. Bono also called the Bible a "plumb line," which is a cord suspending a metal weight that points directly to the earth's center of gravity, used to determine the vertical from a given point. That is how I see the Bible. It determines a direction and keeps us anchored.

For some, this may sound too fundamentalist, but I do have a fundamental belief in the inspired Scriptures being my guide and my authority (I use the word authority in a healthy way here). The Scriptures are used by the Spirit of God to renew my mind, my heart, my life, and to help me walk in the ways of Jesus. I always remember Jesus' words in John 14:23: "Anyone who loves me will obey my teaching." So that means that we need to know what his teaching was in order to obey it. That is why I want to saturate myself in Scriptures, and as a leader in a church, make sure people are being immersed and saturated in the Scriptures as well. Not for knowledge, but for love and also for obedience. Jesus says not only to know his teaching but to obey his teaching. So the Scriptures are for life-change, not just information.

Listening to this verse also means being a good student and understanding the cultural context of the original writers. The Bible was birthed in a specific cultural context, and because of that, there are certain parts we may never really understand. Most Christians, especially conservative ones, will be happy with what I am saying here, but before I end stressing the importance of the Scriptures, let me add a few clarifications.

- *We need to approach the Scriptures with humility.* I believe we need to admit that we are not God, that we are sin-tainted, and that we approach the Bible with our own biases and cultural background.

What this means is that we need to tread more lightly when we view the Scriptures, admitting that we may interpret some things incorrectly. I believe it is actually arrogant to think that our denomination or our church has it all right. You might be wrong on your view of the end times. You might be wrong on your view of women in ministry. You might be wrong on your view of infant baptism. You might be wrong on whether speaking in tongues is a valid gift today. Yet so often in pulpits and on radio ministries, I have heard preachers saying, "God says …," and then they spout off beliefs and make conclusions using Scripture, when I feel we would better approach Scripture with a sense of mystery and humility. Now I am not saying that we need to doubt something like the bodily resurrection of Jesus. We can say with full joyful confidence that God raised Jesus from the dead. But I have heard such stinky, stinky attitudes from people who nail down their theological beliefs with such certainty that there is an "everyone else is wrong but us" attitude. You hear it in their tone of voice, you read it on blogs, you see the cutting remarks made to others who hold different beliefs than they do. It's kind of like when someone says we believe in *sola Scriptura*, but they really mean "Sola-the-way-I-interpret-the-Scriptura." As we hold to our "anchor," I want to remember that there is room to float without letting go of the anchor.

- *We approach the Scriptures more as a narrative than as a science textbook.* The Bible is an inspired story, not a math puzzle, science manual, or how-to-have-a-happy-life manual. So we need to be good students and really listen to what we were supposed to be listening to in proper hermeneutics classes. As we approach the Bible, we must do our best to place ourselves within the story, to understand to our best ability the cultural context of what was happening when it was written, as that frames how we view what we read. Far too often, it seems that we take verses so far removed from their context and historical setting and use them in understanding how we're supposed to live today. I've sat through many sermons that feel more like a "Tony Robbins seminar with a few Bible verses thrown in" (as one twentysomething girl told me she experienced at a certain church), rather than a sermon that moves us into the beautiful and sometimes mysterious narrative of the Bible, helping us become better disciples of Jesus.

- *We can be bold and confident in what the Scriptures do make clear.* Now, I know the phrase "what the Scriptures make clear" is subjective and the cause of so much of what I am talking about. For example, some people say the Scriptures are very clear about teaching there is a pretribulational rapture. But I don't believe the Scriptures state explicitly how and when the return of Jesus and the rapture will happen. If such things were clear, there would not be such wonderful, godly, evangelical scholars who hold different positions. But what is clear is that Jesus will return, something we can say with absolute confidence. I recently heard a pastor make a public comment about how "stupid" the theory of the pretribulational rapture is, since he holds an amillennial partial preterist position. I don't think the pretribulational rapture is the strongest interpretation either, but I am not going to feel that others who believe something different are stupid, nor am I going to harbor an attitude of arrogance or anything but love for my brothers and sisters in Jesus who hold this view. I believe we should hold onto the essential doctrines of the Nicene Creed, and from there be approaching things with humility and respect for other beliefs.

But again, we can have bold confidence about essential core doctrines. In fact, I believe emerging generations are looking for something to believe in. I believe they are looking for "truth," and when we do have something we know is true, we should clearly and boldly say it. But I think the church sometimes says lots of things are "true" when we really aren't certain. Emerging generations respect us when we aren't afraid to say "I don't know" about something. I think it is healthy and honest to do so, and admitting this also creates a wonderful culture of learning as we explore different beliefs about certain doctrines.

## Worshiping the Triune God

As our churches meet to worship each week, we constantly need to be reminded of who it is we are gathered to worship. As A. W. Tozer rightly said, "What comes into our minds when we think about God is the most important thing about us." In the church I am part of, we would state that we are worshiping the triune God—the Father, Son, and Holy Spirit. I know that the word "Trinity" is not in the Bible, and I know it was more formally agreed on in the councils of the early church as they grappled with theological questions of that time period. But even if one approaches the Bible with no former knowledge of the Trinity, you can see God always revealing himself as the one and only God (Deuteronomy 6:4; Isaiah 45:14; James 2:19; etc.). Yet, as you read through the Scriptures, you can't help but find that the Father is God (1 Peter 1:2), and that the Spirit is also recognized as God (Acts 5:3–4). You see Jesus recognized as God when doubting Thomas cries out "My Lord and my God!" (John 20:28), and we see Jesus claiming attributes only God could claim, such as omniscience (Matthew 9:4) and omnipresence (Matthew 28:20). Many places in the Scriptures show the relationship of the Trinity. Can we absolutely know the Trinity and understand it? No, it is so complex and mysterious beyond our human comprehension. But we can say that God has revealed himself as Father, Son, and Spirit.

## Belief in Jesus and the Payment of Sin on the Cross

There has been much discussion lately on different viewpoints of the atonement. I believe there are many facets to the meaning of the death of Jesus. But one that stands out is the substitutionary atonement. I cannot read the New Testament and consider it all inspired and then downplay or ignore the repeated teaching about the blood of Jesus being shed on the cross for the payment of our sin. The atonement is something I cannot completely understand. Thinking about blood sacrifices in the Old Testament is not pleasant, and quite frankly, bizarre-sounding to today's mind-set. Thinking about Jesus dying and his blood paying for my sin is also not pleasant, and what Jesus went through is horrifying. But does it clearly teach these events in the Bible? I can't see any option but to hold that as truth. Because Paul wrote Romans using legal terms familiar to that day, it can all sound coldly technical. But by faith, I believe these events are true, and I then rejoice in the salvation that comes from the blood that was shed as payment on the cross.

I know myself, and I have no problem admitting I am a sinner as the Bible describes. As a sinner, I am so incredibly thankful that God provides a way to atone for our sinful nature. Although I don't understand the mystery, I rejoice that God chose to accomplish it through Christ's death and resurrection. I believe that we are saved through Jesus alone by substitutionary atonement. No human works or religious efforts bring salvation. Only Jesus.

I do, however, wish that worship songwriters would choose to write more songs that focus on the character of God and teachings of Jesus and what we should be like in this life, in addition to the thousands and thousands of songs about the cross and the substitutionary atonement. If we only view worship through the atonement, we don't focus Jesus' teaching on this life and on being a kingdom-minded disciple. I also think we need balance with a holistic Jesus in our teachings; that is, we certainly need to be speaking of Jesus as a friend and full of love, but at the same time we need to focus on him as the Lord of Lords and King of Kings who one day will judge the earth. Too often churches seem to go to polarizing extremes.

## Living in a Post-Christian Global Culture

Many faiths flood our global culture, and many people choose to mix faiths and have a more pluralistic spirituality. So this is a huge issue to wrestle with. If you raised the common question, "Do all religions lead to God?" I would say no. When you examine other faiths, you discover they do have some common truth at a base level, such as loving your neighbor. But the higher you go up the mountain, the more you realize the tremendous difference each has in extremely critical beliefs. For example, the Christian God is one. But in Hinduism, there are hundreds of thousands of gods. Both can't be right. So I choose to believe that God is one, as the Scriptures state emphatically.

Now in practical terms on the mission, I stress Jesus. I don't slam other faiths or discard them or ignore them. I rely on the Spirit to draw people to Jesus as we missionaries do our job being salt and light to those in our communities. When questions arise, we should be prepared to give loving, intelligent answers. In our church we just taught a class on world faiths because we see the world as global, not just local. We can't ignore that or pretend it is only in other countries that people have other faiths anymore. Recently in our church, a twenty-three-year-old Hindu put faith in Jesus. She ended up finding that Jesus was so much more caring and that the God of the Bible was a God who paid personal attention to her, where the Hindu gods and goddesses were more impersonal. After discussion with the friends she knew in our church, one night during a gathering, she prayed to trust in Jesus. I just met and talked with another twenty-four-year-old who was practicing paganism and Wicca but recently put faith in Jesus. In both these cases, we didn't have to give sermons to prove the other faiths wrong; it was a matter of a church community living out the ways of Jesus to them, and they were drawn to Jesus.

As to the question, "What about those in foreign cultures who never hear the name of Jesus?" I don't know—but God does. He is the ultimate and just judge, and I trust he knows what will happen. But I believe the classic and beautiful passage of John 3:16 that "God so loved the world that he gave his one and only Son." I trust that God very much loves the world, and that the people of the world are very much his business and in his heart. I desire our church to be used by God to spread this love and the good news of Jesus in our community and to those around us. I leave the answers to the mysterious questions up to God.

## Approaching the Afterlife with Awe and Wonder

I can't help but conclude this section with a few words on the afterlife, as I get asked about this often. Foremost, I want to focus on this life and on speaking to people about the gospel in terms of the here and now. I don't just focus on the ticket to heaven as I believe this creates a "Glad I'm going to heaven and now I can go back to normal living" attitude in people. We then live managing our sin (as Dallas Willard puts it) as we wait to go to heaven, and how sad that is. We are on a mission here, now, and the kingdom of God is here, now. I think the church has far shortchanged people by focusing just on the afterlife, not on the impact of the gospel for this life.

At the same time, I still do believe in heaven and hell. But even as I write that, I can say that I approach the afterlife with awe, wonder, and mystery. In reading the entire Bible and looking at all the passages on judgment and the resurrection in the New Testament, I believe there is an eternal separation for some (what is called "hell"). Although again, we need to recognize how Greek and Roman culture of the time viewed Hades and how Jesus' metaphors of Gehenna, the garbage dump outside of Jerusalem, incorporated the descriptions of burning fire.

What heaven and hell are like, I do not know, since the Scriptures use so many metaphors, and Revelation needs to be viewed through the lens of apocalyptic Jewish eyes, which we don't have in today's culture. So descriptions seem pointless to try to describe the afterlife in ways we probably wish we could. I see the afterlife as a reality, but as a mystery, and I will never use my views to manipulate people as I have often seen done. Even though I wish I could, I can't dismiss the passages that mention hell, judgment, and eternity. It tears my gut and heart apart to think of hell as a reality. It's a mystery beyond my understanding.

## How We Practice Theology in Our Church

This book focuses on beliefs, not on practice. In both of my books *The Emerging Church* and *Emerging Worship*, I wrote about practice and methodology, including preaching, spiritual formation, evangelism, and related topics. So I won't be going into methodology here. But the fact is that what our churches practice is based on our theology. Anything your church does has a theological backdrop to it. If you have event-driven evangelism with altar calls, that states your viewpoints on salvation. If you have worship that is experiential, that comes from a theological viewpoint and a desire to see people experience God through more than just preaching. If you stress small groups, it communicates your view of ecclesiology and what church and biblical community are. How you set up the rooms you meet in to worship reflects values and a theology of how you see community and the roles of the leaders in where you place them. You can look at a church budget and almost get a feel for how that church theologically views spiritual formation in how they invest their money and what staff they hire. Absolutely everything we do in church is a reflection of what we believe theologically, whether we are consciously aware of it or not. This is a very serious thing to recognize. We also need to be teaching the people in our churches to understand this, so they consider how theology impacts what they do and practice as well.

## A Worshiping Community of Missional Theologians

As a church we use four words to describe our mission and vision. We say that we are asking God to transform us into a "worshiping—community—of—missional—theologians." Because of space, I cannot fully develop all four words we use in our church but will focus primarily on the last word, "theologian." Basically, we start with the word "worshiping" since we first need to be worshipers, and worshiping God is the ultimate goal of all we do. But worship doesn't happen in isolation. We then say "community" because we exist in community, locally and globally. We then use the word "missional," as one of our nightmares would be to become an isolated Christian subculture and lose the mission of why we exist. We theologically believe that Jesus sent his church on a mission (Acts 1:8), so this we will keep as our passion. At a recent staff retreat we each wrote out "missionary letters" like overseas missionaries do when they raise support. We wanted to ask how we are doing as "missionaries" and what stories we would tell. How do we schedule our week as missionaries? The word "missional" is not just evangelism, in the normal usage of the word. It is much broader and much more kingdom focused than just the proclamation of the gospel through words (but this is a whole other topic that I covered in *The Emerging Church*).

If anyone is truly on a mission, as a missionary would be, it means one is prepared for the mission. So, we see our church as being students of the Scriptures. We then use the word "theologians" (not necessarily in the academic sense) as everyone being a serious student of Scripture and deep in thinking about theology together. It is one thing to say you are on a mission as a church, but so many can just go through the motions of church and lose passion. But when someone truly is on a mission somewhere, they can't help but study and discuss Scripture so they respect those they may talk to about their faith. Just as people going on short-term mission trips generally get all excited about the training, we hope to see people in our church have that same zeal and desire to learn for the mission here, as if they were going overseas. We constantly keep the definition of a theologian in our teaching and what we give out to people, as well as try to develop a culture of the church becoming "theologians." We describe it like this in our church literature:

---

**Theologians**

**the • o • lo • gi • an**  *n.* 1. A person who is well versed in the study of the nature of God and inquires into religious questions.

We will set an ethos of deep scriptural study, thinking, and discussion in community for helping us grow in our love for God and people. We desire to develop a lens of viewing the world and culture through the story of the Scriptures.

*2 Timothy 3:15 – 17*

---

In hopes of seeing a culture of theology in our church, we have started a "School of Theology," where we offer classes in various theological and biblical topics. We hope to see the people of our church taking the study of theology and the Bible very seriously. We also primarily teach books of the Bible or sections of books in our preaching. In our mid-week community groups, which are somewhat like house churches, they mainly go through books of the Bible in discussion format. We are trying to create an Acts 17:11 culture, like the Bereans who were studying and looking into Scripture on their own. On occasion, we have think tanks after worship gatherings where we have open forum-like dialogue to discuss the teaching.

We strongly desire to see everyone in the church thinking theologically. We are trying to always teach the theological "whys" behind all we do. We want to develop a culture where people hunger to read the Bible together, to discuss it, to see it transform their lives. We desire to see people able to explain and tell others why they believe what they do (when asked). We cannot imagine that a missionary would not eventually be asked why they believe what they do, so we want everyone to be prepared to answer with intelligence and love. We want to see it as the norm for people to explore theology, to not be afraid to grapple with hard issues and think as a community about theology.

From reading this, you may think we are all cognitive in our approach as a church, but that is far from true. We also balance this study with more experiential approaches to worship, using the arts, prayer stations, and many types of creativity in how we teach and express worship.

## A Chapter in a Book Doesn't Do Justice to the Complex Theology and Practice in a Church

Writing this chapter has been quite difficult. It is so hard to communicate in one chapter what and why a church believes and practices theologically. I tried to highlight a few core beliefs and share my heart about the importance of theology. As someone who is still evangelical in terms of holding to the basics of Nicene Creed Christianity, but also understanding how culture raises perspectives and how emerging issues need to be wrestled with, all this is exciting to me. I love that we can pray, discuss, even debate theology as brothers and sisters in Jesus. All the more today do we need to be open to discussion and more serious about being theologians in community. But with all the theological thinking and discussion, we must always remember that the goal is not knowledge. The goal is to have the Spirit of God transforming our minds and hearts into people who love God more and love people more. The more of a theologian we become, the more humble and awestruck at the greatness and wonder of God we should be. The more "beliefs" we have in our emerging churches, the more we should see the Spirit of God producing "love, joy, peace, patience, kindness, goodness, faithfulness, gentleness, and self-control" in us (Galatians 5:22–23). May we see theology in our churches as a way of being transformed by the renewing of our minds into disciples of Jesus. May God transform us into worshiping communities of missional theologians who walk in the ways of Jesus and bring his good news to the world around us.

# RESPONSE TO
# DAN KIMBALL

## MARK DRISCOLL

I first met Dan in the mid-1990s when he and his very cool hair picked me up at the airport and drove me to speak at a conference at Mount Hermon. Little did I know that the movement that came out of that conference would eventually morph into what is now the emerging church. Before I respond to his chapter, I would like to stress my love for and respect for Dan, whom I consider a friend.

First, I greatly appreciate and agree with much of Dan's chapter. Theologically, I appreciate his emphasis on the exclusivity of Jesus for salvation, human sin, literal hell, and respect for the final authority of Scripture. Practically, I appreciate his personal humility, respect for church history, and desire to see theology as a pursuit of transformation rather than mere information.

Second, Dan provides a very helpful middle way between the seeming theological certainty on all things among fundamentalists and the seeming theological uncertainty on all things among liberals. As a pastor he has rightly learned that there are primary issues that we must hold in a closed hand, and secondary issues that we must hold in an open hand. While Dan's point is wise and good, my fear is that many emerging-type Christians do not have a sufficient love for Scripture, or knowledge of church history, to wisely discern which issues belong in each hand.

Third, because there is uncertainty in the emerging church regarding which issues belong in which hand, emerging pastors will be compelled to add to the good but minimal Nicene Creed. For example, when a gay couple walks in and expects their lifestyle to be accepted, a Wiccan walks in and invites people to attend her pagan eco-spirituality festivals, or *The Da Vinci Code* fans start inviting people from the church to their house to learn about Jesus' wife and kids, the Nicene Creed, though true, is not sufficient because it does not answer any of these sorts of current issues.

Because I know Dan, I know that he regularly deals with these sorts of issues and replies with biblical truth delivered with the tact of a loving pastor. But I also fear that less thoughtful Christians will agree on the need for the kind of Christianity 1.0 that the Nicene Creed provides, but will refuse to also upgrade to Christianity 2.0, 3.0, and 4.0 as needed.

What I mean is that, in reading Dan's chapter, I was reminded of how important it is that emerging Christian leaders acknowledge the various levels of jurisdiction in which theology is done.

First, as different Christian faith communities intersect, they must decide on the handful of essential beliefs they must hold in common, as well as what issues they will agree to disagree on in an agreeable way, so they can maintain unity and truth. This is Christianity 1.0 and is expressed in such things as the Nicene Creed, to which Dan repeatedly appeals. As a Christian, I have friendships with others who agree with me on Christianity 1.0, and as a church, we work together with other churches who also agree with us on Christianity 1.0.

Second, as a Christian leader, there is a set of beliefs that are considered essential to be considered a faithful Christian. These beliefs govern the lives of individuals and families in a Christian community. This is Christianity 2.0 and is expressed in various traditions such as Wesleyanism, dispensationalism, Calvinism, etc. As a new Christian I chose to join an Evangelical Free Church because I agreed with their views on issues such as the authority of Scripture, baptism, and church government, all examples of Christianity 2.0.

Third, there are essential beliefs that a parent wants to impart to their child, while letting their child live out their faith with freedom on secondary matters (e.g., eschatology, charismatic gifts, style of worship) and matters of conscience (e.g., musical taste, clothing style, tattoos). This is Christianity 3.0 and includes such broad Christian teams as the fundamentalists, liberals, evangelicals, etc. In our family, my wife and I are raising our children in Mars Hill Church, which I pastor, because we agree with the views on such things as family structure and cultural engagement. These are a part of our Christianity 3.0.

Fourth, there is a set of personal beliefs and preferences by which someone lives their life of faith that includes far more precise convictions on a wide number of matters. This is Christianity 4.0 and includes a person living their life by their biblical convictions, conscience, general revelation, and church history to the best of their understanding of what it means to be faithful to Jesus. In my personal life, this means that I do not generally travel alone or stay in a hotel by myself when away from home because my conscience commands that I live under continual accountability as part of my Christianity 4.0.

The problem that so many emerging-type Christians are overreacting against is churches where Christianity 3.0 and 4.0 are proclaimed to be Christianity 1.0, so that other faithful Christians are rejected as unfaithful, or the pastor's conscience regarding issues related to Christianity 3.0 and 4.0 is binding on everyone in their church. What I appreciate about Dan's chapter is his emphasis on building faithful, theological-minded Christian churches on Christianity 1.0. The result is that the essentials of our faith, such as the Trinity, human sin, salvation through Jesus alone, eternal hell, and the authority of Scripture, forever remain in the closed hand of certainty.

What I would simply warn other Christians, parents, and leaders to accept, however, is the need for each of these varying levels of conviction and authority, because Christianity 1.0 is not sufficient to answer all of the questions and correct all of the theological errors in our culture today.

# RESPONSE TO
# DAN KIMBALL

## JOHN BURKE

As I've come to know Dan, I've found we have a similar passion for unchurched people, probably because we both came into the church as skeptical seekers. Dan is a leader who longs for the church to be a beautiful bride and a fully functioning body in the world. In his chapter, I hear Dan asking the questions of a leader who loves people far from God: "How do we lead the emerging church to be both true to Scripture and life-giving to our broken world?" I found that I agree with most everything Dan has to say, but I would like to comment on a few very important points he makes.

Although I came to faith apart from involvement in a church, like Dan, my early Christian experience with church came predominately through the tribe of conservative evangelicals. In retrospect, I too have had the same knee-jerk reaction as Dan to some of the "ways of the tribe." I question whether all I inherited from my tribe has been as true to the heart of the Scriptures as we have confidently proclaimed.

Since Christians in America are virtually indistinguishable from those who are not, the emerging church must take a hard look at the theology producing such a lack of fruit and let Jesus ask us, "Why do you call me, 'Lord, Lord,' and do not do what I say?" (Luke 6:46). And I don't just think this means moral, behavioral conformity—Jesus commanded us to love one another in a unified (John 17:21), sacrificial way (John 13:34), so that the world would believe.

We must heed Dan's call to rethink and reimagine how the church can be an attractive bride and an effective body. I don't think any of us leading emerging churches claims to have all the answers, but as Dan indicates, the right answers start with the right questions. If our theology does not lead us to become the kinds of people who look more like Christ, we must reassess our theological priorities and perspectives.

When it comes to the world around us, the emerging church must not be lazy with our theological answers. Dan points out a tendency to defend ourselves with pat answers from the Bible, but people who don't believe in the Bible also don't believe it holds authority. So we must make ourselves uncomfortable theologically by entering into dialogue with the questions of the culture and helping people see why the truth of God is good.

Unfortunately, most pastors speak each Sunday primarily to the already convinced. They don't realize that in almost every church service, there are spiritual seekers who snuck in the back. So many people who found faith at Gateway first tried several other churches nearby. But if pastors don't even know the theological questions those outside the fold are asking, they won't address them.

Consequently, spiritual skeptics listening from the back say, "They don't understand me and I don't understand them." So if we believe the way of Jesus is truth and "good news" for all people, we must work harder to integrate theology with what we know of philosophy, psychology, science, and the arts, to help people "see and taste that the Lord is good" and understand why "putting Jesus' words into practice" is the best foundation on which to build a life.

Dan says we must not "proof text a complex situation" or be afraid to say, "I don't know," but rather "theology needs to be missional." Here's an example of how I have seen that to be true. While teaching a Gateway U class recently, I was asked several questions by people still exploring faith. After I explained the prophetic fingerprint of a suffering Messiah stamped onto the pages of Isaiah 53, one woman asked me, "Why would I want to worship a bloodthirsty God?"

The question of the atonement she had was, "Why is God so fixated on blood—blood sacrifice in the Old Testament, Jesus' cleansing blood in the New Testament? He sounds cruel to me." How often do pastors focus theologically through the lenses of these types of questions? "We've been cleansed by the blood of the lamb" is not a beautiful vision of sacrificial love to her like it is to me.

How do I help her see (through her lenses) that her disdain for cruel, malicious, blood-letting evil *is exactly* why God required the greatest sacrificial payment to appease his justice? How do I help her see that God's will is for loving, peaceful, kindhearted people—yet humanity can't live this way on our own, as history shows. Her concerns are valid, but misdirected against God. So we must think hard theologically and creatively about how to convey the truth in a postmodern, post-Christian context while staying true to what Scripture reveals about mysterious things.

And we must be able to answer in truth and in love without getting defensive. When people sense we're preparing to fight, they too get ready to defend themselves, and soon no one is listening at all and the Evil One wins the war for the heart—regardless of who wins the theological battle. Sometimes the best answer is the true answer that Dan suggests, "I don't know for sure."

As Dan writes, there are some things that are clear and essential in order to rightly relate to God as he has revealed himself. But we will never understand everything. So focus first on getting the core theological questions answered, so that we can decide if we will truly follow Jesus, not just in profession, but also in practice. Then we can wrestle with the peripheral theological questions until Jesus comes back for us (right before the tribulation … or was it in the middle … or maybe after?).

# RESPONSE TO DAN KIMBALL

## DOUG PAGITT

Dan Kimball is one of the finest people I know. I love him and treasure his friendship. If I were ever searching for a pastor, I would look for someone like Dan. In so many ways I have learned from and sought to emulate in my own life, Dan's care, sensitivity, and desire to be faithful. I have had the privilege of being with Dan's family and church community, wonderful people who are a large part of Dan's "success."

Dan and I have known one another for more than a decade, and I have seen him grow, change, and remain faithful. Dan's loyalty is what I admire most about him. This loyalty is expressed in his commitment to his family, church, friendships, and, as is obvious in his chapter, his theology. There is such benefit to being a person of deep loyalty in belief. Above all, it preserves relationships. In dozens of situations, I have watched Dan go to painful ends to be sure people are listened to, encouraged, and helped along the way from whatever point they are starting. This is so admirable.

I can see mixed desires in Dan's writing. His desire to remain faithful, even loyal, and the tug to be adventurous. Fortunately there are categories such as "mystery" and "wonder." These are the places where those who do not want to break loyalty with the past can explore—"I know such and such to be true, but I do not understand it" kind of logic. Or in Dan's words, "But by faith, I believe that the Spirit oversaw and directed the authors to compose what they were supposed to. Of course there are alleged contradictions we may never understand in this life...."

And, "These are mysterious things still to be in wonder and awe about, but they are doctrines that we can have confidence and faith in and believe are truth no matter what culture or time period we are in."

To be honest, I am not sure how useful this sense of mystery is. I am not saying Dan is dishonest, not at all. I am suggesting that at times, there is a bit of word play going on that allows Dan to simultaneously believe (with full assurance of authority) but not have to be responsible for that belief.

I find an interesting ambivalence at work in Dan's acceptance of the creeds and his use of scriptural authority. Dan holds to an authority in the Bible that I believe is better placed in the Holy Spirit. Dan writes:

> I always remember Jesus' words in John 14:23: "Anyone who loves me will obey my teaching." So that means that we need to know what his teaching was, in order to obey it. That is why I want to saturate myself in Scriptures, and as a leader in a church, make sure people are being immersed and saturated in the Scriptures as well.

This verse in John is also one of my favorites that I quote often. I think where Dan and I differ is that I include the next three verses more often than Dan might.

> "Anyone who loves me will obey my teaching. My Father will love them, and we will come to them and make our home with them. Anyone who does not love me will not obey my teaching. These words you hear are not my own; they belong to the Father who sent me.
>
> "All this I have spoken while still with you. But the Advocate, the Holy Spirit, whom the Father will send in my name, will teach you all things and will remind you of everything I have said to you."

It seems that Jesus is indicating that the Holy Spirit will be the teacher and reminder of truth. I am quite certain from previous conversations with Dan that he would argue that this "teaching and reminding" came through the inspiration of the New Testament writings. But I think this kind of argument shows the different emphasis on where our authority comes from. I am not trying to say the Bible is not an important part of our faith and following, but Dan comes from a tradition that places near total authority on the Bible. So for Dan to include the creeds in his authority structure is a true sign of movement and change.

In light of the creeds, Dan writes: "Through time, people have wrestled with and tested these core doctrines in the Nicene Creed, and they apply in any culture of any time period. We would be struggling with these same questions today if they hadn't back then. When we examine the Nicene Creed and its conclusions, we can have confidence that we would reach these same conclusions today. It wasn't just cultural theological response that would later change."

In my words he is asking, "Would we not conclude the same thing, and therefore do we have any concluding to do on these matters?"

This way of thinking suggests that we are not to be struggling with these issues today. We most certainly are, or ought to be. Creeds were never meant to be the end of thinking on such issues; they were meant to be expressions to engage with, or within, as we consider these and other issues in our day. Not to be critical, but the statements of the creeds most certainly were cultural theological responses. To suggest that these creeds constitute some sort of timeless doctrine of finality is to put a pressure on the creeds they were never meant to withstand. Creeds are statements of belief, made in certain contexts. To relegate them to some "frozen" stagnant state is, while seemingly faithful, really anything but.

I am intrigued by Dan's use of the anchor as a metaphor for not "drifting" away from proper belief. While neither of us are seamen, I think this idea of anchoring is a great idea if one wants to stay in port. So, for all who have docked their ships, anchor down, stay put. Don't drift. But what about the times when one wants to, and is even called to move to a new port? In this situation the anchor is a problem. The anchor prevents the ship from drifting, and from sailing. I think that Dan has docked his boat, and this is part of his calling. He is meant to stay put, to be faithful in the port. So to anchor could not be a more appropriate understanding. But that does not mean that we all ought to be "anchored" in that sense.

But with all this friendly "nit-picking" set aside, Dan is a man of deep faith and importance in my life. I am so pleased to be in friendship and ministry with him.

# RESPONSE TO
# DAN KIMBALL

## KAREN WARD

I like Dan Kimball. We've met several times on the emerging "circuit," and I've attended several of the workshops he has led.

I like Dan Kimball's hair. I mean, it must be the most distinctive haircut in the known emerging-church world.

I like the names of Dan Kimball's communities. First "Graceland" and then "Vintage Faith." I really want to visit him in Santa Cruz, as we share an appreciation for things vintage and yet modern, retro and yet "relevant," ancient and yet future, within the emerging church.

I think I'm ready now to forgive Dan for writing a book called *The Emerging Church*, which is the name of my old, and now dated, website (*emergingchurch.org*). Seriously, Dan has made (with Graceland) and is making now (with Vintage Faith) and with all of his books, a great contribution to the diversity and to the generous spirit within the emerging church community.

I like how Dan uses "emerging church" to describe "those who notice culture is changing and are not afraid to do deep ecclesiological thinking as we are on a wonderful adventurous mission together for the gospel of Jesus as new cultures emerge around us."

Again, what is key for me about Dan's writing here and elsewhere is the positive spirit he evidences and the genuine excitement his work expresses.

Dan does a great job of describing the situation and issues around postmodernity in ways others can easily grasp, and he also does a great job of calling for change in how we "do" church without the need to overly critique the views of others coming from non-emerging positions.

I share Dan's distaste for the need to assign people and things related to the church into "categories" of conservative or liberal, to try and pigeonhole them in order to reduce and distill the amazing technicolor palette of Christian viewpoints down into a sterile black or white.

I resonate with Dan's view of his role as "a pastor and leader in a local church community, on a mission striving to be true to Scripture, but also engaged in the culture and thus enjoying wrestling with theological issues our culture raises."

Just as Dan wrestles with being a "conservative evangelical," that is "not one of those conservative evangelicals," I too get tired of being part of two so-called "liberal" mainline denominations, when I am neither a liberal nor a conservative, but a Christian who has an affinity for both the Lutheran clarity in the proclamation of the gospel and for Anglican richness in its liturgical embodiment.

I don't have any glaring differences with what Dan has stated. The differences between us are not so much theological as they are biographical. Really, we just come with different backgrounds, Dan from "conservative evangelicalism" and me from "sidelined mainline-ism," but we still meet up on common ground and have similar views on how the church can emerge within today's postmodern culture.

I also share Dan's disappointment that this meeting of minds is only happening on the printed page ... how very non-emerging! And I echo Dan's words that I will end with here as he says, "I tremendously respect each person contributing to this book. Writing our opinions in this format is difficult, because it is only words without facial expressions; no cup of coffee or a pint of Guinness is on the table as we chat theology here."

Someday, the group of us will all have to come together and do this the real emerging way, face to face, sharing stories, agreeing and disagreeing, but making theology together, over some double-shot lattes or a round of imperial pints.

# THE EMERGING CHURCH AND EMBODIED THEOLOGY

DOUG PAGITT

# THE EMERGING CHURCH AND EMBODIED THEOLOGY

## DOUG PAGITT

I am glad to be involved in this project, but I must confess at the beginning that I have a few concerns. As with all concerns, they come from varied places in my life. Some are from personal apprehension and fear, while others come from hope and desire. All the authors contributing to this book are friends of mine; some I agree with more than others when discussing the topics of this book, but all are friends. I have spent time with all of the contributors, I have met their families, prayed for their churches, as they have mine, and I expect that we will be involved in one another's lives for decades to come. I hope nothing but the best for them and their communities of faith. While a great aspect of this project is our friendship, it is also a bit intimidating. Because they are friends and their opinions matter to me, I want to look good in their eyes and in comparison to them. I am not proud of that desire, but I recognize it. As we all write, we do so in isolation of what the others are contributing. I have attempted to write my section as if I were speaking with each of them. I have imagined they are sitting opposite the table from me as we kick these ideas around in a good conversation. The trouble is, and this is where an additional concern comes in, I know that we are not only talking to one another, but to anonymous readers as well, or even, more importantly. I know that most readers will not know me and will need to make judgments on my content in a "disembodied" way. There may even be some who "will have me all figured out" by what they read. So unlike a coffee-shop conversation, we are not able to lower our voices and whisper the ideas in which we are least confident. In this setting, all ideas are put right here in black and white. So now I need to worry how this sounds to people I don't even know.

I also know that this book is written by practitioners of church-based ministry for other practitioners, and is not intended to be in the academic theological genre. But I still worry what those from the academic world will think of my approach.

In my years as a pastor, I have taken numerous personality inventories and have come to a pretty clear understanding of the way I operate in the world. (Most recently, I have come to understand that I am an Enneagram 8, for those of you who know this type of classification.) I know that I am competitive and a contrarian, and those qualities concern me in this effort, for I do not want to be too much of either. I can only imagine that there are times when I say too much, more from my personality than from conviction, and there are other times when I am working hard not to overstate my beliefs and do not say enough.

I think this is important for you to know about me, and about my view of theology before we get into specifics of my theology. I consider theology a personal venture. I think there is no way to remove ourselves from our theology. We choose our theology for reasons that can be traced to not only our knowledge and faith, but also to our fears and aspirations. I bet most of us construct our theology more from the influences of our personality than we are willing to admit. We believe what we believe because we want it, even need it, to be true. So I, like all the authors (and readers for that matter), come to this with "unclean hands," but in my mind, that makes for a much better discussion (and theology) anyway.

My task for this book, as I understand it, is to put words around my theology in a way that they can interact with the ideas of the other authors. It is not simply to answer a preset list of questions. This process is more dynamic and personal than that. Like the other authors, I am a pastor of a community of faith, and so my theology is embedded in that community. With that being the case, I am not sure how accurately I can describe my theology apart from my community. The assumption that a theology, or better yet, a theological system, can be understood as an isolated endeavor from the community in which it lives, is a shaking one at best. But there certainly must be a level of proximity we can reach. Just as any snapshot photo of my family does not fully represent my family, it does give an outsider a glimpse at what we look like, how old we are, perhaps our ethnic background, and the like. It doesn't tell all, but it tells something, and so it is to that end that I seek in this discussion. But please understand that my

"Impressionist Realism" attempt to explain what I believe and how I view the world is a feeble attempt at best. The true nature of one's theology is in the life lived and the community it is lived within.

So let's get started. Let me begin with a few assumptions I hold, then give a list of a few of the self-diagnosed characteristics of my theology, and finally discuss the kinds of issues I believe Christian theology needs to address in our world today and into the near future.

## Assumptions

### Theology is meant to be temporary

Theology must be at its essence, confessional. It is not enough to simply say what is (or really how we see it to be); theology must come from the life of the one who holds it. We may well have a dead theology, not because the ideas are dead, but because the people who passionately held them and the reasons for their conception have passed. Because theology is connected to real life, answering particular questions, concerns, and opportunities of the day, it will be ever-changing. If it is not so, then it may well not be theology—it may be dogma, history, or a collection of random facts, but not theology. Theology is the living understanding of the story of God in play with the story of our lives.

A year or so ago, a friend gave me a book he discovered in a used bookstore in Stillwater, Minnesota. The title of the book caught his attention: *Reconstruction in Theology*. He told me he thought of me when he saw the book, because of an ongoing conversation we had about how important I feel it is for the emerging church to have a positive contribution to the world and not simply be deconstructing the beliefs of others. So he opened the book and read the following section there in the bookstore. When he gave it to me, he said, "That sounds exactly like the things you were saying":

> The days of the great theological system are doubtless past; not because the great truths do not abide, but simply because the task is differently conceived.... Theology must grow as science grows. The task is endless. Each worker may hope to contribute something to the developing system of theological truth, and, he welcomes the contribution of another; but he does not hope to reach the final system.
>
> In one respect it is even less possible for the theologian than for the scientist to regard his work as final, for it belongs to the very nature of spiritual truth that each age must be its own interpreter in spiritual

things.... Truths therefore, that are to be vital to it require re-statement in these terms, and this re-statement is not to be deplored, but rejoiced in as an unmistakable sign of interest and life. That a generation should be content to say over again precisely as its predecessors any form of truth would mean that that truth was not a living one for them; they did not care to translate it into living thought and language.[1]

John bought the book for $1.25 and gave it to me. I agreed that this section encapsulated my sentiment about theology and was surprised that I have not heard of Henry Churchill King. I was even more surprised to turn to the copyright page of the book and see that it was published in 1899. John knew that the 1890s are a decade I have a fond obsession for, so this made the book an ideal gift. I felt buoyed by the ideas in the book and somehow emboldened that those of my favorite historical decade were thinking similar things. While I had not heard of Henry King at the time and certainly drew different conclusions from him on many matters, I did find the same hope and passion for the personal connection to faith and theology.

This notion that theology must be connected to our lives is not something new; it is, in my opinion, the way it has always been. It was not new in the 1890s either.

Theology functions like an adapter that allows the story of God to connect with the story of our lives.

In the late 1990s, I owned my first portable computer, and in order to connect it to the Internet, I had to insert an adapter card into my laptop and then connect a phone cord to the card. It worked, and worked well. I could get online even though I was tethered to the wall. I now own a computer that has a wireless card in it that still allows my computer to connect to the Internet, but through waves coming from a router and not through a cord connected to the wall. I still want my computer to connect to the Internet, and it does. But I use a different protocol to do so (in this case, a much better way). My desire has not changed but my situation and solutions have.

If I were to suggest that the adapter I used in the 1990s worked so well that I wanted to be sure to use it today, I would have a problem. I no longer have a slot to plug it into; the card is now on the inside of the computer. I could "value" the adapter that served me so well by carrying it around with me or laying it on top of my new computer, or I could tape it to my computer so it would always be there. But this would have nothing to do with connecting my computer to the Internet.

In my view, theology is like the adapter. Theology is not the story of God, and it is not our story; rather, it is the understandings that allow us to connect the two. When my theology no longer serves that purpose, because either my story has changed or my understanding of God's story changes, then the right and faithful thing is for theology to change as well.

I think it is worth saying again that theology is not the same as the story of God. Far too often, in my opinion, this becomes an issue, and when one disagrees with our theology, we can too easily assume they have abandoned Scripture or the story of God. Theology is explanatory—answering certain questions or addressing certain issues. But it must never be confused with the life of God or the story of God.

## Theology is meant to be profession

The importance for a theology of our day is not only found in reaching those on the outside of the faith, but it is profession from those who hold to it. It is to bring life to those inside the faith. In a way, this is what the author was getting at in his admonition to Theophilus in the gospel of Luke: "I too decided to write an orderly account for you, most excellent Theophilus, so that you may know the certainty of the things you have been taught."[2]

Theology that serves to make faith alive for the faithful is certainly prepared to do so for the faithless.

There are far too many people inside Christian faith who feel the need to "give a nod" to the theology of their church or tribe, but it really has nothing to do with their lives. I hear it in comments like, "Well I know such and such but ..." Because theology has so often been seen as permanent inarguable statements of truth that could never change "because God never changes," it has also lost its function to be a profession of faith from the community that is bound by it. In my view, this kind of disconnected theology is not useful nor should it be encouraged.

## Theology is always contextual

To be even more specific, theology is always human. It is people who create theology as a tool of our culture to explain reality as we see it. So we all operate from a context. We think in categories given to us by our language and culture. Theology is not a culturally neutral act.

There is no period of time in which the categories of understanding were ideal, or a time that we ought to return to for our understanding of God. Our culture and language is as sufficient for the theology as any other time.

In many ways, theology is not the point. Theology itself is a category for separating our understanding of God from other "disciplines." The very notion that we can talk about theology as its own venture shows that we are operating in a particular context.

All theology has developed in a context, and those contexts are tenuous at best, so theology must always be developing.

People of the first century certainly understood this. I think I can fairly assert that the New Testament gives us not only the picture of an emerging church (the change from the temple and synagogue model) but an emerging theology (a change from a Hebrew understanding to a Hebrew/Gentile understanding). The question of how the story of God that was embedded so deeply in the Hebrew story could be extended to the "Gentiles" was the setting of the New Testament theology. Much of the writing of that period was directed at that question. The desire to find parallels in our day and to use the arguments of the first century as help in our day is an admirable one, but one that must be carefully done, always keeping in mind that the overriding question of the first century was the Jew/Gentile issue in its relationship to the Law and Spirit discussion initiated by the fullness and completion of God coming in Jesus. To take Paul's arguments that helped explain the blessing of God through Abraham and how it connects to those who are not from the Hebrew genealogy and use them as "pawns" in the fifteenth-century justification and faith debates, or the eighteenth-century predestination debates, or twenty-first-century gender issues, is an unfair and unwise practice. I do believe the story of the New Testament has much to say on those topics, but too often the Bible becomes a patsy for misfit theology.

Those who study the history of the church are aware that the theological presuppositions of any time in history, that many take for granted, were carved from the real-life interaction of people of faith trying to make sense of their world. To take their answers or even their presuppositions without understanding them in their context is not only myopic and limiting, but also potentially fatal to our faith. We are called to more dynamic faith and theology led by the Holy Spirit in our day as the church was in the first century.

## Theology is to be particular

The gospel of Jesus is meant to be good news in its particulars.

We are always living in particular situations and the gospel must meet those situations. This has been one of the most compelling parts of

Christianity—Jesus was not a generic Messiah but was embedded in the life and dirt of culture, and was the fulfillment of particular promises. Christianity does not mandate a singular culture nor a single cultural worldview.

The letters of the New Testament are not generically written moral exaltations—they are practical calls to faith to certain people in certain situations. Many of us who hold the Bible in high regard have the unfortunate habit of trying to theologize, or moralize, the Bible to serve our context. This is quite often seen in the tendency to precede a quote from the Bible by saying, "The Bible says...." rather than acknowledging where it is from, whom it is from, and to whom it was intended. What I find objectionable about this is that it removes the context and places authority in the fact that a statement is in the Bible rather than considering the faith and lives of the people involved. It is yet another attempt to dehumanize the Bible and theology, which I think is a result of a Gnostic bias in certain streams of the church, which thinks we can know certain truths removed from their context, giving us access to God. The canonized Scriptures certainly have authority in our lives and faith, but to rip the quotes from their context and give them generic biblical authority is not helpful, and I believe it disembowels the Bible of the very authority many understand it to have. We can and must do better than this. We are all aware that there are times when things written in Bible passages are meant for certain people in the context in which the letter was written or the event in which the gospel took place. This is what keeps us from walking up to someone who is tending a young donkey and telling them, "Give me that colt, the Lord needs it" even though Jesus told his disciples to do this very thing. And it keeps us from searching nametags at a church event to find a woman named Priscilla from a church in Rome, in order to greet her on behalf of Paul. Yet we take other statements (some in the very sentences before or after those just mentioned) and remove them from their context and quote them as being inarguable Scripture that flawlessly tells us what to do. Worse yet, we build theology around them and then treat our theology as if it has the same function of Scripture.

The gospel is too good for this. We need to have a more contextual understanding of what the Spirit is saying to us in our day in order to live into it.

## Theology is a Spirit-led practice

My contention that theology is led by the work of the Holy Spirit comes from the idea that, when Jesus told his disciples that the Counselor, the

Holy Spirit, would be sent and would remind them of all that Jesus said and taught (John 14:26), this statement has implication for us and is still active today.

Christians have never been intended to be a people only of a book, but a people who are led by the ever-present God, active in our lives, communities, and world. So we do not move into our world feeling that we are searching in the dark to find the way of God. Rather we live as those who profess that the Light has come into the world and that this Light will not be extinguished.

I often wonder what kind of a faith we have if we used the notion of Jesus being Light as often and fully as we have used Jesus as the Word.

> In the beginning was the Word, and the Word was with God, and the Word was God. He was with God in the beginning. Through him all things were made; without him nothing was made that has been made. In him was life, and that life was the light of all people. The light shines in the darkness, and the darkness has not overcome it.[3]

> When Jesus spoke again to the people, he said, "I am the light of the world. Whoever follows me will never walk in darkness, but will have the light of life."[4]

I am not suggesting that Jesus as the "Word of God" is a less-than-valuable way of understanding who he is, but it is also not the only understanding. It is one of many descriptions of Jesus and not the ultimate one. I do think that too often people understand the Christian profession of believing in the Word of God to mean belief in the Bible rather than Jesus, but that is another issue.

I think we would do well in understanding God as Light and recognize that Light of God in each one of us, and shining in all fullness in Jesus. This is the Light that overcomes darkness, not allowing the darkness to prevail. To be a people who fan the flame and brighten the Light of God in the world seems to be Jesus' way as much, if not more than, feeling the need to get the words just right.

### Our theology is taking place in an age of tremendous change

The kind of change that has marked the move from the fifteenth century to the twenty-first is as great as the move from the first century to the third. When one looks at the changes in Christian theology and understandings of the gospel (specifically what makes it good news) from the time of Jesus to AD 300, it is unwise and uninformed to consider it to be simply saying the same things with new words. They were saying new things in the fourth century. There were new questions. There were new problems. And there were new ways in which the good news was good. This in no way is to suggest that it was a total undoing of the Christian understanding from the first century, but the change from the Jewish sect struggling with the Jewish/Gentile question, to the Hellenization and Christian empire, is immeasurable.

The development of creeds, refined statements of belief, and explanation was not driven by a desire to keep the news the same. It was driven by a desire to allow the story of God to make sense in their day to a people with a story different than the Hebrews, and most certainly different than many of our stories today. The Greek converts to Christianity in the first through third centuries had to understand the gospel in their setting, and not only in the first-century Hebrew setting.

We are called to be communities that are cauldrons of theological imagination, not "authorized re-staters" of past ideas. What we have in our communities are not simply people who need to have the gospel applied to their lives, but people who need to know their situation and what the Good News of God means for them. So our job as leaders of communities is not simply to apply the well-founded answers of previous generations' questions or assumptions to the lives of our people, but rather to guide, extract, and join with the hopes and aspirations deeply embedded by God in the lives of our people.

This is what makes the posture of listening to one another in community so important. Community is the place where God dwells. God created in community, is expressed and expresses in community. The goal of Christian community is to be a living place of the hopes and aspirations of God. In this way, Christian community serves as a hermeneutic of the gospel. The lives of the people of the community go beyond individual expressions and become the way that insiders and outsiders experience the life of God.

We have worked hard in our setting to be a community in four ways: global, local, historical, and futurical. We believe that when we talk about being a community, it is not only with the people of our community, but with those who have gone before us, those who are with us in other places around the world, and those who will follow us. But just as in any good community, everyone has something to contribute. We hold that we, even as our little church, have something to contribute to the greater community of followers of God through Jesus. We take seriously the faith of those who have come before us. We also recognize that any tradition that seeks to be faithful to that tradition is often ignorant of other beliefs. Recently this became clear to me in a conversation with church leaders from around the world. When those from the Reformed tradition spoke of "traditional views," they were often not including the Anabaptist or Eastern Orthodox traditions (and the same worked the other way around). Fortunately there were people from many backgrounds, so this kind of "tradition bias" was not allowed to dominate the meeting.

### The song and dance: gospel and culture

I like to think of the relationship of the gospel and culture as a song and a dance. Earlier this summer, our church was spending time during our Sunday night worship gatherings telling the story of the development of Christianity over the centuries. During one week, we discussed the influence of Augustine on the Church (an influence that I believe has too much sway, by the way). We did so in the context of the fourth-century debate between Augustine and Pelagius. Pelagius' understanding of Christianity has been best preserved in Celtic expression, while Augustine's is best seen in the Roman church. The debate between the two was significant during their time in the fourth century, and Augustine eventually used his political influence to have Pelagius excommunicated from Rome as a political agitator and then later excommunicated from his church (I believe on false pretenses and for personal and political, not primarily doctrinal reasons).[5] During our discussion, we attempted to help our community understand the worldview of each perspective so we could better understand the varied conclusions and how we have ended up where we are in thinking today. Pelagius suggested that people were born with the Light of God aflame within them, if even dimly lit. This fit the Druid notions of the Northern Island region of his home. Augustine supported the Greek understanding of God taken primarily from the Greek Pantheon imagery, and proclaimed that people were born separate from God. These differing understandings led each to conclude differently as to the relationship of the church to people, people to God, and people to one another.

In an attempt to help our community understand the relationship of their cultural worldview and their religious understanding, we asked a member of our community, Tim Lyles, to play on his guitar a series of songs, and we asked our people to consider what kind of dance would go with each song. What became obvious was that there were songs and dances that went together and those that did not. Particular dances worked with particular songs.

When Tim played a Spanish tango-style song, our minds moved away from the waltz we were thinking of after his previous selection. When he played an Appalachian tune, our minds conjured yet another image. There was no way one would try to suggest a single dance for all the songs. Songs and dances work together.

So it is with cultural worldviews and understandings of theology. For the Irish of Pelagius' land, the dance that went with the song was Celtic spirituality. This meant finding the goodness in creation and organizing the church to live in harmony with the God of the earth. For the Greeks of Augustine's land, the dance was Roman spirituality. This called for an explanation of how one might appease the removed God living in an "elsewhere heaven."

I am comfortable that different cultures will have different expressions, and to take a Celtic expression to Rome would have met resistance, but so would have the converse.

Having said that, I also have two concerns: One is that people will not allow any other dances to be danced than their own. "No matter what the song, all must dance the tango, for that is what we Christians do!" This view too easily holds that in order to be faithful, the way we have of living the gospel and understanding God must never change. The idea that even if the worldview changes, we will not, is as awkward as dancing the wrong dance to a new song.

The other fear is that we will not allow our song to be expanded. "This is the only music we will listen to, for this is what I know!" The trouble with many Christian expressions is that they feel their worldview or culture is fine and needs no adaptation. The life of God interacts with all worldviews and calls to change what is a static worldview, if not a dead worldview. So as Christians we must never get to the place where we allow our worldview to be stagnant; it must always be able to be changed by the dance. The interplay of dance and song causes both to change, and this is where we find the beauty of the life of God alive within us.

## Theology is for unity, not uniformity

The rich Christian history is rife with examples of Christian unity beyond uniformity. In fact, I would contend that when uniformity becomes the goal, unity ends, and the gospel and the church suffer. In the early days of the first two centuries of Christian faith, there was great regional, ethnic, and cultural diversity. This is why we have four gospels, each written to a particular audience at a place in time. Gospel writers John and Luke even make their intentions deliberate in their versions of the story—Luke was writing to Theophilus and John writes, "Jesus did many other things as well, but these are written that you may believe that Jesus is the Messiah" (John 21:25; 20:31). The Gospels were not intended to be harmonized nor brought into uniformity. Nor was this the intention of the Epistles; they were written by different authors to different people. We need to remember that most Christians of the day had never read or heard the majority of the Epistles. Those in Corinth may have never received the letter to Philemon and those in Rome may not have had access to the writing of James. Paul may have never heard John's telling of the story. The period of uniformity does not set in until there is cultural and political justification for it in the fourth century, when Constantine and others sought to bring about political unity among this newly christened "Christian empire." I think unity beyond uniformity was what Paul was getting at in one section of his letter to the church at Corinth.

It is intriguing to me that in the famous love chapter (1 Corinthians 13), Paul argues for his readers to understand that we are limited in our understanding and that being right is not the goal above love.

I should confess that I am not a particularly love-focused person. I don't think you would find many people who, when listing their recollections of me, would put loving at the top of the list. Quick-thinking, provocative, opinionated, sure, but probably not loving—in the classic sense anyway. So Paul's call for the Corinthians to put love above all is an instructive and challenging call for me. Paul seems to suggest that knowledge, understanding, and being right is of secondary value—something that for my personality is tempting to argue with.

> If I speak in human or angelic tongues, but do not have love, I am only a resounding gong or a clanging cymbal. If I have the gift of prophecy and can fathom all mysteries and all knowledge, and if I have a faith that can move mountains, but do not have love, I am nothing. If I give all I possess to the poor and give over my body [to hardship] that I may boast, but do not have love, I gain nothing.
>
> Love is patient, love is kind. It does not envy, it does not boast, it is not proud. It does not dishonor others, it is not self-seeking, it is not easily angered, it keeps no record of wrongs. Love does not delight in evil but rejoices with the truth. It always protects, always trusts, always hopes, always perseveres.
>
> Love never fails. But where there are prophecies, they will cease; where there are tongues, they will be stilled; where there is knowledge, it will

pass away. For we know in part and we prophesy in part, but when completeness comes, what is in part disappears. When I was a child, I talked like a child, I thought like a child, I reasoned like a child. When I became a man, I put the ways of childhood behind me. For now we see only a reflection as in a mirror; then we shall see face to face. Now I know in part; then I shall know fully, even as I am fully known.

And now these three remain: faith, hope and love. But the greatest of these is love.

Being right, or having right doctrine or theology, must never trump love. Any theology that accomplishes full knowledge or makes accessible the mysteries of the world and is not love is as useless as the sound of pots banging together. This is the kind of statement that ought to rearrange us, not simply be nodded at during a wedding ceremony.

## Theology is to be participatory

My presupposition is that the gospel calls us to participate in the things of God wherever we find them. I find the Bible to be plumb full of stories of people finding the agenda of God beyond both their religion and their culture. This is why the sending of the Messiah/Christ/Savior to the world rings so richly. the declaration of Jesus that "The time has come.... The kingdom of God has come near. Repent and believe the good news!"[6] is a call that is radically Good News in our day. I believe the nearness Jesus speaks of is not only in time, but he is saying that it is close enough that people can step into it.

The call of Jesus is not simply to believe, but to join in and participate.

"As Jesus walked beside the Sea of Galilee, he saw Simon and his brother Andrew casting a net into the lake, for they were fishermen. 'Come, follow me,' Jesus said, 'and I will send you out to fish for people.' At once they left their nets and followed him."[7]

The men invited were people with limited understanding and wrong views on a number of important issues. But they were invited in, and they became participants in the life Jesus initiated. Not only did they live the life, but they created the theology. This call remains today.

I understand that the church has often felt it important to understand and communicate her role in this invitation as both the proprietor of the things of God and at times as the gatekeeper, but I do not find those postures to be best suited for the story of Jesus. By some people's reading,

Jesus seems to give his disciples instructions that could lead us to see their job as gatekeepers more than as gracious hosts and inviters. But I think the Gospels, and the rest of the New Testament (and Old Testament for that matter) do not encourage, or even allow us, to find our roles as the keepers of "truth" that keep others out. We are called to all nations, people, and languages to invite and initiate them into the life of God as fully as possible.

This is the call, from the sending of Abram, through Jesus, right through the "secrets" revealed to John in his revelation. Does this raise significant issues in the global, multicultural world we live in? For sure, that is why we need active, loving, participatory theology.

God's intention for individuals and for collective humanity is to bring together full integration of God's agenda with our world — "Your kingdom come, your will be done, on earth as it is in heaven" (Matthew 6:10). This was a prayer of participation and integration.

Sin is dis-integration, while God's intention is integration. When participation is reduced, we are more likely to disintegrate than to become fully integrated in the things of God. Ironically, I think that too often the church's desire to be righteous has led to the prevention of people's participation.

## Christendom is not the goal

It may be quite necessary for some of us to move forward with the way of Jesus in ways that are not encumbered by the history of Christendom, in the same way the early Christians had to move on with the way of Jesus beyond the temple or synagogue model of Christianity's beginning. For those who think this idea is totally nuts, let me remind you that for the New Testament church, the idea that the agenda of God would come from anywhere but the law of Moses and the temple, was grounds to bring charges against Paul in Jerusalem. I think we find much help in this matter in the New Testament Epistles. For quite often, the Gentiles needed to understand that they need not be encumbered by the requirements of circumcision and the law.

It was really useful to have a bit of Paul's record arguing that the intentions of circumcision were really embedded in the call of Abram and therefore preceded circumcision and the law of Moses. We may well find ourselves in a similar place in relationship to the requirements of Christendom. It may be that in order to be faithful to the gospel that resulted in Christendom, we need not be beholden to Christendom.

A question that must be asked in this conversation is what then are the products of Christendom and what are the elements that necessarily preceded it? This becomes the work of the community of faith—local, global, historical, and futurical.

What kind of Jesus-way would we have if we no longer saw Christendom, or perhaps the church, as being the sole proprietor of the hopes of God through Jesus? What would that do to our understanding of sacraments, authority, our interpretation and application of the Bible, and the general role of the church in our culture? The questions theology must deal with in our pluralistic world are of this nature.

It is my contention that those outside the church have already concluded precisely this—the church, or self-professing Christians, hold no special right to speak for God.

I contend that Christendom was useful when people of faith were having to engage in conversation with a dominant secular worldview. In that setting, it was power versus power (the power of the church and its long-held dogma versus the new power of secular science). It could be argued that the gospel was well served by Christendom in its conflict with secular humanism. "Well-structured" belief countered "well-crafted" critique. But the benefits of Christendom do not transfer into a conversation with a nonreligious, yet spiritual, worldview.

That which allowed Christendom a "place at the table" in the conflict between Christianity and secular humanism may well keep it out of the Christianity and spiritualism conversation. This will continue to be felt as the influence of Eastern religions permeates our world.

## Characteristics of My Theology

I recognize that for many people, this kind of understanding of theology and faith can seem weak, soft, unprincipled, or otherwise dangerous. There have been many situations where I have needed to explain, almost to the point of justifying such a view, to Christian people anyway. When I have this conversation with those who do not claim to be Christians, they often find it quite compelling and hopeful. But again, I believe theology needs to be beneficial to those on the inside of the faith as well as to those on the outside. In an effort to be as helpful as possible, I have, on a number of occasions, put together a short list of what I call "characteristics" of this point of view. I feel the need to qualify the list because it was only created to help answer certain concerns and is not able to fully answer all questions or be definitive of what I believe.

One more qualification if I may. This list was satisfactory at the time I created it, and I guess satisfactory at the time of this writing. It may very well be the case that I will need to add, subtract, or qualify one or all of these characteristics in the future, but as you may well imagine, that is something I find not only acceptable, but preferable. For who would want to have the same characteristics to their thinking for a lifetime? Would we not want to be people who are growing and developing in all areas of life, including or even especially, in areas as important as theology?

## A theology pursuing rhythm with God

A theology of integration with God sits in contrast to systems that are seeking to "bridge the gap" between God and humanity, understanding that was so prevalent in the cultures of early converts to Christianity in the Gentile regions and Greek culture (and that far too often has remained as a "latent disease" in many of our communities of faith). It is my understanding that God creates for the purpose of partnership and collaboration. This is what being created in the image of God is about. A significant theological issue for our culture is to consider what it means to be people who live in deep collaboration with one another, God, and creation. The categories of Greek thought that presented such a problem for the early church are a particular form of Gnosticism, which is not the basis for my understanding of the story of God.

In short, I do not hold to an understanding of the gap between God and humanity based on the notion that the spirit is good and the physical is bad. Rather, I see in the story of the Bible and Christian faith God's love for and engagement in the world in all ways. I certainly believe in sin and forgiveness, but they are not built around a Greek judicial model of separation, rather around a relational call to return to a life in full agreement and rhythm with God. So God does not move away in the midst of our sin, but he moves closer. Sin is atoned for and we are again integrated into the life of God. My understanding of this atonement is shaped more by ideas similar to those prevalent during the time of the biblical story than it is by the Greco-Roman understanding that so influenced some of the early church's understanding. The Jews lived with an understanding of the atonement for sin as a basis of the faith, and this understanding did not require them to claim that God was removed from creation and protected in an isolated heaven as the remnants of Plutonic thought demanded.

From the beginning of the story to the end, God calls, forgives, reunites, and empowers humanity and all of creation to be coconspirators in God's agenda. So what we seek is a life lived in harmony with God. In many ways I find a kinship with Tertullian, who in the early third century famously said, "Free Jerusalem from Athens and the church of Christ from the Academy of Plato." I do not attempt to support all of Tertullian's beliefs, but on this point I believe the church should have listened to his call for freedom.

## A theology of integrated holism

Holism is the goal of God for the world. The Christian story, and I believe any accompanying theology, ought to be one of God's agenda for the entirety of creation. All of creation is to be brought into the fullness of its created purpose. This is what God has in store and works continuously toward. This is the guaranteed future of humanity and creation. In other words, this is creation's predetermined destiny. Paul was seeking to make this point to the Christian converts in Rome, who themselves were having to move away from a Gnostic understanding of God as "the perfect being living in the ether" of heaven and wrongly assuming that God would not have anything to do with the things of earth. Paul argues in the letter to the Romans and in other epistles (especially Galatians) that it is so important to understand that God's intention for the world is not only for the spirit, but for the body and for creation, even going to the point of saying that the body is the temple of God—an idea unheard of for the Gnostics of the day, and unfortunately for some still today. To a culture that was tempted to understand God as the "removed mover," Paul tells the story of the embedded God living out the hope of the world through Jesus. How much do many of our churches, parishioners, and theologies need to be impacted by the same good news in our day?

> We know that the whole creation has been groaning as in the pains of childbirth right up to the present time. Not only so, but we ourselves, who have the firstfruits of the Spirit, groan inwardly as we wait eagerly for our adoption, the redemption of our bodies. For in this hope we were saved. But hope that is seen is no hope at all. Who hopes for what they already have? But if we hope for what we do not yet have, we wait for it patiently.

> In the same way, the Spirit helps us in our weakness. We do not know what we ought to pray for, but the Spirit himself intercedes for us through wordless groans. And he who searches our hearts knows the mind of the Spirit, because the Spirit intercedes for God's people in accordance with the will of God.

And we know that in all things God works for the good of those who love him, who have been called according to his purpose. For those God foreknew he also predestined to be conformed to the image of his Son, that he might be the firstborn among many brothers and sisters. And those he predestined, he also called; those he called, he also justified; those he justified, he also glorified.

What, then, shall we say in response to these things? If God is for us, who can be against us?[8]

The call of God is for that which dis-integrates life (sin) to be done away with. For this dis-integration brings death, but integration brings life. The need to have a more full gospel that jettisons as much as possible the tentacles of Gnosticism that have plagued Christian theology for the centuries has, perhaps, never been more necessary.

## A progressive theology

God's agenda for the world will unfold regardless of who joins in the effort or to what degree they join. And the story of God is never limited. Rather, it is growing. This becomes evident in the story of the Bible. From the creation, to captivity, to a land promised, to a people living under a covenant. From a people wanting a king, to a people wanting to return home, to a people praying for a life beyond this one, to a people hoping for a new David or a new Joshua. This progression continues in the recognition of the Promised One, to the unleashing of the Holy Spirit on the entire community, to the multiple expressions of faith through the ages.

In my reading there is not stagnant theology or faith that is anywhere as beautiful, attractive, or fitting than a progressive agenda of God being guided by his own involvement in the world.

## A theology that includes co-creative humanity

The call given to Eve and Adam in the garden serves as a window into the call given to all humanity—join with God and do as God does. God created, so we are called to create. God brings light, so we are to bring light. God reconciles, so we should make things right. God seeks to put an end to that which kills and destroys, and so ought we.

In the words of Jesus, we are to "be perfect ... as [our] heavenly Father is perfect" (Matthew 5:48). This is not a perfection taken from the mind of Socrates—an attempt to disembark from the body for spiritual perfection, but a perfect partnership with the agenda of God. The Lord's

Prayer is a prayer of co-creative participation. God is the agenda setter. God's agenda be done on earth as in heaven is very much in the vein of "be fruitful and multiply."

## A theology that is evolving

I hold that a reading of history ought to instruct us to create ways of thought that are useful but temporary. Complex understandings meant for all people, in all places, for all times, are simply not possible. Language, situation, specific issues, and people's own preferences and insecurity all are involved in any belief system. There is no way to make a statement of substantive belief without these kinds of issues being at play. So one must make adjustments, even if they are slight, in order to remain faithful.

This was certainly the case for many in the early church, especially Peter. He had a firm and settled view of those God was at work within, and it didn't involve uncircumcised Gentiles. The story of the conversion of Cornelius (and I would argue also the conversion of Peter and the church) gives us a glimpse into this way in which Peter changed a long-held, fundamental belief about Gentiles and God's work within them, "I now realize how true it is that God does not show favoritism but accepts those from every nation who fear him and do what is right" (Acts 10:34–35).

Luke sets this passage in the story of the activities of the apostles in such a way that Jesus-life in the Gentiles becomes the new issue of concern in the book, and consequently for the church.

If Peter had been one who would have allowed his cultural and religious presuppositions to remain firm, and not moved in the way God had led, and in fact even broken the very law of his people, he would have missed out on what God was leading him into. "Talking with [Cornelius], Peter went inside and found a large gathering of people. He said to them: 'You are well aware that it is against our law for a Jew to associate with Gentiles or visit them. But God has shown me that I should not call anyone impure or unclean. So when I was sent for, I came without raising any objection. May I ask why you sent for me?'" (Acts 10:27–29).

This event changed the rules for Peter and became the proof for the church in Jerusalem that God truly is at work among the Gentiles — something the previous version of Christianity could not accept.

Without a temporary view of theology and belief, we are left having to condemn the different beliefs of those who have gone before us. This would include those who excluded the Gentiles, those who argued for a limited role of women in culture or faith, those who believed the world was flat, or that a dome of non-earth matter covered the earth, those who rejected the notion of bacteria, or those who professed a quick end to the current earth. We would not be able to stop disagreeing with those who held these views, and we would have to condemn the people who held such beliefs. If we hold that people are either right or wrong in their beliefs, and leave no place for faithfulness being understood as one being as right as one could be in their day, then we find ourselves standing above and not alongside those who have come before us (or are of a differing opinion near or far from us). We would have to declare there are simply those who are right, in full alignment with the "truth," and that all others are to be condemned.

I am thankful this is not the case for our engagement with those of our history, or those in our current day. I am thankful this is not the case for our own sake. How would any of us like to be held to the understandings of our childhood, or have to settle for the remainder of our lives with the awful choice of never increasing our understanding or calling ourselves wrongful believers in the future?

I believe a much better option is to allow our theology, faith, and belief to progress, to get better. This will mean that someday others will come along and correct our beliefs on issues of great importance, but we need not slump along as if we can believe nothing just because what we believe is not "timeless." Certainly having room for progress allows us to take a wrong turn, making yet another misguided assumption and ending up with a theology that is not closer to the truth at all, but in need of even greater correction. But really, is that so bad considering the other option?

## Theological Questions of Our Day

There seems to be no end to the issues of our day that are pressing theology to continually reconstruct. The notion that the deep theological questions of our day are no different than any other period of time seems to be a perspective shown to be wanting nearly every day. It is not uncommon for someone to suggest, "There is nothing new under the sun." This phrase borrowed from the book of Ecclesiastes is often used to suggest that really nothing has changed. I am not sure at which point these people are suggesting that change ceased, but the general notion is that really all is the way it was in the past. The implication of this sort of comment is most often that the answers of the past are sufficient for today.

I do not see the world this way. I think there are all sorts of things about our world that are new. I think there are things about humanity that are new. I contend that we have ways of understanding our world, living with one another, and opportunities for life in this world that are different from times past.

In the brief time I have left in this discussion, let me mention three such areas. This is meant to be a suggestive list of the opportunities that we must address if we are going to have a theology of Jesus that is useful in our day, and not intended to be a complete list.

## Humanity

We need not only discuss questions of how Christ relates to culture, but of how Christ relates to humanity. I believe we need a far more humane Christianity (not to mention a more feminine Christianity—nurturing, caring, conversational, and process-oriented). Our understanding of humanity will shape our understanding of spirituality.

The theology of the modern church is well equipped to engage with the questions and threats of secularism, but it is not prepared for the engagement with a spiritual world.

The engagement of cultures with one another happening in meaningful ways is taking place in our world like at no other time. Our ability to travel, learn, and communicate has created a landscape of human interaction like never before. These interactions are changing our understanding of who our neighbor is and who our enemy is. It also changes the way we understand truth and authority.

To those living in the late nineteenth century, much of what passes as ordinary medical advancement today would have been mind-bending ideas. That people would be living as not only flesh but as part mechanical, with pacemakers installed in their hearts, or people being part electronic with hearing devices planted in their heads, would have seemed other-worldly. We need a theology that will allow us to consider the changes in humanity that are upon us and will be even greater in the future. What kind of human understanding will we have when babies are born in the confines of a space station? Or are born without development in a human womb? The questions of humanity and genetic research are upon us, and it is new, and we need to be prepared for it.

We now engage in the collaborative process of life creation with God in increasingly wonderful ways. Theology created in a time when our participation in procreation was limited to prayer, sex, and staying healthy will not faithfully inform a world of genetic research, in vitro fertilization, and "nanotechnology" (my use meaning "the willful creation of whole new substances at the atomic level").[9] We need a theology that not only can answer questions produced in this world, but one that is equipped to generate proper questions. Theology must not simply be left to generating correct answers; it must infuse a new kind of question into the mix.

The question of humanity is inexorably linked to sexuality and gender. Issues of sexuality can be among the most complex and convoluted we need to deal with. It seems to me that the theology of our history does not deal sufficiently with the issues for our day. I do not mean this as a critique of past times, but as an acknowledgment that our times are different. I do not mean that we are a more or less sexual culture, but one that knows more about the genetic, social, and cultural issues surrounding sexuality and gender than any previous culture.

Christianity will be impotent to lead a conversation on sexuality and gender if we do not boldly integrate our current understanding of humanity with our theology. This will require us to not only draw new conclusions about sexuality, but will force us to consider new ways of being sexual. For sexuality is not separate from our spirituality. If we have a theology formed in a worldview that sees sexuality as sin, our means, intentions, and explanations of sexuality will be affected. We must engage our entire humanity in our spirituality; this includes our sexuality.

## Creation at the smallest level

Over the last millennium, humans' understanding of our world has changed dramatically. Often our cosmology has not kept up. There have been times when our understanding of the world has allowed us to redefine our thoughts on how God interacts with the world. The Scientific Revolution of the fifteenth century was one of those periods. Christians have long held that Jesus "is the image of the invisible God, the firstborn over all creation. For in him all things were created: things in heaven and on earth, visible and invisible, whether thrones or powers or rulers or authorities; all things have been created through him and for him. He is before all things, and in him all things hold together."[10] But our understanding of how that is and the implications of it continue to change.

We now know that the created world and the spirit are not as distinct as the Newtonian worldview made them out to be. Einstein's theory of relativity may show that theology suggesting God as "wholly other" than creation may be based on an antiquated metaphysical notion. Our theology is called to engage with these kinds of issues. It is simply insufficient to use outdated notions of the cosmos, state them in louder and more certain terms, and then call that theology. This is the kind of thing that has led many to suggest that what we need is a better Christianity and not just a better way to state an eleventh-century version.

In the age of classical physics, when people believed everything could be known precisely, both location and direction, then they could predict the behavior of things. And the "discovery" that the laws of the heavens (in space) are the same as the laws on earth put an end to the notion of earth being a different environment from the "heavenly skies." This was the end of dualism in science.

This world of laws that were predictable through observation gave great confidence and set the groundwork for many advents in science and physics. It was a "clockwork universe" and all we needed to do was observe the world and we would know how it behaves and how it will behave. This secured a notion of the world being determined. Because we know the laws of the universe, at least to a sufficient degree, we can predict how the world will behave, and in doing so, we recognize that what will happen was set to happen. This world of determinism served as a supportive pressure for certain streams of theology to be based on just such a determinism, or "predeterminism."

While some through the ages debated the idea of determinism, it really held sway until the early twentieth century when physicists began suggesting that the rules we use to describe the world at the macro level do not apply at the atomic level.

They began to suggest that the world is not made up of little hard balls of substance at all (picture the rendition of the atom from high school physics class with a proton and electron revolving in perfect symmetry around a nucleus), but rather at the smallest level, there are packets of energy living in dynamic interaction with one another.

Electrons are not like small billiard balls; they are something better described as fuzzy, smeared out, approximate bundles of energy.

Observers of the smallest levels of creation began suggesting that an atom's location and momentum cannot both be determined at the same time, so we cannot know "everything" about it, and therefore future behavior cannot be known.

One of the original voices in this world was a man named Werner Heisenberg, and for the physics world, Heisenberg's uncertainty principle has replaced Newton's determined clockwork universe.

In addition, those studying this world began suggesting that light exists simultaneously as both wave and particle—they use the phrase "Wave-particle duality."

Added to this is the understanding that at the atomic level, the observation of something affects the specimen. In this sense there is no way to be an "objective observer." So if we connect truth to objectivity, we are in a bad place in light of our understanding of the world.

These changes in our understanding of the world create an entirely new landscape for our theology.

When we come to grips with the idea that the world is not made of little hard pieces of substance behaving in determined ways, and that the light exists as both wave and particle, and that it is impossible not to affect the world by living in it, we should be encouraged in our theology.

The idea that, at the smallest level, all matter is made of energy packets and not "little hard balls of matter" is a fascinating notion that requires not only different theological conclusions but different presuppositions. The idea that there is a necessary distinction of matter from spirit, or creation from creator, is being reconsidered. This notion that the difference in waves and particles is not what we assumed allows us to understand the engagement of God in the world and the interrelationality of Father, Son, Holy Spirit, and creation in new and more helpful ways. We are allowed and encouraged to have an understanding that includes creation in the kingdom of God.

I contend there to be no better religious understanding of this world than Christianity. Christianity is ideally suited for our understanding. The presuppositions of Christianity and these discoveries of the "quantum" world will well inform one another.

## Creation at the largest level

We need to have an understanding of creation at its largest level as well. The universe not being what we thought, changes our understanding of everything. What do we do with the fact that there is not a single "verse," a "universe," but rather many "universes," a "multiverse"? We need to be theologians with a full understanding of creation.

We now live in a world where we not only have to consider the basic human instinct, how not to be destroyed by creation (through disease, disaster, or wild beasts), but we need to consider how *we* do not destroy creation. The implications of our theology on our communities when we not only have the ability to subdue the earth, but to extinguish it, are powerful, and our theology needs to engage with these issues.

There is a seemingly ever-growing list in theology of the kinds of things that are calling for a change. I find these issues to be as important as the Gentiles entering the Jewish promise in the first century; or the relationship of Jesus to God and the Holy Spirit in light of the Greek understanding of God in the third century; or as poignant as the question of absolution of sin in the fifteenth-century perspective.

My hope is that the emerging church will be made of communities who engage in the task of theology in ways beneficial to the world in our day and to one another, always doing so in the way of Jesus guided by the Spirit of God and bound together by love. Love for God, for our neighbor, and even for our enemy. May we be communities of faith in rhythm with God in the way of Jesus.

# RESPONSE TO DOUG PAGITT

## MARK DRISCOLL

I find Doug's chapter the most difficult to respond to for two reasons. One, we were assigned to articulate our views on the Trinity, the atonement, and Scripture, and having read Doug's chapter, I remain uncertain of his position on these issues. Two, his chapter is highly conceptual on how theology is not to be done.

But his references to Henry Churchill King and the 1890s are helpful insights. Today, King is an unknown and obscure theologian, but he was at one time among the premier liberal theologians. He began as a professor of mathematics at Oberlin College from 1884 until 1897, when he became professor of systematic theology, and eventually the president of the college until 1927. Oberlin is perhaps best known for Charles Finney who preceded King as the school's first professor of systematic theology and its second president. Finney is a very controversial figure in Christian theology since he denied original sin and believed in the essential neutrality, if not goodness, of human nature.

King rose to prominence when three serious issues were on the minds of liberal Christians. To answer these questions, King wrote *Reconstruction in Theology*, which is the best known of his nineteen books.

First, there is the question of whether Christianity could be reconciled with scientific evolution. King answered that evolutionary theory was in fact compatible with Christianity and that Christianity should accept and trust the findings of modern science. Second, could Scripture be reconciled with historical and literary criticism? King answered that authority is found in internal reason and experience and not in external authorities such as Scripture; therefore, such criticisms must be accepted by Christians. Third, could traditional theology, especially Calvinism, be reconciled with the ethical needs of a world dominated by war and injustice? King answered that theology must be constructed to present Christianity as an ethical way of life. He rejected penal understandings of the atonement in an effort to appeal to modern people who, like him, disdained the thought of God punishing sin and embraced the social gospel movement and political agenda of *The New Republic* magazine with which he was involved.

Perhaps most curious is that King's writings are littered with many of the same phrases commonly used by Doug Pagitt, Brian McLaren, and others involved with the emergent stream of the emerging church. Among them are "emergent evolution," "theology as conversation," "sacredness of the person," "progressive revelation," and "personal relation."[1]

Dr. Walter Marshall Horton, Professor of Systematic Theology at the Graduate School of Theology at Oberlin College, said in a lecture on April 26, 1960, that "*Reconstruction in Theology* is a very important landmark in the history of twentieth-century Christian thought. There is no better book to refer to, if you wish to understand why liberal tendencies in theology grew so rapidly in so many different churches, in the early years of this century."[2] Therefore, in King, Pagitt finds a great articulator of his social gospel liberalism.

There are multiple problems with King's theology as well as Pagitt's. In articulating them I do not seek to be unnecessarily unpleasant. Doug and I have maintained a friendship despite our frequent debates over these matters through the years.

First, by embracing the tenets of evolution, we lose the dignity of the human person as God's image-bearer. Consequently, man is merely the "educable animal."[3]

Second, by denying the human sin nature, the social gospel effort to pursue a utopian dream world of social perfection, including the abolition of what an Oberlin College catalog in King's day called "every form of sin," is rendered impotent.[4] This is because dealing with institutional sins like racism and sexism is impossible until we acknowledge that the problem is not out there in the world, but rather emanates from the sin nature in us. Pagitt embraces this same error in affirming Pelagius, who was denounced as a heretic for denying human sinfulness at the Council of Carthage in AD 418.

Third, the kingdom of God and not the cross of Jesus Christ stands at the center of the liberal theological system. The result is not that we are sinners with our hope in the atoning death of Jesus. Rather, we are essentially good people with our hope in evolutionary progress, faithful living, and moral education leading to utopian social progress. In theological terms this is called an "overrealized eschatology," and it is the same problem that Paul seeks to correct in his letters to the Corinthians.

In King's day there was an overrealized eschatology that believed human goodness and the inevitability of indefinite human progress would lead to the evolution of the kingdom of God on earth in a modified, naïvely optimistic postmillennialism. The overreaction is the presently popular underrealized eschatology of pessimistic dispensationalism. The former overemphasizes the presence of God's kingdom on earth, while the latter underemphasizes the presence of God's kingdom on earth. Pagitt is simply repeating the historical problem of overreacting back to an overrealized eschatology of theological and moral evolution. The solution is Paul's continual language of "already" and "not yet," wherein the kingdom of God is already on the earth wherever the gospel is preached by ambassadors of the King, and not yet fully instituted because King Jesus has not yet returned to place his throne upon the earth.

Fourth, overrealized eschatology and evolutionary assumptions cause social gospel liberals to mistake change for progress. One example of this error includes Pagitt's assertion that "theology must be ever-developing." If theology is evolving, then truth itself is relative and constantly changing. This is exemplified in his vague embrace of new sexualities, which is possibly a tepid approval of homosexuality. Another example of this error is his declaration that the good news of the gospel should not be kept the same, when Paul declared that there is only one gospel and that any alteration to it is damnable (Galatians 1:6–9). Yet another is his assertion that Christians are not keepers of the truth when Paul states that the church is the "pillar and foundation of the truth" (1 Timothy 3:15). And yet another is his statement that sin is not to be articulated in terms of separation because it is borrowed from Greek thought, when it is the Hebrew Old Testament which states that sin has separated us from God (Isaiah 59:2).

Doug may accuse me of proof texting these points as I "rip the quotes from their context," but such a move seems at best a thinly veiled attempt to not deal with the truth claims of Scripture. Every New Testament writer, along with numerous Old Testament writers, quotes from other Bible books without violating their original contexts. Additionally, Jesus commonly quoted Old Testament verses in his teaching.

Perhaps most concerning are Pagitt's declarations that "what we believe is not 'timeless,'" theology will be "ever-changing," and that "complex understandings meant for all people, in all places, for all times are simply not possible." I am left to wonder if his pleading for love is something he also believes should be "ever-changing," and that some future evolution of Christianity could embrace violent injustice yet remain faithful?

In conclusion, Christians are to "contend for the faith that was once for all entrusted to the saints" (Jude 3 NIV). Therefore, the truths of Christianity are constant. But the methods by which truth is articulated and practiced must be culturally appropriated and therefore constantly changing (1 Corinthians 9:22–23). If both doctrine and practice are constant, the result is dead orthodoxy, which Pagitt is reacting against. If both doctrine and practice are constantly changing, the result is living heresy, which Pagitt is contending for. But if doctrine is constant and practice is constantly changing, the result is living orthodoxy, which I propose is the faithful third way.

# RESPONSE TO DOUG PAGITT

## JOHN BURKE

I remember Doug Pagitt and Chris Seay coming down to Austin when we were first launching Gateway, sitting in a car together, praying for our fledgling church core and for me. Even though I'm not sure we've ever agreed on methodology, we've never really disagreed either. I consider Doug a friend and believe his heart is to follow Christ sincerely. As I read his chapter, I find so much I agree with in principle, and yet I do not agree with how it appears he is applying some of those principles.

I understand his concern for honesty about the personal agendas we bring to theology-making. I believe theology must be a Spirit-led practice, or we can be blinded by our knowledge. I agree that theology must address cultural context, and that unity, not uniformity, is an important outcome of that theology. I believe our theology should reflect God's holistic agenda to restore all that was lost to the fall, and that we must teach how sin disintegrates life. I even agree that our theology-making must reflect questions of humanity, biology, and even quantum physics (what does it mean that a photon of light is ageless?).

Having said that, I do not understand why Doug appears to be willing to take everything *but* the Scriptures into account when forming theology. I may be misreading what Doug intends, yet I find no ground or authority given by Doug for the way we are to do theology. He writes, "Many of us who hold the Bible in high regard have the unfortunate habit to theologize, or moralize the Bible to serve our context. This is quite often seen in the tendency to precede a quote from the Bible by saying, 'The Bible says....' rather than acknowledging where it is from, whom it is from, and to whom it was intended. What I find objectionable about this is that it removes the context and places authority in the fact that it is in the Bible rather than in the faith and lives of the people involved."

If I understand Doug correctly, this is where we part ways. If Doug is saying that the ground and authority of emerging theology must be the faith and life of the community first, and the authority of Scripture second, then I wholeheartedly disagree. Even though the Bible is contextual, it is also mysterious. It is the words of people bound by cultural context communicating to people in other particular situations, and yes, we can misrepresent that. Yet if you believe the prophets and Jesus, they claim these Scriptures *do* have authority that can transcend a particular context (in my chapter I explain why I believe they have authority apart from circular claims).

Moses didn't say in Deuteronomy 6, "Keep these commands from God for one generation, then revise whatever you think works best for the faith and life of the next community." Moses said to keep these commandments for generations to come, regardless of the cultural context (which changed drastically in Babylonian captivity).

Jesus didn't have any problem "ripping a quote" from David's context, which was a psalm to be sung, and asserting it had cross-cultural/contextual authority, *because* God mysteriously spoke through David's context:

> [Jesus] said to them, "How is it then that David, speaking by the Spirit, calls him 'Lord'? For he says, 'The Lord said to my Lord: "Sit at my right hand until I put your enemies under your feet."'" (Matthew 22:43–44)

When Jesus was tempted in Matthew 4, he freely quoted Moses in Deuteronomy 6–8, saying, "'It is written'" three times, as if the Scriptures themselves *had authority* not only for the exiles of Israel, but for both Jesus and Satan. When tempted by Satan, he quotes Moses, saying, "People do not live on bread alone but on every word that comes from the mouth of the LORD," as if that quote held authority (Deuteronomy 8:3).

But how do we know which words come from the mouth of God and can feed us with spiritual food for life? Does each community determine that based only on what they perceive God's Spirit is doing, or does the community reflect and respond to the Spirit as they search the Scriptures? Where do we determine the principles God says can guide into faith and life—does each culture determine this? In his Sermon on the Mount, Jesus makes it abundantly clear that the Law and Prophets speak for all humanity and all time and that this is the foundation of all of his teachings (Matthew 5:17–20).

Jesus found authority not only in the words written, but he even took contextual stories of Scripture and reapplied their principles as authoritative. He took the story of David and his companions eating the consecrated bread, which was unlawful to do, and he applied it to his "breaking" of the Sabbath to heal (Matthew 12). But notice, he used Scripture to interpret the authoritative principle that crosses contexts, " '[God] desire[s] mercy, not sacrifice' " (Matthew 12:7).

Jesus asserts that correct interpretation of the meaning *is* essential: "If you had known what these words *mean*," he says (v. 7, italics mine). But again, Jesus quotes Hosea 6:6 without reference to context—God is rebuking Ephraim and Judah for their unrepentant hearts, and he applies the verse's underlying principle to justify picking heads of grain on the Sabbath. Jesus does this because he believes the Hebrew Scriptures came from God and could not be broken (John 10:34–36).

I agree with Doug that theology must be contextual and particular, but not to the exclusion of seeing that God has intervened with words of truth and authority that still have meaning for other contexts or situations. I agree that theology must be Spirit-led or we can fall into the scriptural myopia of the Pharisees, where we dissect and objectify everything but can't see the big picture of what it all means. I appreciate Doug's concerns for our theology answering the questions that emerge as the times change, and I'm not advocating thoughtless quotation of proof texts to answer all questions that may arise, or that we cannot find any truth apart from the Bible.

But the missing factor for me is whether it is the Scriptures from which we derive our theology, or whether Doug is advocating some other source of authority that trumps God's revelation in Scripture. Knowing Doug, I have to believe he is not advocating an overthrow of Scripture as authoritatively from God, but pushing against past abuses of Scripture. I understand these concerns, but I hope in seeking to correct errors of the past, the emerging church will not lose sight of the primary source of our knowledge of God. " 'How foolish you are, and how slow to believe all that the prophets have spoken! Did not the Messiah have to suffer these things and then enter his glory?' And beginning with Moses and all the Prophets, [Jesus] explained to them what was said *in all the Scriptures* concerning himself" (Luke 24:25–27, italics mine).

If we truly are Christ followers, then we must follow Jesus' use of the Scriptures as the source of our "word about God," or our theology. It is these Scriptures we must reflect on as we wrestle with all of the concerns and issues Doug rightfully brings up. Sometimes this reflection will change our theology. Sometimes the theology Scripture reveals must change us. I believe the emerging church needs to tear down some walls built by the church of modernity that constrict the fullness of life Jesus intended, but I pray we won't deconstruct the very foundation Jesus built upon, or in the end, we will find ourselves not following Christ at all.

# RESPONSE TO DOUG PAGITT

## DAN KIMBALL

I love Doug Pagitt and am inspired by him as well as encouraged and challenged by him. I wish I was as tall as he is and as smart as he is. I view him as a very close friend. In regard to theology, I fully agree with him at times and totally disagree with him at other times. As friends, we have had such fun times of arguing and discussion, that after we talk, my head ends up spinning and wondering what just happened.

I have been with Doug many times when we found our voices rising in disagreement about something theological or about church in general. He has the uncanny ability of poking holes in the weak spots of whatever I am saying, which then causes me to fumble around trying to come up with some good answers and defenses to his challenges. Yet, that is the very thing I love about him. Doug causes me to think about things I normally wouldn't think about on my own. He challenges me to become a better thinker who desires to understand theology all the more. I also know that I can't imagine any pastor who truly loves the people of his church or desires to walk in the ways of Jesus more than he does. God has used Doug in many, many ways in my life as a pastor and as a follower of Jesus.

When I read Doug's chapter, it felt like very classic Pagittonian thought (I just made that word up, but I bet there will be an adjective describing his way of thinking one day). Every single time you talk to Doug, you'll generally have a new theological discussion of something he has been thinking about. I suppose that is why the basic theme of his chapter is that theology changes rather than being stagnant. He is always pressing new thinking as he discovers things in quantum physics and other fields that are beyond my scope of reading. He's aware of new discoveries and is always asking how they impact our theology. This I love about Doug and see reflected in his chapter.

I fully agree with Doug that we should be thinking more deeply about the origins of theology. He points out how theology does come out of a context, whether influenced by Greco-Roman thought or Jewish understanding or how Augustine made conclusions influenced by his specific background. I find this so refreshing and invigorating. Without understanding where specific conclusions and thinking arose, we are inclined to be locked into some dogmatic conclusions or philosophy of theology. It is totally enlightening (kind of funny to use that word here) to understand the history of theology rather than just opening up a systematic theology book and taking the concluded statements of a specific theological professor as the way and the truth for all today. No pastor or serious student of the Bible today should be afraid to look at the origins of whatever position they currently hold and consider how it developed. Far too often, we simply grab on to someone else's conclusions without questioning the origins. Not just the denominational origins, but the original train of thought. So I applaud and love that Doug raises this type of thinking in his chapter.

He offers several metaphors, one of which is thinking of theology like a dance, and not being afraid to dance differently to different songs and with different partners. He writes about various new concepts and understandings today that we must dance with. I agree we should not be afraid to explore anything new. I love exploring all types of new thinking and new types of "dances" out there. However, for me, in the midst of exploring and "dancing," there is still the fact that we need some sort of solid floor to be dancing upon. The floor is the constant, the foundation of what we dance upon, though the dance may be different from what we are used to doing and our dance partners may be different than those we are used to dancing with. I understand that words like "foundation" or "constant" are loaded ones and have shortfalls as terms. But I just keep coming back to the floor which would be the core doctrines of historic orthodox Christianity, such as the Nicene Creed. Believing in one God is a constant foundational floorboard. Believing in the bodily resurrection of Jesus is a constant foundational floorboard. Don't we need some constant foundational floorboards to dance on? Otherwise there would be only falling, not dancing. Perhaps one day we will have come up with a way to float and dance without putting our feet on a floor, but then there still will be gravity. We can float and dance and think differently, but gravity is the constant. I know from talking to Doug about this very metaphor that he would tell me the metaphor of having a floor is a weak one, as the floor is only stable in relationship to things on the earth and to us. In other words, it is not constant in relationship to things in space that are moving in relationship to the floor. So "constancy" is relative. He would tell me that to assume gravity is always there just because that is the way it is, is not accurate. That "gravity" is the effect we call the influence of space-time, it is the bending of the cosmos, not a force of its own (these are actually his words). So any metaphor can be broken apart, and Doug is so darn smart, that he is great at tearing apart metaphors.

But I believe there are theological conclusions and beliefs that remain essential whether we are living in AD 285 or in the twenty-first century. No matter what the time period or personality or cultural context, when examining the Scriptures and what God has revealed to us, we would still eventually end up with the same conclusion, even if our choice of words differs, because there is an eventual "floor." So what is the floor? What can we hold to that is constant? We can look at how the doctrine of the Trinity was established, and we can understand the Platonic roots of thinking about God. We can understand the Arian controversy which forced a statement of belief to be written. But if we had no prior knowledge of any of that, would we not still come to the conclusion of the Scriptures revealing a triune God? Maybe we would eventually call it something other than the word "Trinity," but we do see God eternally existing and expressing himself as Father, Son, and Spirit as revealed in the Scriptures. So the Trinity remains part of the floor we dance upon despite who we are dancing with, what kind of dance we're doing, and what music we're dancing to.

Now, as I shared in my chapter in this book, I think a problem with some contemporary evangelicalism is that we haven't merely tried to determine what the floor is. But we go to extremes and have tried to determine the type of wood used for the floor, the age of the wood, or if there is hidden prophetic meaning in the grain patterns of the wood. We want to determine the type and size of the nails used in nailing the floorboards down and develop complex systems of theology about the nails. Our theological dance then becomes this highly detailed and constraining choreographed dance, with people going through predetermined rigid motions, not able to develop anything new or explore different types of dances. So, I am all for dancing, but I don't believe concluding that you have a floor or having an "anchor" (as I also used in my chapter) is limiting at all. Having an anchor, to change metaphors, as part of your boat, still allows you to set sail and explore all types of interesting new places. So by no means does having an "anchor" mean that you cannot be out sailing and exploring new territories. But you always have the anchor, so when you need to dock or not drift somewhere, it is always there for you. I see great freedom in having a floor and don't believe this limits the exploration of new dances and territories. As I type this, I am actually on a plane flying to Nashville where Doug and I will be hanging out. I look forward to our next theological discussion that we will have there as we do some "dancing" together and as he stretches my thinking with some new dance moves. God has used Doug tremendously in my life in this regard. I love Doug Pagitt, and he is my friend and a very important person in my life, even when we disagree on various metaphors and step on one another's toes in our theological dancing.

# RESPONSE TO DOUG PAGITT

## KAREN WARD

Of all the writers in this book, I know Doug Pagitt the best. I've seen Pagitt the most often, and it is not just because he is taller than the rest of us; it is because when it comes to all things emerging, Pagitt seems to be everywhere!

When there are "emerging" jokes on the Internet, Pagitt is much more likely to be the butt of them rather than me, Driscoll, Kimball, or Burke.

I even made up a Pagitt joke myself. I like to speak of us "Emergents" as an order of knights with a big green *E* on our scapulars. We are out there in the Sherwood Forest of the modern church, noble and true and fighting for the right and being led courageously by "the Brian" and "the Pagitt" (as it is a sign of true Emergent royalty when one is known by either a first or last name).

Seriously, Doug has done a huge amount out there to represent "Emergent" the "organization" and "emergent" the "conversation" in ways that are head and shoulders above the average person (green *E* scapulars notwithstanding).

Doug begins with thoughts similar to Dan Kimball. He sees through the paper tiger of the book and longs for the real McCoy of emergence ... the genuine interplay, overlap, and give-and-take conversation that can only happen face to face. Too bad the book does not come with a CD podcast of us all together. But who knows, maybe in the future we will get to record one.

In terms of the content of this chapter, I really resonate with Doug and his views of theology as temporary, professional, contextual, particular, Spirit-led, and taking place in times of change. I also agree that "our job as leaders of communities is not simply to apply the well-founded answers of previous generations' questions or assumptions to the lives of our people, but rather to guide, extract, and join with the hopes and aspirations deeply embedded by God in the lives of our people."

His use of the word "temporary" in reference to theology has a similar function to Clement Sedmak's concept of "little theologies" that I use in my chapter. Little theologies are those developed within local faith communities that help them reflect upon, shape, and live into their lives in Christ within a particular time, place, and set of circumstances, which are unique to them and may not be readily applicable to the times, places, and circumstances in other communities.

These theologies are like fresh-baked loaves of bread that sustain the life (in the way of Jesus) of the communities that bake them, and like the manna that God provided to the children of Israel, they are not meant to be stored, shelved, and transferred out of time, place, and circumstance without becoming somewhat stale and losing some of the nutrient power that fed the originating community.

Seeing the value and validity of temporary and little theologies keeps theology fresh, local, and responsive to real church-life situations and needs, rather than becoming stale, generically universal, unresponsive, aloof, and separated from the real church and community life.

Therein lies the real "emergent family resemblance" between Solomon's Porch and Apostles' communities. We are quite different as the regional cultures we serve are quite different, and we are different in communal temperament, liturgy, music, and even leadership "styles," but what we hold in common is huge. I believe this commonality is the central "ethos" of authentic emerging churches. Our local theologizing has a radical nature, and thus our radical contextualization of Christian faith and practice to our own local times, zip codes, and peoples remains at the same time radically centered and faithful in living into the way of Jesus.

I like how Doug appreciates complexity and how he paints a bigger and broader picture of the locus of theology as he speaks to the overplay of Christendom, as he sees the essential connections between the micro and macro of theology, of how God is at work in the smallest things (at the nano level), and in the big-things realm of the cosmos and in quantum physics.

I also appreciate the clarity of his writing and the categories he uses to outline his theology, and I resonate strongly with his categories of "integrated holism," "co-creative humanity," and that our practice and our theology is "evolving."

In his categories, Doug puts his fingers on the core of what being "emerging" is in my view. There is a movement to it, a recognition that we hold a living faith, and that, as the United Church of Christ's brilliant motto puts it, "God is still speaking."

So theology is not a done deal and a sealed canon written for us by others, that we need to swallow whole and espouse, but instead it is a living "art form" to which we as Christian practitioners are all given a brush.

I also get a strong sense of the transcendence and immanence of God in Doug's theology. A sense of how "omni" is not a word that refers to us in regard to anything, that we don't have "the answers" for Christian faith and practice for all time, but that we do have a critical role in shaping Christian faith and practice for our time, even if all we can do sometimes is give things our "current best guesses" as we continue to love God, serve Christ, live in community, and rely upon the leading of the Holy Spirit to do the rest.

CHAPTER

# THE EMERGING CHURCH AND COMMUNAL THEOLOGY

KAREN WARD

# THE EMERGING CHURCH AND COMMUNAL THEOLOGY

## KAREN WARD

### Theology Made from Scratch with Ingredients from Church of the Apostles' Kitchen Cabinet

> the sous-chef speaks about > the stock recipe

We at Church of the Apostles (COTA) are grateful to accept this opportunity to share stories and swap "recipes" with other emerging Christian communities, and to provide our little Apostles community an occasion to give a wider voice to the ruminating that is coming from our local faith kitchen.

This chapter has been written *in communitas* (in community) as that is how we operate at COTA.

Many people at COTA are bloggers, so in order to have discussions around our theology for this book, the first thing we did was to set up a "COTA theology blog," where our apostles could hash out (in a normal mode that we are used to) the theology that we hold in common.

Within the Holy Trinity (God as Father, Son, and Spirit) we behold "what God is like," and from this beholding we realize that the constitutive nature of all Christian *communitas* is reflective (albeit in broken, fractioned, and dim forms) of God's divine life. Therefore, within our little *communitas*, we seek to pursue all aspects of our life together in ways that reflect and honor Trinitarian *communitas* and our *Imago Dei* (image of God). This includes doing theology together.

To that end, this chapter is dedicated to God and to all the line cooks who make up the household of faith known as Church of the Apostles in Seattle, whose lives provide the local flavors that simmer and the dough that freshly bakes into our communal theology each and every day.

## Artisans for New Humanity

### > making "little theologies" > theology needs everyone! > prolegomenon

A book that inspired us at Church of the Apostles and that describes the calling and task of making "from-scratch" theology is *Doing Local Theology: A Guide for Artisans of a New Humanity* by Clemens Sedmak, Chair of the Epistemology and Religious Studies Department at the University of Salzburg in Austria.

In that book, Sedmak writes about local theology-making:

> Theology has been on loan from the people of God to professional theologians for a long time.... It is about time to ... acknowledge the treasures and gifts of everyone ... the phrase "little theologies" emphasizes theological soundness and situational embededness. Widely known examples of "big theologies" by famous theologians, like Aquinas's *Summa*, Bernard Lonegrans's "Methods in Theology," or Karl Rahner's *Foundations of Christian Faith*, are difficult books. They demand many hours of scholarly work, specialized knowledge, and imply far-reaching claims as to their validity and applicability. These are books with long texts and many footnotes. Little theologies by contrast, are small contributions that serve a local community, or a certain occasion.... Local theologies can do justice to a local context in ways big theologies can't.[1]

Sedmak's book is organized using a set of theses. For this chapter, his Thesis 45 is key:

> Little theologies use local sources of knowledge relevant for dealing with people's lives theologically. Ingredients of little theologies can be found in local rituals and everyday language, in local songs and proverbs, in buildings, and works of art. Using such theological resources means doing "theological field work" living with the people and listening to their voices.[2]

So here we begin ... listen to these little theologies from Church of the Apostles and hear in them our communal theological voice.

## You Are Invited

### > the Gospel "dismembered" > prolegomenon ( putting first things first) > "saved by grace through faith" > the end at the beginning

God "speaks to each of us as he makes us" says a killer poem by Rainer Maria Rilke, which I take to mean that God speaks to us out of our own culture and the stuff of our own lives, no less so than God speaks to us in the canon of Holy Scripture, where the "lyrics" sing:

> The kingdom of heaven may be compared to a king
> who gave a wedding banquet for his son.
> He sent his slaves to call those who had been invited to the wedding
>    banquet, but they would not come.
> Again he sent other slaves, saying, "Tell those who have been invited:
>    Look, I have prepared my dinner, my oxen and my fat calves have been
>    slaughtered, and everything is ready; come to the wedding banquet."
> But they made light of it and went away, one to his farm, another to his
>    business, while the rest seized his slaves, mistreated them, and killed
>    them.
> The king was enraged. He sent his troops, destroyed those murderers,
>    and burned their city. Then he said to his slaves, "The wedding is
>    ready, but those invited were not worthy. Go therefore into the main
>    streets, and invite everyone you find to the wedding banquet."
> Those slaves went out into the streets and gathered all whom they found,
>    both good and bad; so the wedding hall was filled with guests.[3]

The parable of grace above (in both the canonical and in a "dismembered" cultural rendering) is "core" to the content, praxis, and "method" of theology-making at Apostles.

Our theology-making is not driven by the human pursuit of knowledge (which too often puffs up) but instead is our communal response to and reflection upon God's invitation and pursuit of love.

God "proposes" and we respond, God calls to us and we answer, God invites and we accept. We are firstly a community of "God-beloved lovers of God." So our reflection "on God" (theology) and our beliefs "about God" (doctrines) are secondary pursuits to our love of God. And whatever faith (*pistis*: trust) we have within us is born of God's love for us, which *we are invited* to receive, experience, and trust. So it is here, at the end, that we begin.

## The Mystery We're In

### > At-one-ment > Atonement without the "the"

Is there an "emerging" theology of the atonement? I think not. However, I do think that there might be a unique way the emerging church goes about interfacing with the doctrine of the atonement.

### From the COTA Theology Blog

First, we are a bit weary of words. Somehow we don't expect that the latest framing of the atonement will help us any more than the last one did;

instead, we are looking for nonpropositional ways of coming to understand the atonement, ways that involve art, ritual, community, etc.

Second, we are learning to embrace the fact that we are all heretics and idolaters—and bound to be so, because our conception of God inevitably differs from God's true nature. So we'll enter into the dialectic of Christian dogmatics, but with a grain of salt, knowing that if we get saved in virtue of our correct theology, we're all in trouble.

*Posted by: Phil Woodward | October 13, 2005 at 12:16 AM*

It seems to me that concept(s) and doctrinal theorie(s) of atonement ever abound within the church, which we suspect reflects an ongoing (if latent) modernism and preoccupation with the need to define and codify a specific theory of "how God saves." Upon reflection, it seems to us that theories of atonement are just that, theories, which many faithful Christians will continue to posit and then disagree with....

So, we have decided to forgo contributing another espousal of another theory of atonement, and instead, we are excited to contemplate the *welcome* that comes to us as God's gold-leaf, handwritten *invitation* to: gather with the wise men at the manger, stand with Mary at the foot of the cross, fall (face downward) beside the angel and the women at the empty tomb, and drink (face upward) from the life-giving rain of the promised Spirit, the Power from on high, showering and leading us into Truth.

*You are invited* into a mystery.... You are invited to lay down your theories and enter in.... Swallow the red pill, taste and see the "Pascal reality"—the salvific action of Christ—past, present, and future, that is shared with us in the gospel story, and into which *we are invited* to know and experience.

We have been drawn to lay down theories and enter atonement as the totality of what God did, does, and will do in Christ (life, death, resurrection, and return). We have been beaconed to set aside theories and enter atonement as *a happening in God, to God, and through God*, and for our sake, breaking open and making possible a new way to live life. We are being moved, as a community, beyond theories about atonement, to enter into atonement itself, or at-one-ment—the new reality and new relationship of oneness with God which Christ incarnated (in life, cross, and resurrection) and into which *we are all invited* "for all time."

And about "universalism," as a community of Apostles, we are wary of all "isms." Our focus is on God's calling to us and the apostolic work we have been given to do to send out God's invitations to life to everyone we can. We try to do this while maintaining relational integrity, avoiding all forms of "bait and switch" coercion, and with humility that comes from knowing that the invitation we are giving is not our own.

To tell the truth, I have not once thought about the idea of universalism since the formation of Church of the Apostles, until it came up as something to comment on in this chapter. The topic is not that significant to our theological priorities as a community. From our Lutheran and Episcopal tribes, we are always reminded that all our efforts are a response to God's grace. We do not and cannot save anyone as a Christian community. It is God who saves and we who invite. Thanks be to God who is still on the throne, and not the church. Salvation, like everything else concerning God's address to humans, is a relational reality. To be saved or atoned for is to have and experience a love relationship with God that is evidenced by living in a loving manner here upon the earth, as "God is love."

Relationships call for the involvement of the persons in the relationship. Relationships can't be forced. God can invite us into relationship, and we can refuse that invitation, and we often do, but then God has a way of continuing to send the invite over and over again, so the opportunities to enter into this new relationship (to be saved, atoned for . . .) keep coming as long as we are alive, and it is the calling of the church to keep going out to "the highways and byways" to keep giving out God's invitations.

Invitation-giving requires all our energy and does not leave energy for us to worry about who might "opt out" at the end of time, or for fretting that God might "universalize" into the kingdom those who say they don't believe in God or who were brought up in or have chosen to practice a non-Christian faith.

It says in 1 John 4:7 that "Love comes from God," and "Everyone who loves has been born of God and knows God," so anyone who loves God knows God already, even if they know God without a name.

As a church community who knows the name on the invitation (from God through Jesus Christ), what we are doing in giving out invitations, is introducing love to Love, and for those who (for whatever reason) the church cannot "get to" to give them the invitation, but who still live in love, then it is God's place, not ours, to determine if or how these loving non-Christians come into the kingdom. We are not in charge of salvation; we are God's servants and the waitstaff for the kingdom, and our calling is to give and embody God's love and invitation.

## Table Talk
### > Holy Scriptures > Big *C* conversation partner > stories around the fire and into the looking glass > like fish in water

*Posted by: Jon Myers* | October 2005 at 06:46 PM

My main concern with scriptural authority has to do with how it has been abused by some people to oppress other people. We see this kind of thing on street corners, on TV, in the pulpit, and around the globe on what we call the "mission field." By claiming scriptural authority, we can really do a lot of damage, and I've seen more damage than good done in the name of the Bible. This is unfortunate for sure, but I think there could be a corrective—which the ancients held to—and that is a robust theology of the Holy Spirit. Seminaries as well as pop theology found in Christian bookstores often teach that we, as enlightened humans, can indeed stand over the text and extract the true meaning and then apply it to our world. I think this approach leads to arrogance, and when put into the hands of powerful people, it can be used against people rather than for people. What I hope can happen is a revival of the Holy Spirit as the only teacher and possessor of true knowledge. With this posture toward the Scriptures, one is humble and is relying on God, instead of being arrogant and relying on human logic and systems of interpretation. Scripture will have full authority when we stop standing over it, arrogantly trying to figure it out; when we let God hold it over us and interpret for us, and thus let the Scripture flow out of us as we live our lives trying to help humanity and trying to bring the kingdom of God on earth as it is in heaven.

## Comments from Karen

Many of the churches in our Lutheran and Anglican tribes don't have pew Bibles, so I sometimes feel a bit self-conscious when visiting churches that do, or ones where everyone seems to have a Bible in hand, which they may or may not be asked to open within a service. If they do open the Bible, it is usually to follow along with one passage that one person talks about, the one who is up front going through the passage line by line.

Being part of the "mainline" church and coming to our emergence out of the Lutheran and Anglican tribes makes Church of the Apostles kind of odd among other emerging churches, yet our mainline traditions gift us with an ongoing relationship with the Scriptures that is so pervasive and so infusive that it is almost not "known" among our people (who think we don't know Scripture as well as others).

In some ways we are being so immersed in Scripture within liturgy that we are like fish in water. It is all around us, and so we often seem unaware of it.

The *Revised Common Lectionary* (RCL) is an ecumenical system of Scripture readings from the Consultation on Common Texts (CCT). The readings are designed to tell the whole story of Jesus (life, death, and resurrection) in course and over a three-year cycle that moves through the three Synoptic Gospels, the gospel of John, and the Epistles.

In each weekly gathering of our community, we are fed up to four courses of Scripture from the *Revised Common Lectionary*, including a Hebrew Bible passage, a psalm, an epistle passage, and a gospel story. These lections together provide us a scriptural diet that is rich and varied enough to prevent anemia, and one that allows for solid spiritual growth over the long haul in the grace and love of God.

*Note bene*: This book will be released in "menu year" C (the year of Luke) in 2007 of the RCL. The "themes" for our weekly scriptural feast come from here, enabling us to join with millions around the world who have come to appreciate a rich and balanced diet of Scripture that contains all the "food groups," is set within a seasonal menu, and allows us to feast in courses over a year's time.

At Apostles, we call our weekly meeting a "Mass gathering." The micro churches (smaller groups) that make up Apostles' community come together for mass worship. The word "Mass" comes from the end of the ancient Latin liturgy *eta missa est* (the gathering is ended, you are sent forth). So our accent is not on "coming to church," but on leaving, to be Christ's body in daily life and within God's world.

So we come to Mass gathering not so much with heads that are empty and needing to be opened and then filled with scriptural information; but more with stomachs that grumble and seek to be fed, with hearts that are broken and in need of healing, with lives that are confused and complicated and in need of guidance....

We come with the expectation that God will meet us. We come to encounter God in Scripture and in one another and expect that, guided by the Spirit, we will be schooled in the ways of the kingdom and learn together how to become more human.

We come together as children to be gathered around and taken up into the Big Story told by our Father, which we are invited to hear, touch, taste, smell, and see through the life of Jesus. Then we are provided time and open space to talk and share at the table, to eat by the warmth of the Spirit's fire.

At Apostles we call our reflections on the Word the "reverb." Reverb may or may not be a sermon, as a sermon is just one way to break open the Word among many other ways we might use (drama, art, music, discussion, poetry ...).

For us the big thing is the Story, and telling it well, so instead of moving "line by line," we approach the Word "story by story."

We may make use of "line by line" methods for Bible study gatherings, but for our weekly liturgy, we move "story by story" to savor the "whole food" of a scriptural narrative and to allow that narrative itself to speak.

With our stress on the Story in weekly liturgy (rather than on didactic teaching), our speech after hearing the story (a sermon or other response) is more a reverberation of what the Spirit is saying to the church in Scripture, rather than our didactic teaching on the same. To us, this feels like a more natural way of connecting to Scripture each week, where we engage the gospel Story, eat at the Lord's Table, and are sent forth to mission by the Spirit's fire.

In the Apostles' community as a whole, we do not speak of Scripture using the words "inerrant" or "infallible." Instead we speak of Scripture relationally. We honor and treasure the Scriptures as the church's sacred book and as the Word of God. Scriptures provide for us a normative set of stories, telling the story of God which we are invited to find ourselves in, and whose central plot is the revelation of Jesus Christ, who himself is the "Word of God" in our midst.

In some ways the Scriptures are "personified" among us, as each week the lectionary texts are "given." We do not choose the texts, as they have been chosen by the wider church to speak to us, and so we receive them as a gift, set them among us at the table and around the fire, and allow them to speak to us and call us to account on the big Story of God that they contain, and in which we aspire to reflect and live.

Scriptures are also a mysterious stranger in our midst, who like the visitors that came to Abraham at Mamre, come bearing the otherness of God reflected in the various stories of God-encounters that our ancestors in the faith have recorded and handed down to us throughout the ages.

The biblical narrative weaves stories of faith and God-encounters to open up "newness of life" (the reign of God), which we are invited to walk in. The God stories in Scripture are sometimes literal, and sometimes not, but they are always true, that is, truly able to move us to faith by the workings of the Holy Spirit.

## "Church Potluck"

### > offertory > fat things 'R' us > "lay your all on the altar"

The closest image or analogy I have for how we do everything ("preaching," community, and theology-making) at Apostles is the "potluck," as this is how we function at our Abbey community kitchen meals, at our theology pubs, and in our weekly eucharistic gathering and other forms of community life.

A potluck is a curious, fun, risky, and unpredictable way to eat. I remember growing up in my Missouri Synod Lutheran Church in Ohio, where I first discovered, and then was horrified by, the whole concept of the church potluck.

Lutheran church potlucks are things to behold ... six-foot tables covered with red plastic checkered tablecloths lined up in rows in the church parish hall. Each one filled with heaping bowls ("dishes to pass") of often tasteless foods covered with either shredded carrots, raisins, tiny marshmallows, dried french fried onions, or two of the above. Much of which was served up at these suppers was not my idea of fine dining, but what I found to be tasteless, others found to be rich, what I considered too hot, others considered just right, what I considered smelly, others considered pungently gourmet. Yet despite my upturned teenage nose at these suppers, I always managed to find enough dishes to nourish my body and satisfy my hunger, somewhere between the lutefisk and lefse.

Since then, my appreciation for the potluck has only grown and deepened. Somehow, between the tiny wieners and cold sauerkraut, God always feeds us ... likewise are we theologically "fed" at the Church of the Apostles' potlucks.

Eating potluck is not quick or neat, and it also has little need for adding protein bars or other additive "high energy" packaged supplements. Potluck as a metaphor for church and for "renewed human life and community" is a rich one.

In the Danish film, *Babette's Feast*, a serious and pietistic Lutheran family in Denmark is treated to a life-changing feast cooked by the French woman, Babette, who had worked as their cook. The family believed Babette would soon leave them to go back to France after having won ten thousand francs in a lottery.

Then to celebrate an important church anniversary, Babette offers to cook them a feast. Interpreting their strict pietistic practice of Lutheranism to be opposed to such feasting, they allowed Babette to cook it, but vowed themselves not to notice or taste the food as they ate it.

The dinner begins and includes course after course of rich food and choice wines. In the community, conversation and sharing occurs in the context of Babette's artistry, old hurts are provided occasion for healing, old disputes are given space for reconciliation, and breached relationships become whole.

After the feast, the family is saddened at Babette's leaving, but then they learn she is not leaving with her winnings, as she gladly spent the ten thousand francs on the amazing feast.

Each week at Eucharist, God is Babette, providing us with the greatest feast at the cost of God's own self-sacrifice in Christ. And to this feast, God invites us to bring our lives as our participation, as God prepares the table of salvation providing the Bread of Life, the body of Christ, for the world.

To be sure, there are neater, cleaner, more efficient ways to organize a community and to live, but I can't think of a more flavorful way than cooking together. Just as you can eat by ordering from McDonald's or getting prepared food from a professional caterer, there is something special about cooking your own food that makes for unforgettable experiences.

The kitchen at our building (the Fremont Abbey) is often a mess. It seems someone is always in there cooking. Sometimes I wish it were not so. I sometimes wish that the kitchen would stay immaculate, with no crumbs on the countertop, no coffee grounds on the floor, and no half-eaten pies on the table, but then again, you learn to cook best by cooking, and it seems we learn Christian faith and life best by living it, so let the mess and the glory of community and kitchen living go on.

## Escort service

### > a hitchhiking guide to the kingdom > learning to ride in chariots

*Posted by: Ray* | September 09, 2005 at 02:46 AM

P.S.

One crucial aspect of discipleship is the actual PRAXIS (going out and doing) of being a Christ-follower. New Christians as well as those who've hung around for a while will be challenged and will grow in faith by going out and being the hands and feet of Christ to our crazy and chaotic world. I picture this as sort of the reverse of a computer virus. A virus or worm works its way into the system and infects any system that inevitably downloads it. We should be uploading ourselves from our comfy church mainframes out into the world, being "infectious" with the good news of Jesus, not just in words but also in deeds — helping out at homeless shelters, mentoring youth, crying out against social injustices, or (in typical Seattle fashion) taking a new friend to coffee.

## Comments from Karen

Church of the Apostles is now welcoming new Christians into community using an organic and free-range form of the ancient process which the early church called the "catechumenate."

Many folk who come into community with us have come either as de-churched, un-churched, anti-church, or under-churched. Some are looking to delve into the mystery that is life, or they're searching for "values"; some want guidance for building a just society, others are trying to fill an unnamed void left empty by stock portfolios, hobbies, and relationships. Such people are "seekers"—those toward whom many modern churches are striving mightily to be "friendly."

Despite good intentions, some of what the modern church has done in the name of "friendliness" is really what I call "vampire" evangelism; it is done not for the sake of the seeker, but for the needs of the church (to fill pews, make budgets, or feel "relevant" based on numbers of converts and "church growth"). At Church of the Apostles we are not motivated by these things, but by the fact that God's welcome to us is mind-blowing, and we are honored and duty-bound to extend the welcome we have received to other seekers who would be disciples. This is not for our sakes, our needs, or our egos, but truly for their sake and for heaven's sake.

In his whacked-out science-fiction novel *The Hitchhiker's Guide to the Galaxy*, Douglas Adams chronicles the adventures of a ragtag group of interstellar travelers. The two central characters (Arthur Dent and his companion Ford Prefect) find direction for their galactic wanderings by quoting from the *Hitchhiker's Guide*. For those who come to church with little or no Christian background, the world of Christian faith can seem just as strange and foreign as any faraway galaxy, and thus can benefit from such "guides."

For us, the reign of God is a "right-side-up" galaxy in an upside-down world, a realm where the first are last, the lowly are raised up, the mighty are cast down, and where the only way to have life is to lay it down.

So "evangelism" is not something we do to attract seekers; instead we simply invite others to join us and be part of what God is doing in the world around us, and to help us put God's eschatology into practice in doing justice, loving kindness, and walking humbly with God.

We are learning how to be welcoming, but we do so with honesty, knowing that Christianity carries *gravitas*, and that being a Christian calls for a radical shift in loyalties.

We truly believe that following Jesus calls for a reordering of our lives, and because of this, we also provide time and space for seekers to explore and discern what entering into such a life will mean.

What we know of how to be welcoming, we are learning from Scripture, as we see Jesus' way of calling strangers and inviting them to apprentice with him as "would-be disciples." Jesus' approach was "Follow me." Jesus did not ask people to just sit back and ponder theology and espouse doctrine about him; instead, he asked for a "response to him and his way of being in the world that could only be answered with their feet. And as some followed and put their faith in motion (like Philip), their passion and love for him and his way of living compelled them to bid others to "Come and see" (John 1:43–46).

We have observed that as he journeyed deeper into his own mission, Jesus welcomed all would-be hitchhikers in the form of an invitation. "If you want to follow me," he told them, "then follow me." In other words, "If you want to know who I am and what I'm up to in the world, come with me and find out" (Matthew 19:21; Mark 1:17; Luke 9:23).

Those who took up Jesus' invitation and hitched their futures to his did not do so alone. Instead they kept company with a small band of fellow travelers who had embarked upon the same adventure. Their initial following deepened into faith as they traveled with Jesus and tried their hands at the kinds of things Jesus did (with many failures, screwups, and botched assignments along the way). Jesus' way of discipling was messy and "hands-on," because you can't learn to swim from the shore. You have to wade out into the water and get wet.

We resonate with this experience-based pattern which helped seekers become disciples in pre-Christian times, and are finding it useful in assisting seekers to become disciples in a post-Christian culture. The early church called this pattern for discipling the *catechumenate*, which comes from a Greek word *catacheo* that means "to sound in the ear," and also gives us the word "catechism."

Using this third-century-based pattern to welcome postmodern seekers is about as "ancient-future" as you can get!

The catechumenal approach for making disciples is based on apprenticeship, which fits well with the needs of postmodern seekers who don't want easy answers. So instead of giving folk tracts with "spiritual laws" and invitations to pray the "sinner's prayer" off of cards, we try to come alongside seekers and be a community of sound spiritual guidance and good spiritual company as newcomers embark on a life-altering journey into "the grace of our Lord Jesus Christ, the love of God, and the communion of the Holy Spirit."

The goals for this way of discipling differ from the goals of recent past (modern) approaches. Although the following list is simplistic, it gives an idea of the different aims we have in using an ancient-future, apprentice-based path.

| Apprentice path | Modern model |
|---|---|
| Discipleship | Membership |
| Transformation | Information |
| Conversion | Convention |
| Faith as relationship | Faith as knowledge |
| Formation | Orientation |
| Process | Program |
| Length varies | "Six-week" course, or other set time frame |
| Public and communal | Private and individual |
| Members as lay mentors | Pastor's class |
| Incorporation | Indoctrination |

Welcoming seekers into an ancient-future discipling process involves providing:

> time to explore community and ask questions
> time to worship, pray, and reflect on Scripture
> time to prepare for baptism (or affirmation of baptism)
> ongoing Christian living

## Time to explore community and ask questions

Church of the Apostles welcomes newcomers into informal gatherings (like our supper club and theology pubs) to ask questions and inquire into Christian faith. The idea is to come and ask anything you've always wanted to know about God and church, but were afraid to ask.

At this point, the goal is not for the church to give answers, but to honor the seekers by listening to their questions and hearing their stories — the stories of their lives and of what has brought them to inquire into the Christian faith and life.

We do not put newcomers into membership classes, but invite them to take part in all of our normal community gatherings for as short or as long a time as they need, so that they can discern whether or not they wish to continue their exploration of the Christian faith without pressure or any hard sell coming from us to "seal the deal."

## Time to worship, pray, and reflect on Scripture

Whenever they feel ready, seekers can shift out of exploration and be formally welcomed. We do the ancient "rite of welcome" where the community prays over and blesses seekers wanting to commit to following God in the way of Jesus.

Just before the rite of welcome, we pair seekers with a sponsor or companion from our community. This pairing of seekers with companions is modeled on the relationship between Philip and the Ethiopian eunuch in Acts 8, which describes how Philip got into the chariot alongside the eunuch, guided him in his encounter with Christ and the Scriptures, and journeyed with him on the road to baptism.

Companions (mentors or sponsors) accompany seekers to worship and to group gatherings where they learn to reflect on Scripture and to pray. We don't use any packaged curriculum with our apprentice approach. Our primary guidebook for Apostles and would-be apostles is the Bible. We also use the same readings (from the lectionary) that our community gathers around each week in worship. The reason for this approach is that we are welcoming new people to share our life, which means to eat what we eat, do what we do, and hear the same stories of the faith that we hear and are formed by on a weekly basis.

### Time to prepare for baptism (or affirmation of baptism)

After time to experience how we do life in the Apostles' community, those who discern and whom we discern are ready, begin to prepare for baptism (or affirmation) beginning with a "rite of enrollment." At the enrollment, candidates actually sign their names in a book as a sign of commitment before God and community, and then the community vows to take on the responsibility of praying for the catechumens as their journey intensifies. Often the rite of enrollment takes place on the first Sunday in Lent.

Those who prepare during Lent can be baptized or affirmed at our Easter vigil. Other church-year feast days on which we do baptisms and affirmations are: the Baptism of Jesus, the day of Pentecost, Holy Trinity, and Christ the King.

### Ongoing Christian living

Baptism is not the end, but the beginning of life in Christ for new apostles and for all Christians. As the Christian walk lasts a lifetime, it requires community for ongoing formation and nurturing. Among us, this ongoing nurturing takes place in home groups, in intentional Christian community houses, in praying the daily office, in doing our monastic work of service in our Fremont neighborhood, in scriptural study, and in engaging mission in our occupations and places of work, as these are means by which both new and experienced apostles in our community "reach unity in the faith and in the knowledge of the Son of God and become mature, attaining to the whole measure of the fullness of Christ" (Ephesians 4:13).

## Life Together

### > with the Sacred Three > taking the fourth place at the table

*Posted by: Rue* | August 23, 2005 at 02:59 AM

I'm not sure that I need other people (community) to more fully understand God or to become more familiar with the heavenly realm. However, I do think that I can find my place in this world a bit easier with others around.

I speak as one who has had this lack of connection and community. As I open this door to my life, I am very excited to discover the possibilities that come from living in a community of faith and love. But I don't mean to diminish the experiences I've had in solitude. My path has strayed from the metaphorical cities, and yet God was always there. I couldn't feel or see his hand protecting me along the way, and yet looking back, I know it was there. God may not have been able to comfort me through the kind words of a friend as I lived this secluded life, but he was certainly able to provide comfort through other means. Namely, that of nature and his creation.

I don't mean to exclude hermitism as a means for understanding God, or our purpose here on earth. But the presence of other loving individuals in one's life definitely enhances the experience and provides a tool of teaching — by swapping stories of pitfalls and joyfulness with one another.

### Comments from Karen

As we live together in the way of Jesus within community, we see ourselves participating in the very life of God. As God is the source of all relationality, the relationships we have in community that are guided by the Spirit are reflective of the inner relationship that happens in God, even if reflected "in a mirror dimly."

Orthodox churches call this *theosis*. We would modify our view in that we don't believe we are becoming God, but that even here on earth and in small ways, we can mimic God's divinity as we begin to live "in God" and pattern our lives after God's ways.

This is an analogy that tries to describe, in words which fail, the richness of our relationship with God and one another.

In terms of mimicking, it is like us as children, trying to dress and act like our parents, and trying to grow up to be like them. Of course God's shoes are way too big for us, but as we try to stick our feet in them, we are showing our desire to reflect our Father as best we can.

The full consummation and completion of life "in God" is what I suppose heaven must be about. This side of heaven, what we can do is realize that our lives can be reflective of the Trinity as we operate under "The grace of the Lord Jesus Christ, the love of God and the communion of the Holy Spirit."

Using a Trinitarian pulse is the best way we have of discerning the "success" of our community. We do not view success in terms of having large numbers in the community, as we, like the average American congregation, are under five hundred people in size. And as such, our aspirations are to be a faithful, serving, God-reflecting, urban, neighborhood-sized church.

Even though we do not aspire to be a large church, we do aspire to be an effective church. A big reason I believe the early church was effective was because the Trinity reflected the relationality they had and expressed the love they showed to one another and to their world.

I don't think things have changed much since then, as many people in our world today are not so much concerned with *what* we believe as they are with *how* we behave; therefore, what really matters for us is our loving fidelity to the Trinity and our loving deployment in the Trinity.

We pray and work in the Spirit so that we may become reflective of God in ways that welcome others to this same relationship with God. We do this knowing that newcomers will be able to see God more clearly as they see God reflected in the authentic relationships we Christians have with one another and with those in the wider world around us.

Our very favorite icon at Church of the Apostles is by Andrei Rublev, which he painted around the year 1410. It depicts the three angels who paid an unexpected visit to Abraham and Sarah at the Oak of Mamre, but the icon is often interpreted as an icon of the Trinity.

Our version of Rublev's icon of the Trinity is four feet tall and home-made out of wood and paint from Home Depot, by our young artist in residence, Skye Graves.

Our associate pastor, Ryan Marsh, once gave a "reverb" meditation on this icon that included unforgettable insight. Upon describing the depiction of the three angels seated at the table, he commented that with the positioning of the three angels (or Trinitarian figures) seated, there is still an empty place at their table, and that the icon finds completion when the church fills that extra place as we join with God in the work of the kingdom that we have been invited to and equipped for.

## Urban Monks
### > "In the Lord's Boarding House" > tuned in to the rhythms of the saints

*Posted by: Matt Bollinger* | November 21, 2005 at 02:30 AM

Sometimes we learn the most when we speak the least. It is in our times of silence, both corporate and private, that we come to acknowledge the fact that the world does not revolve around us, that there are more important things than what may happen to be on the tips of our tongues. Silence teaches us to be still, to open the ears of our hearts to the whispers of Christ. For when we are truly silent before God, we begin to hear the quiet voice of Christ interceding on our behalf.

### Comments from Karen

One of several streams within the emerging church that we resonate with is the "new monastic" stream. What this is exactly, we are not sure, as it is still emerging and only a small, but growing number of communities resonate with this term.

We call our old urban church building the "Fremont Abbey," and increasingly within the community, I am being called an "abbess."

Alan Roxburgh wrote this in his blog post "On being an abbot":

For leaders, cultivating growth is about becoming an abbot in a congregation rather than a pastor. An abbot is a leader who forms a way of life among a whole people. Missional change is primarily about formation—and formation is about the habits and practices that shape new ways of being the church. Cultivation is an ancient word taken from agricultural practices. It is an organic metaphor rather than one of management or warfare. A gardener or farmer understands that the life and purpose of plants or crops is not something over which the farmer has a great deal of control. And so, leadership as cultivation is not about people fitting into your strategy; it is about providing the environment in which missional imagination buds and develops, and in which the farmer may well be astonished by the results.

We are only just beginning to reflect more on the emerging form of "new monastic" life taking root at Church of the Apostles. We are starting to give more attention to how God is cultivating our life and practices around the things we have always had and used (common prayer, Scripture reflection, and service and liturgy around the rhythm of the church year which mirrors the life of Christ). And only recently have I begun to think of our whole community as a small, local, monastic order in formation. I'm excited to see how this develops and where God will take us as we experiment with being an urban monastery, in service by cultivating the art of life and helping God with community matters here in our artistic Fremont neighborhood.

## On the Road

### > backpacked "road rules" > praxis trumps perfect

Our local theology, composed of our many little theologies, is made "on the go."

Big theologies can be made by other means, as they are not meant to be portable. Like reference cookbooks on the shelf, big theologies can be turned to when the situation calls for research, when we need to mine the knowledge base of master chefs (like Tillich, Barth, Kung, etc.). We consult our big cookbooks as needed, yet most of our theology is made fresh daily, around our community values and spiritual practices.

Listed below are our community "road rules" (our "ruled" way of life) which we can easily pack and carry with us as we move.

> **Mission and friendship.** Because God sent his Son to lay down his life to call us friends, we value the friendship with God that we have in Jesus Christ. Because we too have been far off, we joyously share with others God's invitation to come near by the blood of Christ. We seek to be an organic and missional community, part of God's ever-widening circle of friends and reign upon the earth.

> **Community and hospitality.** Because God's life (as Father, Son, and Spirit) is the source of all relationality, we seek to live in relational community, offering ourselves to God as living members of the body of Christ. Because God has prepared a place for us and welcomes all prodigals home, we honor God's welcome to people from any culture, ethnicity, orientation, economic situation, or social position.

> **Authenticity and economy.** Because Christ came not to condemn the world but to save and reconcile it, we value authentic relationships with God, others, and all creation. We seek to walk lightly upon the earth and to participate in God's creating, redeeming, and sustaining dream for the world.

> **Service and mercy.** Because God sent Jesus into the world, not to be served, but to serve, and because no servant is above the master, we seek to follow in the way of the cross in obedience to the reign of God.

Ever deepening our awareness of the costs of discipleship, we seek to practice (as best we are able) forms of true religion, by aiding orphans and widows in distress and keeping our hearts unstained by the world.

> **Tradition and innovation.** "The wisdom of past ages without a vision of the future is irrelevant, but a vision of the future ignorant of the lessons of the past is irresponsible" (from the COTA website). The practices of those who have come before us in the faith are deep roots that support us as we grow together toward God's future.

We value the traditions handed down to us that are of the gospel. We hold them as treasure entrusted to us for future generations. We will use them creatively to illumine the path we are walking within the emerging culture and toward the kingdom of God.

> **Beauty and wisdom.** Because the fear of God is the start of wisdom, we drink deeply from the well of Scripture, the story of salvation and written testimony to Jesus Christ passed on to us by our ancestors in the faith. The Scriptures form and guide our walk of faith and bear witness to the Word of God who is Jesus Christ.

Because God is beautiful and has made a beautiful world, we value creative and artistic expression in our individual and communal lives. Art, poetry, dance, music — when directed toward God, reflect the beauty and wisdom of God's incarnate word in the person of Jesus Christ.

> **Truth and becoming.** Because God's truth became flesh in Jesus, we seek to be an authentic community in the presence of truth. We do not possess truth or seek to correct the truths of others, but we seek to live faithfully in light of the truth of God in Jesus Christ. We also will attend to the emergence of God's kingdom in our world and in our personal and communal becoming.

> This life is therefore, not righteousness, but growth in righteousness, not health, but healing, not being, but becoming, not rest, but exercise. We are not yet what we shall be, but we are growing toward it, the process is not yet finished but it is going on, this is not the end, but it is the road. All does not yet gleam in glory, but all is being purified.
>
> Martin Luther, *In Defense of all the Articles*, 1521

> **Joy and serendipity.** Because Christ calls us to abundant life, we seek to live joyously in the light of God's presence and celebrate the release and freedom that life in the Spirit brings.

Ever aware that the movements of the Spirit are both uncontrollable and unpredictable, we seek only to surf the holy wind, breathe deep God's holy presence, and enjoy the holy ride.

## Comments from Karen

These values and practices are touchstones for our community life and witness at Church of the Apostles, and we believe that as we purpose our lives (with God's help) to live in this "Way," God will bless these efforts to order our days and our deeds in God's peace.

## The Home Way

### > claiming our religion and moving beyond it > life without shoes > Galilee or bust!

*Posted by: Karen Ward* | December 01, 2005 at 02:30 AM

To me, true "religion" (aiding orphans and widows ...) is not the problem; the lack of love is the problem. Religion without love is bankrupt. I love these words from John Caputo:

> The opposite of a religious person is a loveless person. "Whoever does not love does not know God" (1 John 4:8). Notice I am not saying a secular person because I am out to waylay the usual distinction between religious and secular in the name of what I shall call the "post-secular" or a "religion without religion." I include a lot of supposedly secular people in religion ... a lot of supposedly secular people love something madly, while a lot of supposedly religious people love nothing more than getting their own way and bending others to their own will ("in the name of God"). Some people can be deeply and abidingly "religious" with or without theology, and with or without the religions. Religion may be found with or without religion.[4]

## Comments from Karen

I think we can claim our religion (our *religio* and way of life around Jesus Christ) and still move beyond religion, in terms of it being a source of intolerance and anti-gospel in the world. Mohandas Ghandi is reported to have said, "I like your Christ, I do not like your Christians. Your Christians are so unlike your Christ."

The world we live in tires easily of all forms of loveless religion, yet at the same time, the world longs for a people whose countenance and appearance reflect the face of Jesus Christ. So as we practice our religion, it needs to be re-formed and re-imagined each time it veers away from the call to love in Jesus. The closer we stay to Jesus, the more our faith will be perceived as forming "Christians who are like our Christ."

We view all of Christian life as being lived on "the road to Emmaus," and that all Christian mission is found "in Galilee." Each community of Christians has its own Emmaus and its own Galilee, both local places of "journey destination."

As we journey with Christ, truly we have our reward, and what has been promised is already here. The reign of God is breaking forth even now, and we are called to perceive it. And "the reign of God is within you" (Luke 17:21 YLT). This is what Jesus told his followers. So what would happen if we really believed and perceived this? It is exciting to think about, and even more exciting to try and live it without shoes, because "Earth's crammed with heaven, / And every common bush afire with God; / But only he who sees, takes off his shoes, / the rest sit round it and pluck blackberries, / and daub their natural faces unaware."[5]

## Closing Comments

Thank you for sampling some of the theological soup from Church of the Apostles.

Always starting with the stock God has given us, we will continue to make local theology as we journey toward our local Emmaus and hold base camp each week in our local Galilee.

As we gather we will continue to simmer our little theologies and share holy food and Scripture around a common fire. We will continue to tell others they are invited to join us on this road and at God's banquet. Together we will continue to give thanks at the table and pray for the ordering of our days and deeds in the way of Jesus Christ, the best and only apologetic that each local church can truly make for God.

We have to go now and keep on our journey, but we would like to leave you with blessing words of a favorite poem beloved in our Church of the Apostles community, words we often use as a benediction in our weekly mass gathering. So, go in peace to love and serve the Lord, knowing that:

God speaks to each of us as he makes us,
Then walks with us silently out of the night.

These are the words we dimly hear:

You, sent out beyond your recall,
go to the limits of your longing.
Embody me.

Flare up like flame
and make big shadows I can move in.

Let everything happen to you: beauty and terror.
Just keep going. No feeling is final.
Don't let yourself lose me.

Nearby is the country they call life.
You will know it by its seriousness.

Give me your hand.[6]

# RESPONSE TO KAREN WARD

## MARK DRISCOLL

For the sake of pleasantness, I will begin with what Karen and I hold in common and then explain some of our more significant differences. First, Karen holds to the essential tenets of the Christian faith as articulated in such summaries as the Apostles' and Nicene Creeds. Second, Karen planted her church, something that is the logical outgrowth of a truly missional theology, and curiously, one of the few things that each of the contributors share as a common experience.

Karen's church is in many ways very much like the average American church. Its size of roughly eighty people is average, and its affiliation with large mainline denominations is also typical of a large percentage of churches. And her admitted affinity for such modern theologians as Tillich, Barth, and Kung is also common in many typical mainline Christian churches.

What distinguishes Karen, however, from the mainline church is her affiliation with the emergent stream of the emerging church. She has sought in many ways to refashion the mainline church with a makeover that includes renaming churches as new monastic communities, renaming church leaders as abbesses instead of pastors, and exchanging the church bulletin for a blog. And while I would be reticent to endorse a departure from biblical words for biblical concepts, I generally agree with the need for God's people to continually pursue culturally creative ways to make the gospel and the church of Jesus Christ most accessible to as many people as possible. Paul taught this in 1 Corinthians 9:22–23 and modeled it in his interactions with people from various cultures.

But what also concerns me is whether or not emerging church leaders also believe that the propositional truths of our faith are timeless, unchanging, or as Jude 3 says, "once for all entrusted to the saints."* Karen's chapter

---

*All Scripture quotations referenced by Mark Driscoll are from the *New International Version.*

raises a number of very important theological questions that have become more sharply debated in recent years because of the rise of the postmodern mood. Therefore, I will note each of these questions and explore them briefly.

First, what is the appropriate role for a woman to hold in the leadership of a church? A hierarchical would say that women and men are created to operate in different ministry spheres, that women are unable to hold a church office and should focus solely on ministries for other women and children. A complementarian would answer that men and women are partners in every area of ministry, and that all church leadership is open to women with the singular exception of the office of elder/pastor. An egalitarian would answer that a woman can hold any church leadership position. As an unmarried woman who is the senior and only ordained leader in her church, Karen models this last position.

I hold the complementarian position for four reasons. First, the foundational government upon which church and state rest is the government of the home, which the man is created to lovingly lead (Titus 2:3–5; Ephesians 5:21–33; Colossians 3:18; 1 Peter 3:1–6). Second, the Old Testament's highest spiritual office of priest was only open to qualified men. Third, Jesus chose only qualified men as his senior leaders. Fourth, the New Testament states that only a qualified man should hold the senior church leadership position of elder/pastor (1 Timothy 2:1–15; Titus 1:5–9). And, while many will welcome this position as happily as a cat does water, it is the position of the early church fathers John Chrysostom and Augustine, Catholic theologian Erasmus, Lutheran reformer Martin Luther, Presbyterian reformer John Calvin, and Baptist theologian John Gill.

Second, Karen's chapter raises the important question of what exactly is the level of authority that Scripture holds in the church. Karen's chapter uses only three Scripture references, an old worship song, an indie rock band, a postmodern philosopher, a church blog, a movie, an obscure theologian, and Hindu Ghandi as her authorities. And while quoting various cultural references is not inherently bad, since Paul was also known to quote law codes and mainstream poets, it is concerning when the final authority of Scripture is questioned. She quotes the poet Rilke, saying, "God speaks to us ... out of our own lives, no less so than God speaks to us in the canon of Holy Scripture ..." at the risk of stating the obvious, before we drop the authority of Scripture, we need a better reason than a poem from a non-Christian whose mother wanted a girl so badly that she called him Sophia and made him wear girls' clothes until the age of five.

Third, Karen's chapter raises the crucial question of what place the cross has in the life of the church. She says, "We don't expect that the latest framing of the atonement will help us ..." I find this point naïve because the reason there are multiple biblically grounded perspectives regarding Jesus' substitutionary death is not because none are helpful, but rather because all are helpful. This is why Paul boasted only in and preached only of the cross as literally the crux of his pastoral ministry (Galatians 6:14; 1 Corinthians 2:2). Practically, I find the doctrine of expiation (the cleansing of sin's stain upon one's soul by Jesus' blood) to be a great comfort to many people, for instance, those who have been sexually abused and made to feel defiled. Simply, apart from the cross, the church has nothing unique to offer the world that they could not get from a psychologist or self-help seminar with principles for community and self-esteem.

Fourth, her chapter raises the question of the limits of our knowledge of God. She says, "We are learning to embrace the fact that we are all heretics and idolaters ..." Because the first commandment tells us not to be idolaters and 2 Peter 2:1–12 says heretics go to hell, idolatry and heresy are not something we should "learn to embrace." The Bible is clear that God has secrets and that we see dimly (Deuteronomy 29:29; 1 Corinthians 13:12). This does not mean that we cannot know the truth, but rather that we cannot know it fully and must live humbly with partial knowledge and faith.

Fifth, Karen's chapter raises the question of whether Christians should have confidence in their beliefs and seek to alter the beliefs of others. She says, "We do not possess truth or seek to correct the truths of others, but we seek to live faithfully...." Yet, Jesus said he is the truth and called Scripture truth (John 14:6; 17:17). Paul said Scripture existed in part for correction, and that the church is the possessor of truth (2 Timothy 3:16; 1 Timothy 3:15). He also commanded church leaders to teach and preach sound doctrine, which includes refuting and demolishing error (1 Timothy 3:2; 2 Timothy 4:2; Titus 1:9; 2 Corinthians 10:5). And entire New Testament books such as 1 Corinthians, Galatians, and 1 John were written to refute false teaching.

Sixth, her chapter raises the question of whether there should be authoritative teachers in the church. The quote from the church blog pining for "a revival of the Holy Spirit as the only teacher" and the claim that church services should have only Scripture readings without any human teacher clarifying their meaning, defies the entire ministry of the Holy Spirit who gifts teachers to teach the Scriptures that the Holy Spirit inspired. This illogic is espoused on a church blog where anyone can appoint themselves as a teacher and teach others that teaching is a bad thing, of course with the exception of when they are teaching. Without clear teaching, the church is vulnerable to false teachers and wolves. Furthermore, Jesus was murdered because he claimed to possess the truth, taught with authority, and corrected the false beliefs of others.

In conclusion, Karen's chapter never speaks of sin, which is the root of all trouble. Without an awareness of human sin, the pursuit of loving community and nonjudgmental dialogue becomes unprofitable because it is no longer tethered to truth. Without clear Jesus-centered Bible teaching, the church drifts on a sea of uncertainty, because faith comes by hearing God's Word and not by seeing an icon, painting, or interpretive dance (Romans 10:17).

# RESPONSE TO
# KAREN WARD

## JOHN BURKE

I like Karen's creative chapter and prolegomenon as a reminder that God invites all willing guests, both good and bad, to his party. Not all will reply, not all are suitable to stay, but his church's theology must pragmatically be lived out with this open party invitational approach.

As far as Karen's take on the Scriptures, Karen says, "God speaks to us out of our own culture and the stuff of our own lives, no less so than God speaks to us in the canon of Holy Scripture." One of the most important understandings for me has been the realization that God does speak to us and guide us in very personal ways. I agree with Karen that God communicates to us in ways other than the Scriptures, but if she's saying those other ways hold the same weight of authority as Scripture, I disagree.

God does not need a voice or airwaves or eardrums to get his thoughts into my head; he can just put them there. But I must learn to listen because I can hear things that are not from God—Peter's "leading" came straight from hell as can mine (Matthew 16:23). Plus, my own cultural and sociological biases can create "selective hearing" in me.

For that reason, we teach our church to listen for and follow the leadings of the Spirit, but to be always checking those leadings against the authority of Scripture, and against the wise counsel of the community of other Christ followers.

I do agree with Jon Myers' concern for past scriptural abuses, and I agree with his suggested remedy of a humble, Spirit-led response, putting ourselves under the authority of Scripture as we read and seek understanding. I was taught how to study Scripture by dissecting, diagramming, tracing logical flow, and reading the original Greek and Hebrew.

This can become a very head-filling but soul-draining experience if we are not humbly listening to the "so what" personal nudging of God's

Spirit. We need to "make every effort" to grow in knowledge as Peter tells us, but only if our knowledge leads to life-changing practices that consummate in love. Peter says this reflective posture of growth will "keep you from being ineffective and unproductive in your knowledge of our Lord Jesus Christ" (2 Peter 1:5–8).

Karen says, "The God stories in Scripture are sometimes literal, and sometimes not, but are always true." The word "literal" has a Pandora's box-worth of connotation, so I'm not sure what Karen means by this. Some advocate the "literal interpretation" of Scripture in very selectively "literal" ways. Maybe her statement means to correct this malpractice.

For instance, some assert that the earth cannot be millions of years old, despite the fossil record, despite plate tectonics, despite radiometric dating, despite astrophysics, and despite the geological record that indicates a very old earth. They point to Genesis saying, "God created in six 'literal' days." Never mind that the Hebrew word for "day" is used in Genesis 2:4 in a "non-literal" (as in non-twenty-four-hour) way: "In the *day* that the LORD God made earth and heaven ..." (NASB). Obviously this is more than twenty-four hours, and God has apparently not finished his seventh-day rest (Hebrews 4:3–5). This is just one example of selective "literalism."

On the other hand, I do think we must approach Scripture taking it as inspired and seeking to understand what God's Spirit intended, which sometimes we only see by letting Scripture interpret Scripture. This task gets messy and requires interpretation that must subject itself to the wider community of faith—our culture and those of the past—to best get at what God intended.

This sometimes causes me to struggle. Moderns and postmoderns often want to explain away Jonah surviving in a gigantic fish as a "story" meant to make a point, rather than it being "literal," as in "it actually happened." Yet Jonah writes about it seeming to intend it as God's miraculous deliverance of not only Jonah, but Ninevah as well. And Jesus seems to treat it as a miraculous work of God that forecasted his miraculous third-day resurrection from the belly of the earth. Though this doesn't explain well, I must wrestle with what it seems Scripture intended, even when it causes me to squirm.

Do all people have to hold my view of creation or Jonah's story to be right with God through Christ? I don't think so. I'm open to correction and debate, and there are people on our staff and Christians in our church who disagree with me on these issues. These are not central beliefs necessary for following Christ.

On the other hand, I agree in part with Karen on the atonement question of "who is in and who is out" when it comes to salvation. Karen says, "It is God who saves and we who invite ... God can invite us into relationship and we can refuse that invitation ... and it is the calling of the church to keep going out to the 'highways and byways' to keep giving out God's invitations."

I agree that too much sitting around speculating, and at times playing judge, of who God will or won't save is not the most important task of the body of Christ.

If we are to re-present his body, we must be about his business: "The Son of Man came to seek and to save what was lost"; "The Son of Man did not come to be served, but to serve...." (Luke 19:10; Mark 10:45). If we spend more time and energy debating questions that involve mysteries not fully revealed (Deuteronomy 29:29) than we do thinking about how to serve, invite, and be instruments of healing and restoration to our broken world, then we've missed the heart of God.

Again, as Karen says, we need to focus on inviting all people, both good and bad, "to join us and be part of what God is doing in the world around us ... and provide time and space for seekers to explore and discern what entering into such a life [of following Jesus] will mean."

I know some theologians reject this idea. They think it wrong to include spiritual seekers into the community of faith as Karen suggests.

At Gateway we have seen hundreds of spiritual seekers find faith as they experience the "body of Christ." I think this approach of including unbelievers among the community of the church reflects Jesus' community of disciples. Didn't Jesus include skeptics, like Thomas, who would find faith? Didn't Jesus include even those who would remain unbelievers to the end? Didn't Jesus treat Judas as "one of us," and even appoint him as treasurer? Jesus gave Judas every opportunity to repent and follow—yet his heart hardened to the point of betrayal. There will be Thomases and Judases drawn into the community of faith, and we must still be like Jesus to all of them.

# RESPONSE TO
# KAREN WARD

## DAN KIMBALL

I was quite envious of Karen's very refreshing and creative approach to writing her chapter. Using the kitchen metaphor and looking at theology as a recipe with various chefs involved in its formation certainly put the other chapters to shame in regard to artistic expression. Quite honestly, her chapter was the one that moved me most emotionally and also caused a stronger desire to create some soup or a potluck with the other cooks in her church. It made me want to be part of her worship gatherings and experience how her church expresses their worship to God and how they teach Scripture. I also really admire her desire to see not only her own views written, but to allow the other "cooks" in her church to contribute to the chapter's content. This obviously lines up with what she is saying about how her church approaches theology.

Amidst the creative and poetic form, I found myself resonating with the things Karen said about the acknowledgment of "mystery" and the importance of community and relationships determining theology. Far too often, I feel that the people in a local church, except for the pastor or leader, are not involved in theology. They passively sit and listen to someone else spouting out what they learned in the seminary they attended. Most people aren't asked to be thinking theologically for themselves; they are just watching and listening like one watches a television show. So to hear that Karen's church views theology like a potluck with contribution and discussion is so incredibly refreshing. I can only imagine from this approach how the people of the church might grow deeper in their theological views and scriptural knowledge—which in turn should transform them into more loving disciples.

At the same time, however, I would be curious to find out a couple things about this. I would like to learn how the church having a "potluck" that is open to everyone with many "cooks" to participate, is able then to screen out the potato salad that was added to the table that was left in the sun too long and isn't healthy to eat. Or if someone brings some chicken salad to the potluck that wasn't refrigerated and is unhealthy to consume, what do they do? How can one person cook and allow everyone to contribute, but still ensure that healthy soup and food is being served? Karen did say that cooks learn best when cooking, so it seems that her community is thinking through the systems and ways of training people in this regard. I also saw her high value for Scripture and church history and also her crediting the Holy Spirit for the process of spiritual transformation.

I went to Church of the Apostles' website and found that they posted the Nicene Creed as their statement of belief. So from that, I then assume there are theological conclusions they hold to no matter what is brought to the potluck or put into the soup.

Being grounded in the Nicene Creed, with a pretty meaty content of ingredients already determined in there, I would then also assume that her church understands they aren't cooking something entirely new. If we hold to the Nicene Creed, then we are cooking with some recipes that stem back to the early church. There are a lot of things that aren't included in the Nicene Creed that I would have liked to hear more about from what they believe. But it is hard to know a church's theology from merely a chapter. Overall, through the poetic and creative approach of Karen's chapter, I was refreshed and happy to see that a church doesn't just teach theology in a one-way format, but allows people to be in dialogue and discuss it and "cook" it together. If this happens, and if the "cooking" is monitored and somehow grounded in the Nicene Creed, I imagine that the people of the church really will have their lives changed. The Spirit will then use the intense discussion of Scripture to move from the academic nature that theology normally has, to more of a heart and mind and body life-changing nature. If people are engaged in theology and grounded in the historical creeds, then I can only imagine the result would be seeing their minds sharpened by the Scriptures used, and their hearts softened and shaped into disciples of Jesus who grow in their love for God and other people.

# RESPONSE TO KAREN WARD

## DOUG PAGITT

Karen Ward is a friend of mine and a mentor in many ways. She has worked hard and effectively at making the story of the church inform how her community lives today.

In some ways, Karen's view of theology and practice are different from mine, but in more ways, our perspectives are similar.

The way Karen leads her community is an inspiration for me. From the start of this project, she was saying that she wanted her contribution to be from a collective voice and not only from her. I find this impulse at play not only in her writing, but also in her daily life in her community.

I find great hope that Karen allows her community to speak for itself. When I encourage people to be part of the Apostles' community, I try to tell them all I can about it, and they are often excited about what they hear. The best sign of the Apostles' community is that my glowing endorsement is overshadowed by the beauty of the actual experience.

While I find most hope in the future of what God is creating in the world, Karen and her community find similar encouragement in the history of the church.

I also find it wonderful that Karen has chosen to allow her theology to flourish within the context of her denomination. Karen is effectively seeking to bring change from within, which active theology ought to do. She highlights this in her use of the word "and." Church of the Apostles is an "and" kind of community. There are certainly issues in an "and" world, but these are the challenges we ought to take.

Karen and those at Church of the Apostles are pioneers. Pioneering new expressions of worship, new paths for women in leadership, new paths of community engagement and dialogue. This kind of expression will need to carefully navigate the past and the future.

Her notion of "Apostles' Theological Soup" is a terrific image. Soup warms and comforts. It heals and nourishes. It is made from small contributions of many ingredients. It gets better as it simmers. It can be the main course or a side item. When talking about our theology in the emerging church, we would have every right to quote Mary, the mother of Jesus, by saying, "All generations will call [us] blessed" as we live with the Christ among us. Just as Mary was honored to be part of the fulfillment of God's promise, so do I see Karen creating this involvement in her community as they live the gospel. In the same way the church of the New Testament had a life (theirs and that of Jesus) to point to as the evidence of their faith, Karen's perspective points toward living, breathing "temples of faith." Hers has the feel of the Jesus of Jeremiah 31 — the Word of God not written on tablets of stone, but on the living tablets of the hearts of the people.

# CONCLUSION:

# ASSESSING EMERGING THEOLOGY

## ROBERT WEBBER

The sudden appearance of the emerging church and its widespread embrace by many, especially the young, has already provoked a considerable amount of assessment. Perhaps the most crucial and widely read evaluation is that of Don Carson, who argues, "The movement embraces a number of worrying weaknesses."[1]

One weakness of emerging theology is what Carson calls "porous borders."[2] Because of its "porous borders," people are not sure what the emerging church is, what it stands for, or how to think about it. Interested students frequently ask me at conferences, "What are they saying?" or "What is the fuss about?" or "I have listened, and I still don't get it." It may very well be that you have read these chapters and feel the same way. The truth is that these writers, except for Mark Driscoll, have not really addressed the theological issues in a way that many evangelicals are used to. The language of the writers does not have the clarity most desire. They do not speak in familiar categories. Their thoughts on theological issues seem slippery and difficult to pin down. So we ask, "Are they really evangelicals?" or "Are we witnesses to an emerging evangelical liberalism?" if indeed those two words can be comfortably used together.

My task in this conclusion is to go behind the scenes, so to speak, and to uncover the theological perspective of the emerging church, to inquire what is going on underneath these writings, and to assess the theological thinking expressed in the attitudes, words, phrases, and stories that appear in these chapters. The primary evaluation I seek is not of this or that individual, but of the emergent movement as a whole, represented by these five contributors. Rather than deal with an individual writer, I seek to create a conglomerate picture. However, I ask you to keep in mind that the emerging church is too young to have produced a full-orbed theology. It is as Brian McLaren insists, a "conversation." You don't analyze a conversation as you would an artifact of history. Instead you enter the conversation without a full grasp of where it came from or where it is going. My approach is to enter this conversation by sitting at the same roundtable in order to provide a commentary on the conversation. My commentary is very basic and addresses three questions:

1. Who are these conversationalists?
2. What are they saying?
3. What do we need to hear?

## Who Are These Conversationalists?

We all are aware that to understand someone's perspective, we must know something about where that person is coming from. Postmodern philosopher Hans George Gadamer tells us that true conversation can only take place when we understand each other's prejudices. By the word "prejudice" he does not refer to the negative connotation of the word, but to those influences that have gone into making a person think and act the way they do. Questions such as, What is your family of origin like? Where did you grow up? Where did you go to school? and What is it that has formed you to be the person you are? These questions are important ingredients of a conversation. Obviously the limits of this book do not allow us an in-depth study of the origins of each of these conversationalists. However, there are several influences that are common to each, and common to most other emerging leaders. Naming these commonalities will help us understand their theological outlook.

First, and very importantly, the contributors to this book are pastors, not professional theologians. They are not called to the classroom, but to the pulpit. Therefore, we must read them as pastors reflecting on how theology forms and shapes their ministry. We should not look for insights into biblical, historical, philosophical theology, but for applied theology. *What does theology have to do with ministry?*

Second, they all approach ministry with a common educational background. There may be slight differences in the schools they attended, but they all have in common a *modern* curriculum emphasizing a critical study of the Bible in the original languages of Greek and Hebrew; a study of Systematics with an emphasis on a particular system (such as Lutheranism, Calvinism, Wesleyanism, dispensationalism); and an overview of church history that neglected the ancient and medieval period but emphasized the Reformation and modern movements such as Pietism, the evangelical awakenings, and the missionary movement, all precursors to twentieth-century evangelicalism. In addition, they have taken courses in homiletics, evangelism, counseling, and church polity, but no courses in worship or spirituality. I find each writer (except Mark Driscoll) distancing himself or herself from modern theological education and evangelical theological speak.

The third matter these five writers have in common is that their backgrounds, and particularly their seminary educations, have not prepared them for ministry in a postmodern world. In particular, they share three problems inherent in modern seminary education. The first is the compartmentalization of the seminary curriculum. Traditional seminary education provides very little integration between biblical, historical, and theological courses. Consequently, their theological training has been toward abstract, heavily academic concepts, and somewhat unrelated to the cultural issues of the postmodern world. Second, their seminary training has been strongly analytical and oriented around evidential apologetics, logic, and reason. And third, little attempt has been made in seminary to show the relationship between theology and ministry. Ministry, particularly worship and spirituality, having been cut loose from their origins in theological reflection, has become formed by the cultural narrative of programs (for worship), and the narcissistic pursuit of self-focused experience (spirituality).

What then are we to understand about the writers? What prejudices do they bring to ministry? I see three:

1. They all have backgrounds in modern twentieth-century thought.
2. They all are educated in the modern, compartmentalized seminary curriculum.
3. Their education did not train them to minister in the realities of the postmodern, post-Christian, neo-pagan world of the twenty-first century.

In order to understand how emerging pastors think theologically, we must stand in their educational formation and see the task of ministry in the new world from the perspective of what they seek to overcome.

## What Are They Saying?

Most who make judgments about the theology of emerging leaders do so through the eyes of a traditional evangelical background—with its modern compartmentalized, analytical, and scientific theology.

In my opinion, it is more beneficial to judge emerging beliefs not by what the leaders are not saying, but by asking what they *are* saying.

First, these leaders remind us that we live in a new world. This assertion doesn't mean that emergents feel the old modern world is completely gone. They acknowledge we live in two worlds—the modern and postmodern. What they ask of us is to get ready for the new world, to recognize that we live in a time of transition, where the old Christendom is dying and the new postmodern world is emerging. So move from a contextualized theology that fits the certainties of the Newtonian world toward a contextual theology that speaks into the uncertainty of the Heisenberg world; acknowledge that we now live in a global village; a new cultural era has arrived; people know and learn differently; we now live in a culture of pluralistic worldviews and religions; the church is in a new missional setting.

Second, emergents are concerned that evangelicals have not been trained to minister in this world. They remind us that Christianity is no longer the idea to be defended. The modern method of contextualizing theology doesn't connect with this new world; it does no good to answer questions that are no longer asked; Theology, they tell us, is not meant to be professional. Instead, systems of theology must be temporary; the outcome of theology must impact a hurting world.

Third, emergents are saying theology and practice must be brought back together again. They call on us to find a better way of doing theology; because theology is not abstract, ethereal answers. Instead, theology must be contextual, particular, Spirit-led, a song and dance with culture, participatory. It must be integrated with God's agenda for the world; it must seek to answer the questions being asked in today's culture; it must interface with world religions; it must speak to the mission of the church; it must form worship and spirituality and all the ministries of the church. Clearly the emergents are standing on the rooftops calling us to listen, to be aware of the crumbling foundations of modernity, and to see the new emerging culture that dominates the landscape.

What I sense is a *cultural clarity*, a call to a new missiological situation with an equal call not to depart from the historic faith, but to rediscover the faith afresh for this new world. The latter call is a process, a conversation in which we must all engage.

## What Do We Need to Hear?

You may have read this book to "check out these emerging pastors to see if their theology is sound." If you have done that, looking, for example, for the words and phrases that are commonly used in evangelical-theological speak, you probably have been disappointed. Emerging theology, as I have indicated above, is in a rediscovery or reapplication mode. So what do we find here?

First, the emergent movement is marked by *diversity*. All these writers are viewed as emergent pastors. Yet the diversity is striking. Mark Driscoll holds unwaveringly to a Reformed Biblicist theology with which most traditionalists would by happy; John Burke, like many pastors, affirms all that any evangelical holds but is looking for new ways to make it real; Dan Kimball wants to go back and find unity in the common faith of the Nicene Creed; Doug Pagitt and Karen Ward, more edgy than the others, are asking us to find language, symbols, and actions that connect with this generation. Underneath this diversity is the common faith of the church. No one denies what has always been essential to the faith. However, except for Mark Driscoll, no one has articulated the faith the way most modern evangelicals want the Good News to be stated.

I believe there is a reason for these contributors to articulate their faith the way they do. Emerging pastors are coming to theological questions out of practice, not out of abstraction. And this is the second thing we need to hear. The title chapters show the search for the relationship between practice and theology. Consider, for example, the implications of a theology that is incarnational or missional or embodied or communal. These are terms that imply the connection of ministry with theology. In recent years, the practice of ministry has been pragmatic, driven by needs, by the market, and by advertising. Emerging leaders, as in the titles to these chapters, are saying, "Let us connect ministry to the essential convictions of the faith."

Third, in the demand for an applied theology, the contributors unconsciously call us to *theological roots*. Stop doing ministry shaped by this or that cultural narrative and go back to the story of the triune God in history, authoritatively recorded in Scripture and summarized in the Nicene Creed (AD 325).

Fourth, however, emerging leaders do not want a closed theological system all neatly tied together by reason and logic. They call us to a more open view of theology with room for mystery. Theology is "an adventurous exploration of new horizons." Theology is more like a "mysterious adventure than a mathematical puzzle."

Fifth, a crucial component of this call is the plea to recover the missiological dimension of the church, to be the church in *this* culture, finding "a new job description," which is to cease and desist from a theology that is a mere science and a practice of faith captured by civil religion or the status quo.

Sixth, this call to be missional is in a world that is no longer secular, but at a horizon now shaped by an incredible appetite for *worship and spirituality*. We live in a time of spiritual awakening, but one dominated by the practices of New Age and Eastern religions. Therefore, the emerging church is recovering ancient Christian liturgies and spirituality formed by the ancient church in the crucible of a culture steeped in pagan practices, much like ours.

For those who have read this book to gain clarity on emerging beliefs, I have to say that what you are looking for is not here, except in Mark Driscoll. However, I also have to say that the other four do not deny the faith, they simply ask you to join the quest to figure out how the faith speaks into a new culture. And in this invitation, there are no clear formulaic answers, only dangers and challenges.

## The Dangers and Challenges That Lie Ahead

Space does not permit a detailed analysis of the dangers and challenges that lie ahead, but a few comments are in order.

There are two dangers the emerging church needs to avoid. The first danger is to fall back into the common abstract theology of the evangelical church that seeks to validate the authority of the Scriptures and the Christian faith through rational arguments and evidential apologetics. The Christian faith does not need outside verification. It stands on its own as the true story of the world and the meaning of human existence. The second danger facing the emerging church is to perpetuate the Christian pragmatism (with a new postmodern twist) arising during the *awakening* (1964–1984) and dominant through the *unraveling* (1984–2004).

Perhaps it could be said that traditional evangelicalism is theology weak in applied ministry, whereas pragmatic evangelicalism is practice weak in theology. The danger is falling back into one of their incomplete expressions of the faith.

The challenge that lies before the emerging church is to bring theology and practice together once again. As I have indicated above, the healing of the division between theology and practice is evident in the writings of the contributors to this book. The ancient church had a saying for this kind of applied theology: *lex orandi, lex credendi*. The literal translation of this Latin phrase is, "The rule of prayer is the rule of faith" or, another way of putting it is to say, "Show me what you practice, and I will show you what you believe." In the traditional evangelical approach to theology, this saying was reversed. We were taught, "Get your theology straight and it will inform your practice." But that approach failed. It never built the bridge between theology and practice. Theology became a thing in itself. And starting in the eighties, the pragmatists introduced practices of the Christian faith shaped by the market, by entertainment, by narcissistic self-focused interest, by psychology, and by business. Now, the emerging church leaders are saying, "Stop! Look at what you've done. Christian practice is no longer formed by theological reflection." Considering the problems inherited from evangelicalism since WWII, emerging leaders have a formidable task before them.

## Summary Thoughts

I have attempted in both the opening and closing sections to provide a historical framework to understand the phenomena of the emerging church. My conclusion is that the emerging church must be interpreted against the background of the historical cycle of crisis, stability, awakening, unraveling, and back again to crisis. As such, emerging concerns differ from the concerns of a traditional evangelicalism that was born in secularism where it experienced the need to prove itself. Emergent concerns also differ from contemporary and pragmatic evangelicals who responded to the awakening revolution and to the unraveling of society, by swinging the pendulum away from an intellectualized theology toward pragmatic solutions taken from the marketplace of culture.

What is happening among emerging leaders is a desire to return ministry to the story of the triune God from which the story derives. So the question we should be asking the emerging church is not, "Is your theology straight?" but, "Where will your current practices of ministry take you theologically?" Maybe in ten to twenty years, a more seasoned and mature emerging leadership will be able to answer that question more clearly than it can be answered now.

In the meantime, rather than perpetuate the divisions that exist between the traditionalists, the pragmatists, and the emergents, the best we can all do is to join the conversation and learn from each other, affirming that we all do stand in the historic faith as we seek to understand it and apply it to the new world in which we minister. Who knows where this might take us?

# CONTRIBUTORS

## JOHN BURKE

John is founding pastor of Gateway Community Church in Austin and the author of *No Perfect People Allowed*. Gateway was formed out of the emerging post-Christian, postmodern culture and grew during the first six years from a house church of a few people to two thousand attendees. The majority of people at Gateway were not Christ-followers before coming, 75 percent are under forty, and over half are single. John also started Emerging Leadership Initiative (ELI), an organization devoted to partnerships that empower planters of emerging churches. Prior to starting Gateway, John was on the management team of Willow Creek Community Church. Along with overseeing the ministries of Willow, he helped start Axis, a next-gen church-within-a-church, and he supervised the development of Extension partnerships to inner-city Chicago and the two-thirds world. He and his wife Kathy led a campus ministry in California before pioneering a work in St. Petersburg, Russia, for a year after the collapse of communism. Prior to ministry, John worked as a project manager for Chevron. He studied engineering at the University of Texas and did his graduate work at Trinity University in Chicago. John loves playing drums and soccer with his son, Justin; playing guitar and sailing with his daughter, Ashley; and he loves doing everything with his wife of sixteen years, Kathy.

## MARK DRISCOLL

Pastor Mark Driscoll was born in 1970, raised Irish Catholic, and was born again in late 1989. In 1996, he founded Mars Hill Church in Seattle, which has grown to almost five thousand attendees in one of America's least churched cities, becoming one the nation's sixty fastest growing churches (*www.marshillchurch.org*). Pastor Mark is president of the Acts 29 Church Planting Network (*www.acts29network.org*). He also founded and leads the Resurgence Missional Theology Cooperative (*www.theresurgence.com*). Pastor Mark has been named one of the twenty-five most influential pastors in America by *The Church Report*, and one of the most influential young preachers in America by Christianity Today Incorporated. He was also named one of the twenty-five most powerful people in Seattle by *Seattle Magazine*. His writing includes two books, *The Radical Reformission: Reaching Out without Selling Out* and *Confessions of a Reformission Rev.: Hard*

*Lessons from an Emerging Missional Church.* He is also a staff columnist for the *Seattle Times, Rev!* magazine, and *The Church Report.* He and his high school sweetheart Grace have five young children.

## DAN KIMBALL

Dan Kimball is the author of *The Emerging Church: Vintage Christianity for New Generations,* which received the *Christianity Today* Book Award in the church/pastoral leadership category. He also has authored *Emerging Worship: Creating Worship Gatherings for New Generations* and *They Like Jesus, but Not the Church* and *I Like Jesus, but Not the Church* (Zondervan, 2007). Dan served as a high school pastor at Santa Cruz Bible Church in Santa Cruz, California, for eight years, then in the same church started "Graceland" which was a young adult ministry and alternative worship gathering. He recently launched Vintage Faith Church as a church plant of Santa Cruz Bible Church in Santa Cruz (*www.vintagefaith.com*). Dan is married to Becky, has two daughters, and drives a rusty 1966 Ford Mustang. He is currently pursuing a Doctor of Ministry at George Fox Evangelical Seminary where he also serves as adjunct faculty mentor. Dan's personal blog can be found at *www.dankimball.com.*

## DOUG PAGITT

Doug Pagitt is the founding pastor of Solomon's Porch in Minneapolis, Minnesota—"an holistic missional Christian community." Doug has authored four books, *Church Re-Imagined: The Spiritual Formation of People in Communities of Faith, Preaching Re-Imagined: The Role of the Sermon in Communities of Faith, BodyPrayer: The Posture of Intimacy with God,* and *An Emergent Manifesto of Hope,* and contributed to a half a dozen other books.

Doug is married to Shelley, and they have four teenage children. Shelley and Doug adopted their two youngest children through the Foster Care System.

Doug was one of the founding organizers of a network of friendships called Emergent (*www.EmergentVillage.com*), and he spends a significant amount of time and energy in the relationships that are Emergent.

## KAREN WARD

Karen M. Ward is the abbess and founding pastor of Church of the Apostles, Seattle, Washington (*www.apostleschurch.org*), a four-year-old emerging, monastic, incarnational Christian community of the Episcopal Church USA and the Evangelical Lutheran Church in America (ELCA).

Karen is a columnist on church and culture for *Worship Leader* magazine, sits on the Board of Directors of Emergent, and speaks and consults in North America and beyond on emerging missiology, liturgy, leadership, community formation, and spiritual practices with her congregation's mission center, *praxisctr.org.*

Karen enjoys drinking yerba mate, listening to glitch and idm music, Apple computer geeking, pod-casting, and blogging on church and culture at *www.submergence.org.*

## ROBERT WEBBER

Robert Webber is Myers Professor of Ministry at Northern Seminary in Lombard, Illinois; President of the Institute for Worship Studies, a long-distance graduate school located in Orange Park, Florida; and professor of Theology Emeritus, Wheaton College. He is the author of more than forty books, including the Ancient-Future series published by Baker Books.

# RESOURCES RECOMMENDED
# BY CONTRIBUTORS AND EDITOR

## JOHN BURKE

Anderson, Norman. *Christianity and World Religions*. Downers Grove, Ill.: Inter-
Varsity, 1984.

———, ed. *The World's Religions*. Grand Rapids, Mich.: Eerdmans, 1976.

Bloesch, Donald. *Holy Scripture: Revelation, Inspiration, and Interpretation*. Downers Grove, Ill.: InterVarsity, 1994.

Burke, John. *No Perfect People Allowed*. Grand Rapids, Mich.: Zondervan, 2005.

Emerging Leadership Initiative, *www.elichurchplanting.com*.

Gateway Community Church, *www.gatewaychurch.com*.

Newbigin, Lesslie. *The Gospel in a Pluralist Society*. Grand Rapids, Mich.:
Eerdmans, 1989.

## MARK DRISCOLL

The following recommended books do not technically qualify as emerging. However, they each incisively contribute to a better understanding of and resolution
for emerging theological issues, and therefore are "must-have" volumes for every
library.

### Historical Theology

Brown, Harold O. J. *Heresies*. Peabody, Mass.: Hendrickson, 1998.

McGrath, Alister. *Historical Theology*. Malden, Mass.: Blackwell, 1998.

———. *Christian Theology*. Malden, Mass.: Blackwell, 2001.

### Theological Method

Bloesch, Donald. *A Theology of Word and Spirit*. Downers Grove, Ill.: InterVarsity,
1992.

### The Gospel

Piper, John. *God Is the Gospel*. Wheaton: Crossway, 2005.

### Doctrinal Controversies

Erickson, Millard J., ed. *Reclaiming the Center*. Wheaton: Crossway, 2004.

### Liberalism

Machen, J. Gresham. *Christianity and Liberalism*. Grand Rapids, Mich.: Eerdmans,
2001.

### Incarnation

Machen, J. Gresham. *The Virgin Birth of Christ*. Cambridge, Eng.: James Clark
and Co., 2000.

### Atonement

Morris, Leon. *The Apostolic Preaching of the Cross*. Grand Rapids, Mich.: Eerdmans, 1984.

Stott, John R. W. *The Cross of Christ*. Downers Grove, Ill.: InterVarsity, 1986.

### New Perspective of Paul

Stuhlmacher, Peter. *Revisiting Paul's Doctrine of Justification*. Downers Grove, Ill.: InterVarsity, 2001.

### Hell

Morgan, Christopher, and Robert Peterson, eds. *Hell under Fire*. Grand Rapids, Mich.: Zondervan, 2004.

### Open Theism

Ware, Bruce. *God's Lesser Glory*. Wheaton: Crossway, 2000.

———. *Their God Is Too Small*. Wheaton: Crossway, 2003.

### Apologetics

Carroll, Vincent. *Christianity on Trial*. San Francisco: Encounter Books, 2002.

Tennent, Timothy C. *Christianity at the Religious Roundtable*. Grand Rapids, Mich.: Baker, 2002.

Zacharias, Ravi. *Jesus Among Other Gods*. Nashville: W. Publishing, 2000.

### Hermeneutics

Vanhoozer, Kevin. *Is There a Meaning in This Text?* Grand Rapids, Mich.: Zondervan, 1998.

### Secular Critiques of Feminism

Crittenden, Danielle. *What Our Mothers Didn't Tell Us*. New York: Simon & Schuster, 1999.

Graglia, F. Carolyn. *Domestic Tranquility*. Dallas: Spence, 1998.

Sommers, Christina Hoff. *The War Against Boys*. New York: Touchstone, 2000.

### Evangelical Responses to Feminism

Grudem, Wayne. *Evangelical Feminism and Biblical Truth*. Sisters, Ore.: Multnomah, 2004.

Piper, John. *Recovering Biblical Manhood and Womanhood*. Wheaton, Ill.: Crossway, 1991.

### Women in Ministry

Gundry, Stanley, ed. *Two Views on Women in Ministry*. Grand Rapids, Mich.: Zondervan, 2005.

### Homosexuality

Gagnon, Robert. *The Bible and Homosexual Practice*. Nashville: Abingdon, 2001.

**Next Generation**

Smith, Christian, and Melinda Denton. *Soul Searching*. New York: Oxford Univ. Press, 2005.

**American Culture**

Prothero, Stephen. *American Jesus*. New York: Farrar, Straus & Giroux, 2003.

## DAN KIMBALL

Gibbs, Eddie, and Ryan K. Bolger. *Emerging Churches: Creating Christian Community in Postmodern Cultures*. Grand Rapids, Mich.: Baker, 2005.

Kimball, Dan. *The Emerging Church: Vintage Christianity for New Generations*. Grand Rapids, Mich.: Zondervan, 2003.

———. *Emerging Worship: Creating Worship Gatherings for New Generations*. Grand Rapids, Mich.: Zondervan, 2004.

———. *They Like Jesus, but Not the Church*. Grand Rapids, Mich.: Zondervan, 2007.

———. *I Like Jesus, but Not the Church*. Grand Rapids, Mich.: Zondervan, 2007.

*Vintage Faith*, Culture and Church Website, *www.vintagefaith.com*.

Webber, Robert. *The Younger Evangelicals: Facing the Challenges of the New World*. Grand Rapids, Mich.: Baker, 2002.

Witherington, Ben III. *The Problem with Evangelical Theology: Testing the Exegetical Foundations of Calvinism, Dispensationalism, and Wesleyanism*. Waco: Baylor Univ. Press, 2005.

## KAREN WARD

Ashley, Jennifer, ed., with Mike Bickle, Mark Driscoll, and Mike Howerton. *The Relevant Church*. Orlando: Relevant Books, 2004.

Ward, Pete. *Liquid Church*. Peabody, Mass.: Hendrickson, 2002.

Flory, Richard, and Donald E. Miller, eds. *Gen X Religion*. New York: Routledge, 2000.

## ROBERT WEBBER

Altson, Renee. *Stumbling Toward Faith: My Longing to Heal from the Evil That God Allowed*. Grand Rapids, Mich.: Zondervan, 2004.

Anderson, Ray. *An Emergent Theology for Emerging Churches*. Downers Grove, Ill.: InterVarsity, 2006.

Baker, Jonny, and Doug Gay, with Jenny Brown. *Alternative Worship: Resources from and for the Emerging Church*. Grand Rapids, Mich.: Baker, 2003.

Beckhan, William A. *The Second Reformation*. Houston: Touch Publications, 1995.

Bell, Rob. *Velvet Elvis*. Grand Rapids, Mich.: Zondervan, 2005.

Boersma, Hans. *Violence, Hospitality and the Cross*. Grand Rapids, Mich.: Baker, 2004.

Burke, John. *No Perfect People Allowed: Creating a Come-as-You-Are Culture in the Church*. Grand Rapids, Mich.: Zondervan, 2005.

Burke, Spencer, with Colleen Pepper. *Making Sense of Church: Eavesdropping on Emerging Conversation about God, Community, and Culture*. Grand Rapids, Mich.: Zondervan, 2003.

Carroll, Colleen. *The New Faithful: Why Young Adults Are Embracing Christian Orthodoxy*. Chicago: Loyola Press, 2002.

Carson, Donald A. *Becoming Conversant with the Emerging Church: Understanding a Movement and Its Implications*. Grand Rapids, Mich.: Zondervan, 2005.

Clapp, Rodney. *Tortured Wonders: Christian Spirituality for People, Not Angels*. Grand Rapids, Mich.: Brazos, 2004.

Driscoll, Mark. *The Radical Reformission: Reaching Out without Selling Out*. Grand Rapids, Mich.: Zondervan, 2004.

Fitch, David E. *The Great Giveaway: Reclaiming the Mission of the Church from Big Business, Parachurch Organizations, Psychotherapy, Consumer Capitalism, and Other Modern Maladies*. Grand Rapids, Mich.: Baker, 2005.

Frost, Michael, and Alan Hirsch. *The Shaping of Things to Come: Innovation and Mission for the 21st-Century Church*. Peabody, Mass.: Hendrickson Publishers, 2003.

Gibbs, Eddie. *ChurchNext: Quantum Changes in How We Do Ministry*. Downers Grove, Ill.: InterVarsity, 2000.

Green, Joel B., and Mark D. Baker. *Recovering the Scandal of the Cross: Atonement in New Testament and Contemporary Contexts*. Downers Grove, Ill.: InterVarsity, 2000.

Green, Joel B., and Michael Pasquarello III, eds. *Narrative Reading, Narrative Preaching: Reuniting New Testament Interpretation and Proclamation*. Grand Rapids, Mich.: Baker, 2003.

Green-Mathewes, Frederica. *The Open Door: Entering the Sanctuary of Icons and Prayer*. Brewster, Mass.: Paraclete, 2003.

Greer, Robert C. *Mapping Postmodernism: A Survey of Christian Options*. Downers Grove, Ill.: InterVarsity, 2003.

Harink, Douglas. *Paul among the Postliberals: Pauline Theology beyond Christendom and Modernity*. Grand Rapids, Mich.: Brazos, 2003.

Lindbeck, George A. *The Nature of Doctrine: Religion and Theology in a Postliberal Age*. Philadelphia: Westminster Press, 1984.

Long, Jimmy. *Emerging Hope: A Strategy for Reaching Postmodern Generations*. Downers Grove: InterVarsity, 2004.

McLaren, Brian. *A Generous Orthodoxy*. Grand Rapids, Mich.: Zondervan, 2004.

———. *More Ready Than You Realize: Evangelism as Dance in the Postmodern Matrix*. Grand Rapids, Mich.: Zondervan, 2002.

———. *A New Kind of Christian: A Tale of Two Friends on a Spiritual Journey*. San Francisco: Jossey Bass, 2001.

McLaren, Brian, and Tony Campolo. *Adventures in Missing the Point: How the Culture-Controlled Church Neutered the Gospel*. Grand Rapids, Mich.: Zondervan, 2003.

Miller, Donald. *Blue Like Jazz: Nonreligious Thoughts on Christian Spirituality*. Nashville: Thomas Nelson, 2003.

Myers, Joseph R. *Organic Community*. Grand Rapids, Mich.: Baker, 2007.

Okholm, Dennis, and Timothy R. Phillips. *Four Views on Salvation in a Pluralistic World*. Grand Rapids, Mich.: Zondervan, 1995, 1996.

Pagitt, Doug. *Preaching Re-Imagined: The Role of the Sermon in Communities of Faith*. Grand Rapids: Zondervan, 2005.

Pagitt, Doug, and the Solomon's Porch Community. *Church Re-Imagined: The Spiritual Formation of People in Communities of Faith*. Grand Rapids, Mich.: Zondervan, 2003, 2005.

Penner, Myron B., ed. *Christianity and the Postmodern Turn: Six Views*. Grand Rapids, Mich.: Brazos, 2005.

Seay, Chris. *Faith of My Fathers: Conversations with Three Generations of Pastors about Church, Ministry, and Culture*. Grand Rapids, Mich.: Zondervan, 2005.

Smith, James K. A. *Introducing Radical Orthodoxy*. Grand Rapids, Mich.: Baker, 2004.

———. *Who's Afraid of Postmodernism?* Grand Rapids, Mich.: Baker, 2006.

Smith, James K. A., and Henry Isaac Venema. *The Hermeneutics of Charity: Interpretation, Selfhood, and Postmodern Faith*. Grand Rapids, Mich.: Brazos, 2004.

Sweet, Leonard, ed. *The Church in the Emerging Culture*. Grand Rapids, Mich.: Zondervan, 2003.

Taylor, Steve. *The Out of Bounds Church?: Learning to Create a Community of Faith in a Culture of Change*. Grand Rapids, Mich.: Zondervan, 2005.

Tomlinson, Dave. *The Post-Evangelical*. Grand Rapids, Mich.: Zondervan, 2003.

Vanhoozer, Kevin J. *The Drama of Doctrine: A Canonical Linguistic Approach to Christian Theology*. Louisville, Ky.: Westminster John Knox Press, 2005.

Webber, Robert. *Ancient-Future Faith: Rethinking Evangelicalism for a Postmodern World*. Grand Rapids, Mich.: Baker, 1999.

Yaconelli, Mike, ed. *Stories of Emergence: Moving from Absolute to Authentic*. Grand Rapids: Zondervan, 2003.

Yong, Amos. *The Spirit Poured Out on All Flesh: Pentecostalism and the Possibility of Global Theology*. Grand Rapids, Mich.: Baker, 2005.

# APPENDIX 1:

# THE COMMON CREEDS OF THE CHURCH

The common creeds defend God as Creator, the incarnate one, and the Redeemer (fully God and fully man) of all things.

## The Apostles' Creed

An ancient creedal summary of the Christian faith for instructing catechumenates (converts) in the Christian faith. Recognized as a basic statement of faith at baptism. Affirmed by the Protestant Reformers of the sixteenth century. It is now being used, once again, to instruct new Christians in the essentials of faith.

> I believe in God, the Father Almighty,
>> Creator of heaven and earth.
>> I believe in Jesus Christ, his only Son, our Lord.
>
> He was conceived by the power of the Holy Spirit
>> and born of the Virgin Mary.
>> He suffered under Pontius Pilate,
>> was crucified, died, and was buried.
>
> He descended to the dead.
>
> On the third day he rose again.
> He ascended into heaven,
>> and is seated at the right hand of the Father.
>> He will come again to judge the living and the dead.
> I believe in the Holy Spirit,
>> the holy catholic Church,
>> the communion of saints,
>> the forgiveness of sins,
>> the resurrection of the body,
>> and the life everlasting.
> Amen.

## The Nicene Creed

The fourth-century creed defending the word "incarnate" as the true God against Arianism, which argued that the word "incarnate" was not God, but of a different essence. It was "God of God" who became incarnate, the Nicene Creed affirms, "for us and for our salvation."

We believe in one God,
>   the Father, the Almighty,
>   maker of heaven and earth,
>   of all that is, seen and unseen.
We believe in one Lord, Jesus Christ,
>   the only Son of God,
>   eternally begotten of the Father,
>   God from God, Light from Light,
>   true God from true God,
>   begotten, not made,
>   of one Being with the Father.
>   Through him all things were made.
>   For us and for our salvation
>       he came down from heaven:
>   by the power of the Holy Spirit
>       he became incarnate from the Virgin Mary,
>       and was made man.
>   For our sake he was crucified under Pontius Pilate;
>       he suffered death and was buried.
>       On the third day he rose again
>           in accordance with the Scriptures;
>       he ascended into heaven
>           and is seated at the right hand of the Father.
>   He will come again in glory to judge the living and the dead,
>       and his kingdom will have no end.
We believe in the Holy Spirit, the Lord, the giver of life,
>   who proceeds from the Father and the Son.
>   With the Father and the Son he is worshiped and glorified.
>   He has spoken through the Prophets.
>   We believe in one holy catholic and apostolic Church.
>   We acknowledge one baptism for the forgiveness of sins.
>   We look for the resurrection of the dead,
>       and the life of the world to come. Amen.

## Council of Chalcedon, AD 451

The fifth-century clarification that Jesus Christ is fully God and fully man united in the person of Jesus "without confusion, without change, without division, without separation." Affirming thereby that our Savior is fully God and fully man.

Therefore, following the holy fathers, we all with one accord teach men to acknowledge one and the same Son, our Lord Jesus Christ, at once complete in Godhead and complete in manhood, truly God and truly man, consisting also of a reasonable soul and body; of one substance (*homoousios*) with the Father as regards his Godhead, and at the same time of one substance with us as regards his manhood; like us in all respects, apart from sin; as regards his Godhead, begotten of the Father before the ages, but yet as regards his manhood begotten, for us men and for our salvation, of Mary the Virgin, the God-bearer (*Theotokus*); one and the same Christ, Son, Lord, Only-begotten, recognized in two natures, without confusion, without change, without division, without separation; the distinction of natures being in no way annulled by the union, but rather the characteristics of each nature being preserved and coming together to form one person and subsistence, not as parted or separated into two persons, but one and the same Son and Only-begotten God the Word, Lord Jesus Christ; even as the prophets from earliest times spoke of him, and our Lord Jesus Christ himself taught us, and the creed of the Fathers has handed down to us.

# APPENDIX 2:

# WHAT IS THE ANCIENT-FUTURE VISION?

Because the Ancient-Future Vision has been associated with the emerging church, I am including a brief response to the frequently asked question, "What is an Ancient-Future Vision?" For more information, go to *www. ancientfutureworship.com* to read the *Call*.

The Western world is currently passing through an enormous cultural shift. This shift may be described as a movement away from historic religious sensibilities to a new condition of life. The phrase "historic religious sensibilities" encompasses the Christian worldview of the ancient church and the Reformers who sought to restore classical Christianity in the face of late medieval corruption. "Movement away" is the process of secularization that has occurred over the last three hundred years, through which God and the Christian faith have been marginalized. The "new condition of life" is the advent of a postmodern, post-Christian secular and spiritually pagan New Age world.

Since the 1960s the church has been caught in the turmoil of this great paradigm shift. For the most part, the traditional church has been ministering to the remnants of the old worldview while the contemporary church movement has been ministering to the unraveling culture. Yet all of us have been caught in the tension between the old and the new.

In this struggle between the old and the new cultural realities, the traditionalists have been out of touch with cultural changes, and the contemporaries who have become so thoroughly enmeshed with and catechized by culture are out of touch with the traditions. This reality has created what seems to be an unalterable division between devoted Christians.

What are we to do? Should we encourage the split? Or is there a new direction for us all? In the pattern of history, opposite positions will inevitably harden and go their own way in an either/or position. Will that mentality rule today or will we seize the opportunity for a both/and future? An Ancient-Future faith calls upon us all to embrace a both/and future. What will it take to create an Ancient-Future faith in this time of current cultural upheaval? I believe there are three commitments we must all make.

First, an Ancient-Future faith calls us to return to our ancient roots in the first centuries of the church. Christianity emerged in a culture somewhat similar to ours—very religious, very secular, very pagan. In these centuries of turmoil and religious persecution, the most fundamental realities of the faith forged by the Spirit reflected on the cosmic events of the incarnation, death, resurrection, ascension, and coming again of Jesus Christ. Early church worship proclaimed and enacted God's saving work; established the church as community; affirmed and wrote the universal creeds; determined the church's relation to culture; developed forms of evangelism, discipleship, and spiritual formation; and laid down Christian ethics of behavior. In the face of religious, spiritual, and ethical relativism, the church cried, "We believe, we belong, we behave." This proclamation of absolutes and exclusivity resulted in the rapid and widespread growth of the church and determined the common roots of the whole church — Orthodox, Catholic, Protestant. It is to these roots that an Ancient-Future faith will return.

Second, an Ancient-Future faith is characterized by connection. While there is a common tradition that defines us all, there are particular traditions that characterize the diversity we experience within our unity. Throughout history, divisions have existed because of particulars. Then, too, reforms have emerged again and again to renew the church. These divisions and new movements are to be understood and affirmed in their cultural settings. It is all right to be Orthodox, Roman Catholic, Lutheran, Reformed, Anabaptist, fundamentalist, evangelical, Pentecostal, charismatic, or a contemporary Christian. While there are differences, Christians are not to be divided over them, but are to seek understanding in particulars while affirming unity in the common tradition. Because there is one Lord, one faith, and one baptism, we are brothers and sisters connected to the same family. This ecumenical conviction is central to an Ancient-Future Vision.

Third, an Ancient-Future faith seeks to be authentic in a changing world. The truth of the Christian faith does not change because we live and minister in a new cultural era. How faith is communicated and defended, however, does change. In today's postmodern, post-Christian, secular, and pagan world, the church must emerge as a countercultural movement in its message, its community, and its ethics. Yet, authentic Christianity affirms and relates to many cultural changes: The shift in science, from a mechanistic view of the world to the world as a web of interconnections; in philosophy, from rationalism to mystery; in globalization, from monoculture to multiculture; in historical consciousness, from anti-historical to nostalgia for the past; in language, from propositional to performative; in communication, from monologue to dialogue; in technology, from word to image; in society, from individualism to community; and in the rise of terror that moves us from a state of stability to personal vulnerability. Christians can and do affirm these new cultural realities and speak an unchanging faith through them.

In the midst of all these cultural changes, we are called to be an authentically transformed people, conforming to the image of Christ, conducting ourselves as salt and light in the political, economic, educational, institutional, and family life of our neighborhood, the state, the nation, and the world. Here we witness to Christ as victor over the powers of evil—the powers that were bound at the temptation, dethroned at the cross, and to be destroyed at the end of history.

Finally, let it be said that these changes suggested by an Ancient-Future faith will not be brought about except by the Holy Spirit leading us all into a deep study of Scripture and the ancient tradition, a penetrating analysis of the whole church, historical and global, and careful analysis and study of the current cultural situation. Indeed what lies before us is an arduous task, a journey through perilous waters that must be navigated with great care and embraced with anticipatory joy.

Those who are called to an Ancient-Future Christianity will do so with humble dependence on the Spirit; by affirming the ancient roots of faith, a connection to God's people in all times and everywhere; and a commitment to an authentic engagement with culture.

**ROBERT WEBBER**

## Resources

*www.ancientfutureworship.com*: Receive a free monthly email newsletter by Robert Webber.

### Books, education, etc.

Interested in worship education or graduate education in worship? Check out:

The Institute for Worship Studies: *www.iwsfla.org*
Northern Seminary: *www.seminary.edu*

# APPENDIX 3:

# A CALL TO AN ANCIENT EVANGELICAL FUTURE

## Prologue

In every age the Holy Spirit calls the Church to examine its faithfulness to God's revelation in Jesus Christ, authoritatively recorded in Scripture and handed down through the Church. Thus, while we affirm the global strength and vitality of worldwide Evangelicalism in our day, we believe the North American expression of Evangelicalism needs to be especially sensitive to the new external and internal challenges facing God's people.

These external challenges include the current cultural milieu and the resurgence of religious and political ideologies. The internal challenges include Evangelical accommodation to civil religion, rationalism, privatism and pragmatism. In light of these challenges, we call Evangelicals to strengthen their witness through a recovery of the faith articulated by the consensus of the ancient Church and its guardians in the traditions of Eastern Orthodoxy, Roman Catholicism, the Protestant Reformation and the Evangelical awakenings. Ancient Christians faced a world of paganism, Gnosticism and political domination. In the face of heresy and persecution, they understood history through Israel's story, culminating in the death and resurrection of Jesus and the coming of God's Kingdom.

Today, as in the ancient era, the Church is confronted by a host of master narratives that contradict and compete with the gospel. The pressing question is: who gets to narrate the world? The *Call to an Ancient Evangelical Future* challenges Evangelical Christians to restore the priority of the divinely inspired biblical story of God's acts in history. The narrative of God's Kingdom holds eternal implications for the mission of the Church, its theological reflection, its public ministries of worship and spirituality and its life in the world. By engaging these themes, we believe the Church will be strengthened to address the issues of our day.

1. **On the Primacy of the Biblical Narrative**
   We call for a return to the priority of the divinely authorized canonical story of the Triune God. This story—Creation, Incarnation, and Re-creation—was effected by Christ's recapitulation of human history and summarized by the early Church in its Rules of Faith. The gospel-formed content of these Rules served as the key

to the interpretation of Scripture and its critique of contemporary culture, and thus shaped the church's pastoral ministry. Today, we call Evangelicals to turn away from modern theological methods that reduce the gospel to mere propositions, and from contemporary pastoral ministries so compatible with culture that they camouflage God's story or empty it of its cosmic and redemptive meaning. In a world of competing stories, we call Evangelicals to recover the truth of God's word as *the* story of the world, and to make *it* the centerpiece of Evangelical life.

2. **On the Church, the Continuation of God's Narrative**
   We call Evangelicals to take seriously the visible character of the Church. We call for a commitment to its mission in the world in fidelity to God's mission (*Missio Dei*), and for an exploration of the ecumenical implications this has for the unity, holiness catholicity, and apostolicity of the Church. Thus, we call Evangelicals to turn away from an individualism that makes the Church a mere addendum to God's redemptive plan. Individualistic Evangelicalism has contributed to the current problems of churchless Christianity, redefinitions of the Church according to business models, separatist ecclesiologies and judgmental attitudes toward the Church. Therefore, we call Evangelicals to recover their place in the community of the Church catholic.

3. **On the Church's Theological Reflection on God's Narrative**
   We call for the Church's reflection to remain anchored in the Scriptures in continuity with the theological interpretation learned from the early Fathers. Thus, we call Evangelicals to turn away from methods that separate theological reflection from the common traditions of the Church. These modern methods compartmentalize God's story by analyzing its separate parts, while ignoring God's entire redemptive work as recapitulated in Christ. Anti-historical attitudes also disregard the common biblical and theological legacy of the ancient Church.

   Such disregard ignores the hermeneutical value of the Church's ecumenical creeds. This reduces God's story of the world to one of many competing theologies and impairs the unified witness of the Church to God's plan for the history of the world. Therefore, we call Evangelicals to unity in "the tradition that has been believed everywhere, always and by all," as well as to humility and charity in their various Protestant traditions.

4. **On Church's Worship as Telling and Enacting God's Narrative**

We call for public worship that sings, preaches and enacts God's story. We call for a renewed consideration of how God ministers to us in baptism, eucharist, confession, the laying on of hands, marriage, healing and through the charisms of the Spirit, for these actions shape our lives and signify the meaning of the world. Thus, we call Evangelicals to turn away from forms of worship that focus on God as a mere object of the intellect, or that assert the self as the source of worship. Such worship has resulted in lecture-oriented, music-driven, performance-centered and program-controlled models that do not adequately proclaim God's cosmic redemption. Therefore, we call Evangelicals to recover the historic substance of worship of Word and Table and to attend to the Christian year, which marks time according to God's saving acts.

5. **On Spiritual Formation in the Church as Embodiment of God's Narrative**

We call for a catechetical spiritual formation of the people of God that is based firmly on a Trinitarian biblical narrative. We are concerned when spirituality is separated from the story of God and baptism into the life of Christ and his Body. Spirituality, made independent from God's story, is often characterized by legalism, mere intellectual knowledge, an overly therapeutic culture, New Age Gnosticism, a dualistic rejection of this world and a narcissistic preoccupation with one's own experience. These false spiritualities are inadequate for the challenges we face in today's world. Therefore, we call Evangelicals to return to a historic spirituality like that taught and practiced in the ancient catechumenate.

6. **On the Church's Embodied Life in the World**

We call for a cruciform holiness and commitment to God's mission in the world. This embodied holiness affirms life, biblical morality and appropriate self-denial. It calls us to be faithful stewards of the created order and bold prophets to our contemporary culture. Thus, we call Evangelicals to intensify their prophetic voice against forms of indifference to God's gift of life, economic and political injustice, ecological insensitivity and the failure to champion the poor and marginalized. Too often we have failed to stand prophetically against the culture's captivity to racism, consumerism, political correctness, civil religion, sexism, ethical relativism, violence and the culture of death. These failures have muted the voice of Christ to the world through his Church and detract from God's story of the world, which the Church is collectively to embody. Therefore, we call the Church to recover its counter-cultural mission to the world.

## Epilogue

In sum, we call Evangelicals to recover the conviction that God's story shapes the mission of the Church to bear witness to God's Kingdom and to inform the spiritual foundations of civilization. We set forth this *Call* as an ongoing, open-ended conversation. We are aware that we have our blind spots and weaknesses. Therefore, we encourage Evangelicals to engage this *Call* within educational centers, denominations and local churches through publications and conferences.

We pray that we can move with intention to proclaim a loving, transcendent, triune God who has become involved in our history. In line with Scripture, creed and tradition, it is our deepest desire to embody God's purposes in the mission of the Church through our theological reflection, our worship, our spirituality and our life in the world, all the while proclaiming that Jesus is Lord over all creation.

This *Call*\* is issued in the spirit of *sic et non*; therefore those who affix their names to this *Call* need not agree with all its content. Rather, its consensus is that these are issues to be discussed in the tradition of *semper reformanda* as the church faces the new challenges of our time. Over a period of seven months, more than three hundred persons have participated via email to write the *Call*. These men and women represent a broad diversity of ethnicity and denominational affiliation. The four theologians who most consistently interacted with the development of the *Call* have been named as *Theological Editors*. The *Board of Reference* was given the special assignment of overall approval.

If you wish to sign the *Call*, you can do so by going to *www.ancient futureworship.com* where the *Call* is hosted and where signatures may be affixed.

---

\* © Northern Seminary 2006 Robert Webber and Phil Kenyon. Permission is granted to reproduce the *Call* in unaltered form with proper citation.

# NOTES

## Introduction: THE INTERACTION OF CULTURE AND THEOLOGY
### ROBERT WEBBER

[1] William Strauss and Neil Howe, *The Fourth Turning: What the Cycles of History Tell Us About America's Next Rendezvous* (New York: Broadway Books, 1997), 2.

[2] Ibid., 3.

[3] Ibid., 173.

[4] Ibid., 204.

[5] Ibid., 206.

[6] Ibid., 6.

[7] Ibid., 7.

[8] Ibid., 22.

[9] Ibid., 6.

## Chapter 1: THE EMERGING CHURCH AND BIBLICIST THEOLOGY
### MARK DRISCOLL

[1] 1 Cor. 15:1–4

[2] Luke 24:44

[3] Matt. 5:17

[4] Matt. 19:4–5; Mark 10:6–8

[5] Luke 11:51

[6] Matt. 24:37–39; Luke 17:26–27

[7] John 8:56

[8] Matt. 10:15; 11:23–24; Luke 10:12

[9] Luke 17:28–32

[10] Matt. 8:11; Luke 13:28

[11] John 6:31, 49, 58

[12] John 3:14

[13] Matt. 8:4; 19:8; Mark 1:44; 7:10; 10:5; 12:26; Luke 5:14; 20:37; John 5:46; 7:19

[14] Luke 6:26

[15] Matt. 12:40

[16] Mark 7:10

[17] Matt. 13:14; Mark 7:6

[18] Mark 12:36

[19] Matt. 24:15

[20] Matt. 5:17–20; 22:29; 23:23; Mark 12:24

[21] Matt. 4:1–11 cf. Deut. 8:3, 6:16, 6:13; Matt. 27:46 cf. Ps. 22:1; Luke 23:46 cf. Ps. 31:5

[22] Matt. 11:10; 26:24, 31, 53–56; Mark 9:12–13; 14:21, 49; Luke 4:21; 18:31–33; 21:22; 22:37; 24:25–27, 44–47; John 5:39–47; 13:18; 15:25; 17:12

[23] Matt. 5:18; Luke 16:17; John 10:35

[24] Matt. 5:17–20; Luke 24:25–47

[25] John 5:39

[26] John 14:25–26; 16:13

[27] John 10:4, 27; 18:37

[28] 1 Cor. 2:13–14

[29] Matt. 21:42; 22:29; 26:54, 56; Luke 24:25–32, 44–45; John 5:39; 10:35; Acts 17:2, 11; 18:28; Rom. 1:2; 4:3; 9:17; 10:11; 11:2; 15:4; 16:26; 1 Cor. 15:3–4; Gal. 3:8, 22; 4:30; 1 Tim. 5:18; 2 Tim. 3:16; 2 Peter 1:20–21; 3:15–16

[30] Gen. 12:3 cf. Gal. 3:8; Ex. 9:16 cf. Rom. 9:17

[31] Gen. 2:24 cf. Matt. 19:4–5; Ps. 2:1 cf. Acts 4:24–25; Ps. 2:7 cf. Heb. 1:5; Ps. 16:10 cf. Acts 13:35; Ps. 95:7–8 cf. Heb. 3:7–8; Ps. 104:4 cf. Heb. 1:7; Isa. 55:3 cf. Acts 13:34

[32] 1 Cor. 2:12–13; 1 Peter 1:10–12

[33] Luke 1:1–3; John 20:30–31; Acts 1:1–3, 9; 10:39–42; 1 Cor. 15:6–8; 1 Peter 5:1; 2 Peter 1:16; 1 John 1:1–3

[34] 2 Tim. 4:11

[35] Luke 1:1–4

[36] 1 Peter 5:13

[37] 1 Cor. 14:37; 2 Cor. 13:3

[38] 1 Tim. 5:18 cf. Deut. 25:4; Luke 10:7

[39] 2 Tim. 3:15

[40] 1 Cor. 14:37; 1 Thess. 2:13; 2 Peter 3:2

[41] 2 Peter 3:15–16

[42] Col. 4:16; 2 Thess. 3:14

[43] Acts 2:42; 15; Eph. 2:20; 1 John 4:6

[44] Isa. 7:14; Matt. 1:18–23

[45] Mic. 5:2; Luke 2:1–7

[46] Hos. 11:1; Matt. 2:13–15

[47] Mal. 3:1; Luke 2:25–27

[48] Zech. 11:12–13; Matt. 26:14–15

[49] Ps. 22:18; John 19:23–24

[50] Ps. 22:16; Luke 23:33

[51] Isa. 53:8–9; Matt. 27:57–60; Luke 23:50–53

[52] Ps. 16:10; Isa. 53:10–12; Acts 2:25–32

[53] John 6:27; 17:3; 1 Cor. 8:6; 2 Cor. 1:3; Eph. 1:3; 1 Peter 1:3

[54] Isa. 7:14; Matt. 26:63–65; 28:19; John 1:1–4, 14; 5:17–23; 8:58–59; 10:30–33; 12:37–41; 19:7; 20:28–29; Acts 20:28; Rom. 9:5; 1 Cor. 8:4–6; Phil. 2:10–11; Col. 1:16–17; 2:8–9; 1 Tim. 6:15; Titus 2:13; Heb. 1:8; 1 John 5:20; Rev. 1:8, 17–18; 17:14; 19:16; 22:13–16

[55] Isa. 7:14; cf. Matt. 1:18–23; Isa. 9:6; Rom. 8:3; Phil. 2:7; 1 John 4:2

[56] Mic. 3:8; Acts 1:8; Rom. 15:13, 19

[57] Heb. 9:14

[58] Isa. 40:13–14; 1 Cor. 2:10

[59] Gen 1:2; Ps. 104:30

[60] Ps. 139:7

[61] John 14:16; Acts 5:3–4; 2 Cor. 3:16–18

[62] Eph. 4:30

[63] Acts 7:51

[64] Heb. 10:29

[65] Rom. 1:7; 1 Cor. 1:3; 2 Cor. 1:2; Gal. 1:3; Eph. 1:2; 6:23; Phil. 1:2; 1 Thess. 1:1; 2 Thess. 1:1–2; 1 Tim. 1:1–2; 2 Tim. 1:2; Titus 1:4; Philem. 3; James 1:1; 2 Peter 1:2; 2 John 3

[66] John 3:17; 5:31–32; 8:16–18; 11:41–42; 12:28; 14:31; 17:23–26; 2 Cor. 1:3–4; Gal. 1:1; 4:4; 1 John 2:1; 4:10

[67] Luke 3:22; John 14:16; 15:26; 16:7

[68] John 14:15–16; 15:26; Rom. 8:11, 26–27

[69] Matt. 3:16–17

[70] Eph. 1:3–14

[71] Deut. 32:21; 1 Sam. 12:21; Ps. 96:5; Isa. 37:19; 41:23–24, 29; Jer. 2:11; 5:7; 16:20; 1 Cor. 8:4; 10:19–20

[72] Deut. 32:17; Ps. 106:37; 1 Cor. 10:18–22; Gal. 4:8

[73] Col. 1:15

[74] Isa. 14:11–23; Ezek. 28:1–19

[75] 2 Peter 2:4; Rev. 9:1; 12:3–4

[76] Hos. 6:7; Rom. 5:12–21; 1 Cor. 15:21–22, 45–50

[77] Ps. 51:5; 58:3; Rom. 3:23; see also Ps. 53:3; Isa. 53:6; 64:6; 1 John 1:8

[78] Ps. 51:5; Rom. 3:10–18; 8:7–8

[79] Heb. 4:15

[80] 1 John 1:8

[81] Ps. 14:1–3; Isa. 53:6; Rom. 3:10, 23; 1 John 3:4

[82] Prov. 4:23; 17:20; 20:9; Matt. 6:21; Luke 6:45

[83] Rom. 8:18–27

[84] Gen. 1:26; 9:6; James 3:9

[85] Eph. 4:18

[86] Rom. 6:16–17

[87] Titus 3:3

[88] Rom. 8:10

[89] Ps. 29:2; Rom. 3:23; 11:36; 16:27

[90] Matt. 7:17–18; Rom. 8:7–8

[91] Ex. 3:5; Lev. 19:2; Ps. 5:4–6; 99:5; Isa. 6:3; 8:13; 57:15; Hab. 1:12–13; 1 Peter 1:14–19; 1 John 1:5

[92] Ex. 34:7; see also Gen. 18:25; Deut. 32:4; Acts 17:31; Rom. 2:11

[93] Ps. 5:4

[94] Prov. 6:16; Zech. 8:17

[95] Isa. 59:2; 64:7

[96] Gen. 6:5–6; Isa. 63:10; Eph. 4:30

[97] Ex. 4:14; 15:7; 34:6–8; Lev. 26:27–33; Num. 11:1; 12:9; 22:22; 25:3; 32:13; Deut. 9:20; 13:17; 29:24–29; Josh. 7:1; Judg. 2:14; 2 Sam. 24:1; 1 Kings 14:15; 15:30; 16:2; 22:53; 2 Kings 13:3; 17:11; 23:19; 1 Chron. 13:10; 2 Chron. 28:25; Ps. 7:11; 11:4–7; Hos. 12:14; Mark 10:14; Heb. 10:27; Rev. 2:6

[98] Ps. 5:5; Hos. 9:15; Amos 5:21; Mal. 1:3; Rom. 9:13; Rev. 2:6

[99] Isa. 53:6–12; John 3:16; 11:50–51; 15:13; Rom. 3:25–26; 5:6–8, 17–19; 1 Cor. 15:3; 2 Cor. 5:4–15, 21; Gal. 3:13; 1 Tim. 1:15; Heb. 2:17; 9:28; 10:10–12; 1 Peter 2:24; 3:18; 1 John 2:1–2; 4:10

[100] 2 Cor. 5:21; Heb. 4:15; 7:26; 1 Peter 2:22

[101] Isa. 53:10–12; John 11:50–51; 15:13; Rom. 5:17–19; 2 Cor. 5:14–15, 21; Gal. 3:13; 1 Peter 3:18

[102] Gen. 2:16–17; Ezek. 18:20; Rom. 6:23; James 1:15; Rev. 21:8

[103] Matt. 12:38–40; Mark 8:31; 9:31; 10:33–34; John 2:18–22

[104] Matt. 20:28; Mark 10:45

[105] Lev. 4:13–20; 16; 17:11; Jer. 31:31–34; Matt. 26:26–29; Mark 14:22–25; Luke 22:19–20; John 1:29, 36; Rom. 3:23–25; 5:8–10; 1 Cor. 5:7; 11:23–25; Eph. 5:2; Heb. 7:22; 8:3–13; 9:26–27; 10:10, 12; 1 Peter 1:18–19; 1 John 1:7; Rev. 1:5

[106] Matt. 26:26–29

[107] Rom. 3:25–26

[108] John 12:20–28; 13:30–32; 17:1

[109] John 1:18; 3:16; 15:12–13; Rom. 5:8; 1 John 4:9–10

[110] Isa. 53:10; Eph. 1:3–14

[111] Rom. 11:33–36; 1 Cor. 1:7–2:5

[112] Isa. 53:11; Matt. 25:31–33, 46; Luke 18:9–14; Acts 13:38–39; Rom. 2:13; 3:20, 23–28; 4:2–5, 25; 5:1, 9–21; 8:33–34; Gal. 2:16–17; Titus 3:7

[113] The wrath of God appears nearly six hundred times in the Old Testament, and these concepts are also found in Luke 18:13; John 8:34; Rom. 1:18, 24, 26; 3:25; Heb. 2:17; 9:5; and 1 John 2:2; 4:10.

[114] Ex. 6:2–8; 15:1–18; Deut. 7:8; 15:15; 2 Sam. 7:23; 1 Chron. 17:21; Neh. 1:10; Ps. 74:2; 77:15; Isa. 43:11; Jer. 31:11; Titus 2:14; Heb. 2:14–15; 9:12; 1 Peter 1:18–19; Rev. 1:5

[115] Rom. 5:18; 6:6; 8:1–4; 1 Peter 2:24

[116] Rom. 8:1

[117] Gal. 3:13

[118] Rom. 7:1–5; 1 Cor. 9:20–24; Eph. 2:15; Col. 2:14–23

[119] Col. 1:13–17; 2:13–15

[120] Isa. 59:2; Hos. 5:6; Rom. 5:10–11; 2 Cor. 5:18–21; Eph. 2:16; Col. 1:22; 1 Peter 3:18

[121] Luke 4:1–13; John 12:31; 16:11; Acts 26:18; Rom. 6:6, 14; 7:4; 8:2, 20–23, 37–39; Gal. 3:13; 6:14; Col. 1:13; 2:13–15; Heb. 2:14–15; 1 John 3:8; 4:4

[122] Mark 10:45; 1 Tim. 2:5–6

[123] Rom. 3:21–22; 4:4–6; 5:12–21; 10:4; 1 Cor. 1:30; 2 Cor. 5:21; Phil. 3:8–9; 1 Peter 2:24; 3:18

[124] Matt. 16:24–25; 2 Cor. 5:14–21; Phil. 2:5–8; 1 Peter 2:19–25; 1 John 3:16; 4:9–11

[125] Isa. 53:6; John 3:16; Rom. 5:6–8; 2 Cor. 5:14–15, 19; 1 Tim. 2:1–6; 4:10; Heb. 2:9; 2 Peter 2:1; 3:9; 1 John 2:2; 4:14; Rev. 5:9

[126] Matt. 20:28; 26:28; Rom. 5:17–19

[127] John 10:11, 15

[128] Acts 20:28; Eph. 5:25

[129] Rom. 8:32–35

[130] Matt. 1:21

[131] John 15:13

[132] 2 Cor. 5:15; Titus 2:14

[133] 1 Cor. 1:18
[134] Gal. 5:11
[135] Phil. 3:18
[136] Gal. 1:6–10
[137] 1 Peter 2:7–8
[138] Gal. 6:14
[139] Rom. 1:16
[140] 1 Cor. 3:18
[141] Ex. 6:6; Deut. 7:8; 15:15; 2 Sam. 7:23; 1 Chron. 17:21
[142] 1 Cor. 15:3–4
[143] Gal. 1:11–12, 15–17
[144] 2 Cor. 11:3–4; Gal. 1:6–9
[145] Rom. 5:9–10
[146] Rom. 2:5; 3:5; 5:9; Eph. 5:6; Col. 3:6; 1 Thess. 1:10
[147] Ex. 34:6–8; Deut. 29:24–29; 32:21–22; Ps. 11:4–7; John 3:36; Rom. 1:18–32; Eph. 5:6; Col. 3:6; Rev. 14:9–11, 18–20; 19:11–15
[148] John 1:13; 6:44; 10:28; Rom. 5:5–8; 1 Cor. 1:30; 2 Cor. 5:18–20; Col. 1:21–22; James 1:18
[149] Heb. 9:27
[150] John 1:29; 3:17–18; 4:42; 5:19–23; Acts 4:12; 1 John 2:2; Rev. 5:9
[151] Acts 13:48; Eph. 1:3–11; 2 Thess. 2:13
[152] Acts 3:19; 11:21; 14:15; 20:21; 26:18, 20; 1 Thess. 1:9; James 5:20
[153] John 1:13; Rom. 9:16; Eph. 2:8–10; Titus 3:5–6
[154] Matt. 25:46
[155] Isa. 66:22–24; Dan. 12:1–2; Matt. 5:22–30; 10:28; 25:46; John 3:36; Rom. 1:18–32; 2 Peter 2:4–22
[156] Matt. 20:12–15; Rom. 9:20–21
[157] John 15:16; Acts 9:15; Rom. 3:1–2
[158] 2 Peter 2:4
[159] Isa. 66:22–24
[160] Dan. 12:1–2
[161] Matt. 8:11–12; 13:40–42, 49–50; 22:13; 24:50–51; 25:30; Luke 13:27–28
[162] Matt. 8:29; Mark 1:24; 5:7
[163] Matt. 13:40–42, 49–50; 22:13; 25:30
[164] Matt. 13:49–50; 18:8–9; 25:41; Mark 9:43–48; Luke 16:19–31
[165] Matt. 18:8–9; Mark 9:43–48
[166] Matt. 24:50–51
[167] Matt. 25:41
[168] Mark 9:43–48
[169] Luke 12:46–48
[170] Luke 16:19–31
[171] 2 Thess. 1:6–9
[172] 2 Peter 2:9
[173] Rev. 14:9–11
[174] Rev. 19:20; 20:10–15; 21:8
[175] These sermons are available for free at *www.marshillchurch.org*.
[176] For more information, go to *www.acts29network.org*.

## RESPONSE TO MARK DRISCOLL

### DAN KIMBALL

1 Ben Witherington III, *The Problem with Evangelical Theology* (Waco, Tex.: Baylor Univ. Press, 2005), 3.

## Chapter 2: THE EMERGING CHURCH AND INCARNATIONAL THEOLOGY

### JOHN BURKE

1 Notice in Acts 15:15–19 how the theological conclusions are tested against the words of the prophets.

2 Bruce Shelley, *Church History in Plain Language* (Dallas: Word Publishing, 1982), 113.

3 John Burke, *No Perfect People Allowed: Creating a Come-As-You-Are Culture in the Church* (Grand Rapids, Mich.: Zondervan, 2005).

4 Acts 15:19

5 George Barna, *The Second Coming of the Church* (Nashville: Word Publishing, 1998), 68.

6 Romans 2:14–15

7 C. S. Lewis, *Abolition of Man* (New York: MacMillan, 1947), 95–121.

8 Excerpt adapted from *No Perfect People Allowed*, 134–36.

9 Deuteronomy 32:16–17

10 Note also how many times "sin" in the Old Testament is equated with adultery or unfaithfulness, rather than merely wrong behavior (though it manifests itself in behavior against God's will): Jeremiah 3:6–10; 5:7–8; Ezekiel 16, 23; Hosea.

11 1 Corinthians 9:22

12 Acts 14:17

13 Acts 17:28

14 Galatians 3:23–24 (NASB)

15 Daniel 4:28–37

16 Hebrews 11:31

17 Matthew 12:42

18 Matthew 2:1–2

19 Adapted from *No Perfect People Allowed*, 140.

20 Galatians 2:11–12

21 Deuteronomy 18:21–22

22 Isaiah 46:9–10

23 Matthew 22:43

24 Luke 24:27 (italics mine)

25 Matthew 5:17–19

26 Matthew 11:25

27 These messages are available online at *www.gatewaychurch.com* in Weekend Message Archives: *Prophesies of the Messiah: Divine Humility* series.

28 Adapted from *No Perfect People Allowed*, 170–71, 180.

29 Matthew 9:13

30 Genesis 18:18 (italics mine)

31 1 Kings 8:43 (italics mine)

[32] Isaiah 52:10 (italics mine)

[33] 1 Timothy 2:3–6 (italics mine)

[34] Christian Week Online, "No Discernible Difference," July 4, 2000, vol. 14, issue 7. *www.christianweek.org/stories/vol14/no07/record.html.*

[35] I hope Romans 2:23–24 is not our indictment also: "You who boast in the law, do you dishonor God by breaking the law? As it is written: 'God's name is blasphemed among the Gentiles because of you.'"

[36] John 12:47–48

[37] Matthew 22:8–10 (italics mine)

[38] Yes, I know, Bono said it in the song, "Grace." U2, "Grace," on *All That You Can't Leave Behind* Audio CD (Santa Monica: Interscope Records, 2000).

[39] Ephesians 2:8–10 reminds us that God's grace restores us into the masterpiece he created us to be, doing the good works he created us to do. But grace must come first. It's not by works that we are restored!

[40] Adapted from *No Perfect People Allowed*, 93–94.

[41] 1 Corinthians 3:6 (italics mine)

[42] John 15:5 (italics mine)

[43] Matthew 13:24–30

## Chapter 3: THE EMERGING CHURCH AND MISSIONAL THEOLOGY
### DAN KIMBALL

[1] Bruce Larson and Ralph Osborne, *The Emerging Church* (Waco, Tex.: Word Books, 1970).

[2] This imagery of evangelicals disturbs me so much that I wrote an entire book that addresses this: *They Like Jesus, but Not the Church* (Zondervan, 2007).

[3] "Bono: The Rolling Stone Interview," *Rolling Stone*, Issue 986, November 3, 2005.

## Chapter 4: THE EMERGING CHURCH AND EMBODIED THEOLOGY
### DOUG PAGITT

[1] Henry King, *Reconstruction in Theology* (New York, 1899).

[2] Luke 1:3–4

[3] John 1:1–5

[4] John 8:12

[5] Pelagius was tried for heresy on multiple occasions and never found guilty until he was unable to return to Rome to defend himself. I am not seeking to justify Pelagius' position as much as to highlight the issues at hand in the fourth century.

[6] Mark 1:15

[7] Mark 1:16–18

[8] Romans 8:22–31

[9] Jack Uldrich with Deb Newberry, *The Next Big Thing Is Really Small* (New York: Crown Business, 2003).

[10] Colossians 1:15–17

## RESPONSE TO DOUG PAGITT
### MARK DRISCOLL

[1] Gary Dorrien, *The Making of American Liberal Theology: Idealism, Realism, and Modernity: 1900–1950* (Louisville: Westminster John Knox, 2003), 65.

[2] Dr. Walter Marshall Horton, "Henry Churchill King and Oberlin Liberalism," *Oberlin Today* 18, no. 3 (1960): 8–9.

[3] William Fraser McDowell and Henry Churchill King, "The Moral and Religious Phases of Education," Liberal Education 90, no. 1 (Winter 2004): 26–30.

[4] Horton, Ibid., 4.

## Chapter 5: THE EMERGING CHURCH AND COMMUNAL THEOLOGY
### KAREN WARD

[1] Clemens Sedmak, *Doing Local Theology* (Maryknoll, N.Y.: Orbis, 2002), 3, 121, 123.

[2] Ibid., 146.

[3] Proper 2, Revised Common Lectionary Year A, Matthew 22.

[4] John D. Caputo, *On Religion* (New York: Routledge, 2001), 2–3.

[5] Elizabeth Barrett Browning, *Aurora Leigh*, lines 61–65.

[6] Rainer Maria Rilke, "God Speaks to Each of Us," *The Book of Hours: Love Poems to God* trans. Anita Barrows and Joanna Macy (New York: Riverhead Trade, 1997).

## Conclusion: ASSESSING EMERGING THEOLOGY
### ROBERT WEBBER

[1] Donald A. Carson, *Becoming Conversant with the Emerging Church* (Grand Rapids, Mich.: Zondervan, 2005), 10.

[2] Ibid., 9.

# INDEX

*Page references in italics indicate information contained in a table.*